Terrorism:
Theory and Practice

Other Titles in This Series

Self-Determination: National, Regional and Global Dimensions, edited by Yonah Alexander and Robert A. Friedlander

International Terrorism: An Annotated Bibliography and Research Guide, Augustus R. Norton and Martin Greenberg

Victims of Terrorism, edited by Frank M. Ochberg

Westview Special Studies in National and International Terrorism

Terrorism: Theory and Practice
edited by Yonah Alexander,
David Carlton, and Paul Wilkinson

The use of sporadic and relentless nongovernmental political and ideological violence—principally, but not exclusively, as part of a parochial or transnational revolutionary strategy—is characteristic of our "Age of Terrorism." This volume presents theoretical and practical aspects of this phenomenon, with a view toward understanding current challenges and implications for the future. The contributors represent a wide range of backgrounds and disciplines.

Yonah Alexander is professor of international studies and director of the Institute for Studies in International Terrorism at the State University of New York at Oneonta. He is the editor of *International Terrorism: National, Regional, and Global Perspectives,* and editor-in-chief of *Terrorism: An International Journal.* David Carlton, senior lecturer in diplomatic history at the Polytechnic of North London, is the author of *MacDonald versus Henderson: The Foreign Policy of the Second Labour Government.* Paul Wilkinson is senior lecturer in politics at University College, Cardiff. He is the author of *Political Terrorism* and *Terrorism and the Liberal State.*

Published in cooperation with
The Institute for Studies in International Terrorism
State University of New York

Terrorism:
Theory and Practice

edited by Yonah Alexander,
David Carlton, and Paul Wilkinson

Westview Press / Boulder, Colorado

Westview Special Studies in National and International Terrorism

Copyright © 1979 by Westview Press, Inc.

Published in 1979 in the United States of America by
Westview Press, Inc.
5500 Central Avenue
Boulder, Colorado 80301
Frederick A. Praeger, Publisher

Library of Congress Cataloging in Publication Data
Main entry under title:
Terrorism: theory and practice.
(Westview special studies in national and international terrorism)
Bibliography: p.
Includes index.
1. Terrorism—Addresses, essays, lectures. I. Alexander, Yonah. II. Carlton, David, 1938- . III. Wilkinson, Paul. IV. Series.
HV6431.T5   301.6'33   78-14491
ISBN 0-89158-089-1

Printed and bound in the United States of America

Contents

vii

Preface

The study of terrorism has now "arrived" internationally, as evidenced by the birth of a new international multidisciplinary journal, *Terrorism*; the proliferation of scientific conferences and papers; and the growth of university research and teaching on the subject. Historians, social scientists, lawyers, criminologists, administrators, and political leaders are showing an increasing awareness of the need for more informed scholarly analysis of the growing international incidence of acts of terrorism perpetrated by extremist groups of almost every ideological hue and in every continent.

Our book offers a cool, long-term appraisal of terrorist phenomena. It relates the theory and practice of terrorism both to wider changes in social behavior, attitudes, and conditions and to advances in scientific knowledge and technology. A valuable feature of many of the contributions is the effort to assess the development and implications of modern terrorism against the broader canvas of trends in international relations and conflict.

The first three parts of the book survey theories of terrorist motivations and underlying and precipitative causes of terrorism, social scientific theories of violence, and the characteristics of terrorist movements and their modus operandi. Part 4 contains essays on topics of current interest, such as terrorism in Northern Ireland, hostage negotiation, and the relationship between terrorism and the media. The two concluding contributions offer wide-ranging and objective discussions of possible future trends in terrorism and explore some of the implications of this assessment for policymakers and the public.

Although, thus far at least, no mass casualties and widespread destruction have resulted from a single terrorist attack, it is suggested by experts that future incidents could be much more costly. First, there is the extremely difficult problem of protecting people and property. The security of a state depends on the goodwill of the people within its borders. The terrorist, however, has the advantage of surprise. Police and citizenry cannot check everyone and every place. Second, new technology is creating new dangers. Today, conventional weapons, including machine guns and modern plastic and letter bombs, are used by terrorists. Highly sophisticated weapons, such as the SA-7 surface-to-air rockets, which can destroy an airplane and kill hundreds of passengers, are now relatively easily available to various terrorist groups.

It is also possible that in the future, terrorist groups will have access to biological, chemical, and nuclear instruments that have the potential to kill large numbers of people. An entire city's water supply can be poisoned with lethal chemicals. Nerve agents can cause hundreds of thousands of fatalities. A single incident involving biological agents, both toxins and living organisms, or nuclear bombs would obviously produce many casualties and mass destruction. Thus, the advances of science and technology are slowly turning the entire modern society into a potential victim of terrorism; there is no immunity for the noncombatant segment of the world population or for those nations and peoples who have no direct connection to particular conflicts or to specific grievances that motivate acts of violence.

In view of our physical and societal vulnerabilities to the dangers of contemporary terrorism, we decided to organize a multilateral research project dealing with some theoretical and practical aspects of this serious and complex problem. Our two-year effort produced this volume, which includes papers presented at two academic seminars sponsored by the Institute for Studies in International Terrorism (State University of New York) and held at the Polytechnic of North London in January 1976 and December 1977, as well as several invited contributions. Each author bears sole responsibility for his approach, views, and conclusions.

The editors wish to thank their colleagues in the United States, Canada, and the United Kingdom for their cooperation and to gratefully acknowlege the assistance provided by the State University of New York (College at Oneonta). We hope that this book will stimulate further dialogue among students of the problem of terrorism and thereby contribute to a deeper understanding of the issues.

Yonah Alexander
David Carlton
Paul Wilkinson

The Contributors

Yonah Alexander (co-editor) is professor of international studies and director of the Institute for Studies in International Terrorism at the State University of New York at Oneonta and, concurrently, research associate at The Center for International and Strategic Studies at Georgetown University. He is the editor of *International Terrorism: National, Regional, and Global Perspectives,* co-editor of *Terrorism: Interdisciplinary Perspectives,* and editor-in-chief of *Terrorism: An International Journal.*

David Carlton (co-editor) is senior lecturer in diplomatic history at the Polytechnic of North London. He is the author of *MacDonald versus Henderson: The Foreign Policy of the Second Labour Government,* and co-editor of *The Dynamics of the Arms Race, International Terrorism and World Security,* and *Arms Control and Technological Innovation.*

Paul Wilkinson (co-editor) is senior lecturer in politics at University College, Cardiff. He is the author of *Social Movement, Political Terrorism, Terrorism and the Liberal State,* and *The Defense of the West.*

Bowman H. Miller, Leon J. Banker, Jr., and *Charles A. Russell* have worked together in the Counterintelligence Directorate of the U.S. Air Force Office of Special Investigations and have studied terrorism for the past ten years. Together they have contributed articles to various military publications and journals. They have lectured at the U.S. Air Force's Air Command and Staff College, the Air War College, the FBI National Academy, and the California Specialized Training Institute, and to various military and law enforcement audiences in

s and abroad. Mr. Miller has been a Fulbright fellow
a doctoral candidate at Georgetown University. Mr.
ɾney, is a graduate of St. Michael's College, University
d of the Dickinson School of Law. Dr. Russell, also an
ɾed his Ph.D. in international relations from American
ɛ retired from the U.S. government in June 1978 and is
liated with Risks International, Inc., an Alexandria,
ı engaged in computer analysis of terrorist incidents.

Amy Sands Redlick has worked in the Office of the Special Assistant
to the Secretary of State and Coordinator of Activities to Combat
Terrorism and in the Naval Communications Command. From 1977
to 1978, she was a visiting lecturer in the Political Science Department
of Boston College where she taught courses on political development
and guerrilla warfare and terrorism. She is currently assistant director
of the Office of Sponsored Programs at Boston University.

Alan O'Day has taught political science at the University of Salford,
economic history at the University of East Anglia, and American
studies at the Universitat Giessen (Germany); he is now senior
lecturer in history at the Polytechnic of North London. His
publications include *The English Face of Irish Nationalism* and *The
Edwardian Age*. At present, he is completing *The Many Coloured
Coat: Irish Home Rule, 1867-1914*.

Abraham H. Miller, professor of political science at the University of
Cincinnati, was a visiting faculty fellow with the U.S. Department of
Justice, Law Enforcement Assistance Administration, from 1976 to
1977. His work on collective violence won the 1975 Pi Sigma Alpha
Award of the Western Political Science Association for best research,
and he wrote the commemorative editorial for the eleventh
anniversary of the Watts riots for the *Los Angeles Times.* He has
contributed numerous articles to academic journals and is co-editor
of *Black Power and Student Rebellion.*

L. C. Green is university professor at the University of Alberta,
Canada, and a member of the ILA Terrorism Committee. He is the
author of numerous journal publications and several books: *International Law Through the Cases, Law and Society,* and *Superior
Orders in National and International Law.*

Robert A. Friedlander, associate professor of law at the Ohio
Northern University College of Law, is the author of thirty articles

and review essays dealing with domestic and international law and politics and a two-volume study of international terrorism. He is a life member of Delta Tau Kappa (International Social Science Honor Society), a life fellow of the Academy of Diplomacy and International Affairs (Cologne, West Germany), a member of the Committee on International Terrorism of the World Association of Lawyers, and on the Advisory Board of the *Denver Journal of International Law & Policy*.

Part 1

Overview

1
Out-Inventing the Terrorist

Charles A. Russell
Leon J. Banker, Jr.
Bowman H. Miller

"What to do until the terrorist comes": in an unpublished paper so entitled, Robert H. Kupperman and Harvey A. Smith discuss a threefold plan of action involving an improvement in and acceleration of intelligence collection, the development and implementation of adequate physical security safeguards in critical areas, and above all the creation of a crisis management capability focused specifically upon the terrorist problem. Looking toward new and qualitatively significant changes in future terrorist operations, motivations, group structure, and tactics, these authors also argue "some continuing research and development expended on the invention of new terrorist schemes (and their counters) by imaginative official pseudoterrorists would appear to be a worthwhile effort."[1] It is toward this goal of "out-inventing the terrorist" that the present discussion is dedicated.

In examining the problem of terrorism as it may develop in the future, we approach the subject from three separate but interrelated points of view. The first, termed *traditional analytical*, is essentially that used in intelligence analysis. Utilized to examine the contemporary terrorist phenomenon, it proceeds from known capabilities to possible intentions, operates on and from an established data base, and is essentially pragmatic in nature. It focuses on the increasingly transnational aspects of terrorism, the groups involved in such activity, their capabilities, known intergroup linkages, motivations, and finally targets. From this springboard of relatively hard data, the second approach, termed *speculative*, reverses the

An earlier version of this paper was presented by Dr. Russell at the conference on Research Strategies for the Study of International Terrorism on May 30, 1977, at Evian, France. The views expressed are those of the authors and do not necessarily reflect the view of the United States government or any of its agencies.

capabilities-to-intentions progression and begins with an evaluation of optimum terrorist targets. It moves from this point into the areas of future terrorist motivation, capabilities, and finally the possible configuration of terrorist groups themselves. The final approach, called *crisis management: nontechnical threat assessment*, probes those informational areas wherein data must be sought and rapidly provided to the individuals responsible for decision making in the face of a stated terrorist threat to inflict high-order (nationally significant) disruption or destruction.

In applying the threefold methodology outlined above, the authors are aware of shortcomings inherent in each of the three approaches. From the traditional analytical point of view, the methodology tends to assume that "past is prologue." It is factbound in orientation, conservative in outlook, and tends to be nonpredictive. Recognizing, however, that the terrorists of the future may not be the same as they have been in the past, the speculative technique is used to counterbalance traditional analysis. But it, too, has drawbacks. Among these are its inability to prove conclusions based on hard data and a tendency toward "worse case" scenarios. The final approach poses questions as yet unanswered. These are, nonetheless, questions and avenues of exploration that must be addressed and carefully considered if we are ever to be successful in countering terrorism. Cognizant of the potential problems in these three approaches, yet desirous that this discussion be of some practical consequence, we have endeavored to meld the three approaches while intentionally weighing the scales toward reasoned analysis and away from creation of purely imaginative scenarios. In the final analysis, however, the discussion anticipates that significant qualitative changes will occur in future terrorist activity. In this light, it offers some basic guidelines as we begin the challenge of out-inventing the terrorist.

The Contemporary Phenomenon: A Traditional Analytical Assessment

Terrorist Groups

The roots of modern terrorism (we define terrorism as the threatened or actual use of force or violence to attain a political goal through fear, coercion, or intimidation,[2]) appear to lie largely in the rising tide of student and radical unrest so evident in most nations of the world during the early 1960s. From this almost international groundswell of dissatisfaction with then extant political establishments, various antiestablishment organizations formed, splintered, and eventually spawned elements dedicated to destruction of "the system." Terrorism, a means to an end, was the tactic primarily and sometimes exclusively employed.

National in composition, political orientation, and scope of operations (which are generally limited to the geographic confines of a single state), these "national" terrorist groups are epitomized today by organizations such as the Armed Proletarian Nuclei and the Red Brigades in Italy; the Basque Fatherland and Liberty Movement (Euzkadi ta Azkatasuna—ETA) and the First of October Anti-Fascist Resistance Group in Spain; and the People's Strugglers and People's Sacrifice Guerrillas in Iran, among others. Also included in this category are the numerous terrorist elements in Latin America as well as those in Greece, Turkey, and South Asia and such groups as the Weather Underground and New World Liberation Front in the United States.[3]

In the late 1960s, terrorist group activities took a quantum leap from those purely national in scope to those involving operations across national boundaries, virtually anywhere in the world, often at great distance from the terrorists' homelands. Characterized by many authors as "transnational" terrorist groups, these small, highly professional and disciplined, tightly compartmented, and highly dedicated cadres capitalized quickly on the mobility afforded them by expanding international transportation and communication systems. Exploiting the absence of international agreement[4] concerning the legitimacy of terrorism, such groups have operated literally at will throughout the Western world, utilizing sympathetic safe-haven states from which to launch and terminate their operations. In contrast with "national groups," they have no standard modus operandi and vary their techniques from aircraft hijacking and kidnapping to assassination, hostage-taking, stand-off attack, arson, and bombing.[5] In brief, transnational terrorist groups have increased significantly the problems and frustrations of security and police agencies worldwide; it is all but impossible to determine with assurance where, when, why, or against whom their next assault may be launched. This unhappy realization in the first line of defense (intelligence) and the resulting complications in the security and crisis resolution phases of counterefforts coalesce to make the consequence of terrorism international.

Although the origins of terrorism itself probably antedate recorded history, the beginning of contemporary transnational operations can be traced directly to 1968 and a conscious decision by certain Palestinian elements to move the focus of their attacks outside Israel proper—to Israeli targets abroad where risks were least and Israeli vulnerability greatest. Thus, the 23 July 1968 hijacking of an El Al flight from Rome to Tel Aviv[6] by the Popular Front for the Liberation of Palestine (PFLP) represents the first application of the transnational "third country operation" concept in modern terrorism. Although a careful assessment of the potential available to terrorists through an expansion of their operations into an international arena of noncombatant nations should have been anticipated, few analysts foresaw the full impact of this development and the truly qualitative change it brought to the terrorist operational capacity.

Following the PFLP lead, the Black September Organization and other less well publicized Palestinian groups—as well as various non-Arab entities—moved into transnational activity. Among these were the Japanese Red Army (JRA) and remnants of the West German Baader-Meinhof group and Movement Two June. Almost all other transnational terrorists—working either as individuals or within their respective groups—have been affiliated operationally with the PFLP. The September 1977 presumably Iranian operation in France directed at the shah's sister may mark yet another entry into the transnational category.

In considering both national and transnational terrorist groups, most authors estimate there are approximately fifty such groups active today. Total action cadre[7] ranges from one to three thousand persons. Within the purely transnational category, however, there are only seven to nine groups with total membership in the hundreds. In general, these entitites include the PFLP and its operational partners: the JRA, Baader-Meinhof/Movement Two June successor elements, and the apparatus directed by Venezuelan-born Ilich Ramirez Sánchez (Carlos). Also included are other Palestinian elements such as the PFLP–General Command, the Black September Organization, the Iraqi-based Black June and its Syrian counterpart Saiqa, as well as the IRA, the only group with no known firm operational tie to the Palestinians.

The worldwide mobility of transnational groups and the absence of significant international restraints on their activities has facilitated their operational capability. There is no hard evidence as yet of any formalized coordination of terrorist operations by the equivalent of an international board of directors—despite the inferences and conclusions of some commentators that behind the malady lies Moscow, which would appear to benefit from terrorism in the West. The existence of shared support apparats, the use of certain specialists and their expertise by more than one group, and occasional interchange of personnel are established facts. Thus, in 1970, handguns stolen from a U.S. Army facility in Butzbach, Federal Republic of Germany, subsequently found their way into the hands of Baader-Meinhof group members and ultimately were used by Japanese Red Army terrorists in the September 1974 takeover of the French embassy in The Hague. In a similar manner, explosives stolen in West Germany during 1971 apparently were used in the May 1972 Baader-Meinhof operations against U.S. Army facilities in West Germany. Grenades known to be in the hands of Baader-Meinhof members during 1971 later found their way into the possession of both JRA and PFLP cadres and were also used by the JRA in the September 1974 barricade operation in The Hague. Additionally, similar grenades moved from the hands of Baader-Meinhof members to the Venezuelan terrorist Carlos and were used in the 14 September 1974 attack on Le Drugstore in Paris.[8]

Cooperation among terrorist cadres in West Germany, Switzerland, Italy, Spain, and Latin America also is a matter of record. During early 1974, ETA, a revolutionary Basque organization, dispatched one of its members to Argentina where he was trained in terrorist tactics and the construction of "people's jails" by the Revolutionary People's Army (ERP). That same year, the ERP loaned the Chilean Movement of the Revolutionary Left (MIR) 5 million of the 14.2 million dollars obtained from the kidnap ransom of ESSO Argentina executive Victor Samuelson.[9] Countless other examples of limited but attested cooperation among similar groups can be cited. An examination of the Carlos apparatus alone sheds substantial light on the nature and extent of such intertwined linkages.

Terrorist Capabilities

Among national and transnational terrorist groups, the most crucial area of cooperation is in the training sector. It is here, in the shared instruction provided to various terrorist elements by the PFLP and previously by the Fatah, that a truly cohesive catalyst emerges, binding together otherwise seemingly diverse groups. In short, Palestinian training and its outgrowth provide what might well be called the glue holding together many of today's transnational and national terrorist elements. In a very real sense, these terrorists studied with the same faculty and are graduates of the same academy. Some first met one another in these schools. Here, directly or indirectly, they have learned their basic skills along with the sophisticated PFLP modus operandi, organizational structure, excellent security practices, and clandestine tradecraft.

Since its inception in approximately 1968, Palestinian instruction has been provided at least to the IRA, JRA, West German personnel from at least three groups, and to Turkish and Iranian terrorist cadres.[10] In 1976, training also was given to at least fifteen members of the Dutch Red Help (Rode Hulp) in the People's Democratic Republic of South Yemen.[11] Coupled with this group-level instruction has been training for various single terrorists including a number of Latin Americans. Notable among these have been the self-styled "super terrorist" Ilich Ramirez Sánchez and Patricio Arguello, a Nicaraguan killed in the September 1970 attempted hijacking of an El Al airliner by a PFLP team, which included Leila Khaled.

While shared training experiences have been an instrumental ingredient in the mortar binding together the various national and transnational terrorist groups, also important is the similarity in social, political, and philosophical backgrounds of these individuals. With few exceptions, these individuals conform closely to a relatively consistent profile.[12] They are, in the main, single, male, 22 to 25 years old (an increasing tendency toward younger recruits is evident of late), university-trained, reared in an urban environment, middle to upper class in social origin, and anarchist/Marxist in ideology (with a steadily increasing nihilist ingredient). While variations from this basic pattern obviously exist (among German groups, approximately one-third of the operational cadre are female while both German and Japanese terrorists are somewhat older than the 22- to 25-year-old norm), the pattern is remarkably consistent for virtually all groups regardless of national origin. Even in terms of education—a notable exception is the IRA—the vast majority of terrorists with university backgrounds have studied in the humanities or nontechnical fields. Minor exceptions occur, for example, among Iranian and Turkish terrorists where a number are technicians, engineers, and physical scientists.

Terrorist Motivation

Although separatist and nationalist objectives are important motivators for the Palestinians, the IRA, and ETA, almost all terrorist groups active today either find or rationalize their raison d'être in Marxist ideology or anarchist schools of thought. Also evident in many groups is an accelerating trend toward nihilism.[13] The few operative right-wing organizations such as Croation nationalists, Ordine Nero and Ordine Nuovo in Italy, and counterterrorist forces of the right in Spain and Latin America are the obvious exceptions.

If the sociological profile outlined above is representative, the link between Palestinian "national liberation" objectives and the political aims of like-thinking non-Arab groups is obvious. As a result, the close relationships that have grown between George Habbash's PFLP and the groups or individuals it has trained and used in operations are not difficult to understand. Suffice it to say that groups receiving PFLP training have benefited significantly. In return, the PFLP has increased its pool of personnel available for use in transnational operations while at the same time raising the level of terrorist activity generally. In keeping their end of the bargain—and probably as a form of quid pro quo—shortly after completion of their training, the JRA, Turkish groups, Latin Americans, and Germans all have attacked targets selected *purely* from a Palestinian viewpoint. The May 1971 assassination of Israeli Consul General Ephraim Elrom in Istanbul by Turkish terrorists, the JRA May 1972 assault at Lod Airport, and German terrorist attacks on Israeli facilities in Frankfurt and Berlin are all evidence of this "payment" procedure.[14]

In addition to the abovementioned "proxy type" operations carried out by PFLP-trained national groups, a joint PFLP cadre of terrorists (joint in the sense of nationality) also has developed. This cadre can consist of separate groups performing various phases of an operation as in the Baader-Meinhof/Carlos/JRA cooperation in the September 1974 assault on the French embassy in The Hague or the late 1976 Dutch Red Help intelligence-gathering operation conducted for the PFLP against the Air France route between Paris, Tel Aviv, and Bombay.[15] The cooperative cadre also can take the form of multinational operational teams. Since 1970, when the Nicaraguan Patricio Arguello and PFLP member Leila Khaled worked together in the attempted hijacking of an El Al flight, the following joint operations involving the PFLP have taken place:

May 1972: JRA/PFLP/German collaboration in attacking Lod Airport, Israel.

July 1973: PFLP/JRA/Latin American cooperation in hijacking a Japan Airlines 747 in Europe.

January 1974: PFLP/JRA operation against Shell Oil facilities in Singapore.

September 1974: JRA/PFLP/Baader-Meinhof collaboration in assaulting the French embassy, The Hague.

January 1975: PFLP/German/Carlos cooperation in an attack against an El Al aircraft, Orly Airport, Paris.

December 1975: Carlos/German/Palestinian collaboration in the

Vienna assault on the ministerial conference of the Oil Producing
and Exporting Countries (OPEC).
June 1976: PFLP/Latin American/German effort culminating at
Entebbe.

As a result of the commonalities in sociological background and
political outlook, a shared ideology and training experience, and
the meandering membership of individual terrorists between and
among groups—as well as their participation in joint and proxy
operations—links between individual terrorists and terrorist groups
have increased significantly. Through these ties and the channels
they create, documentation, weapons, and operational aid all have
been exchanged.

To a significant degree, this same type of assistance is provided
by states supporting terrorism and several key leftist apparats that
seek to further Trotskyite or orthodox Marxist political objectives
on a broad front. Ulrike Meinhof—before soliciting Palestinian
training—reportedly sought the aid of North Korea for such instruction in November 1971.[16] In this same context, it is generally assumed
the nine Japanese Red Army Faction terrorists who hijacked a Japan
Airlines jet to Pyongyang in 1970 received training there, as have
subsequent cadres before and since that date. Similar instruction
has been provided by Cuba and the Soviet Union under the guise of
military training for national liberation.[17] Additionally, Palestinian
training camps are or have been located in Iraq, Libya, Lebanon,
Somalia, and the People's Democratic Republic of Yemen.[18] During
late 1976, it also was reported that possibly as many as one hundred
Basque terrorists were trained in Algeria.[19] In most support activities
of the type described above, however, Libya has been the primary
source for Palestinian terrorist support, providing finances, weapons, training, safe haven, and an operational staging area. Two
examples in the latter category are the August 1975 JRA attack at
Kuala Lumpur and the 11 August 1976 PFLP attack on passengers in
Istanbul's Yesilkoy Airport, both of which either ended or originated
in Libya.[20]

Additional evidence of how diverse nationalities can and do
collaborate within an assault team was seen in both the OPEC attack
and the Air France hijacking to Entebbe. The West Germans, for
example, showed in the persons of Hans-Joachim Klein and
Gabrielle Kroecher-Tiedemann how they could work effectively with
Venezuelan Ilich Ramirez Sanchez (Carlos) as their team chief at
OPEC. At Entebbe, Wilfred Boese and Brigitte Kuhlmann, longtime

cohorts of Klein, led the assault in the air but yielded operational control to others on the ground, possibly to the South American Antonio Dages Bouvier, former London-based chief of the apparatus headed by Carlos.[21]

In addition to a similar personal background, shared ideology and training, intergroup links, and the assistance of support states, transnational terrorist operations also require a variety of weapons and high-quality false or stolen documents. Although terrorist weapons have ranged from handguns to the man-portable SA-7 missile, the timed bomb and automatic weapon have remained the mainstays of the terrorist arsenals. Both provide effective destructive potential and relative ease of transport and concealment, and thus enhance operational security. Such weapons and explosives also can be readily acquired from benefactor states through theft, purchase, or even simple fabrication. Equally important in both transnational and national terrorist activity are quality false documents. Again, as in the case of weaponry, the same basic avenues of supply—benefactor states and sympathizers—are available; false documents are also obtained through theft, alteration, and outright purchase. All these methods of acquisition are in regular use and are reliable. In this context, "national liberation" broker networks, such as the Paris-based "Curiel apparat" formerly directed by the late Henri Curiel, also should not be discounted. These reportedly have been involved in the production of some of the better false documents recently available to terrorist cadres.[22]

Terrorist Targets

Despite occasional setbacks, the appeal of contemporary terrorist activity accounting for its continued widespread use is quite simply its apparent success. It is a cost effective, manageable, and operationally sound tactic useful to small groups of highly dedicated, well-trained, and resourceful personnel. The motivation for using terrorism lies largely in the notion "propaganda by deed"[23] and the recognition afforded its users. They recognize its value to them as well. Along with a common sociological background, most terrorist groups share the same general political goals: negatively expressed, to destroy a government, alter a policy or law, oust a foreign power or economically dominant class, attack imperialism/colonialism/ Zionism, and so on. As long as this motivation is rooted in an ideology with universal applicability or is without ideological roots at all, national-level objectives can easily be subordinated to international political goals or melded with them. Thus, the Japanese Red

Army could readily support the PFLP as one phase in its ultimate plan for "simultaneous world revolution." In a similar manner, the purely national goals of such groups as the Turkish People's Liberation Army, the Iranian People's Sacrifice Guerrillas, or the various German terrorist organizations can be melded easily with the broader revolutionary aims of the PFLP or even the JRA.

Of particular concern in this dilation of group-specific motivations is the fact that as motivation ceases to function on a purely national plane, the constituency for whom the terrorist group operates may begin to fade in favor of some vague worldwide constituency—if, in fact, constituency continues to play any role at all. Such a change could have a direct impact upon the nature and degree of terrorist violence, assuming that a constituency (real or imagined) acts as a moderating influence on the type, targets, and level of violence in terrorist operations. Put another way, if the terrorist feels a need to avoid alienating certain groups of people or sectors of society (the masses, "the little man," the proletariat, the innocent victims of exploitation, and so forth), then this factor must enter his deliberations on target selection and the type of operation to be conducted.

Such may be the rationale for choosing facilities rather than people as targets in certain instances. In terrorist incidents recorded since the benchmark PFLP hijacking in 1968, whether carried out by national or transnational groups, the actual number of casualties has been relatively small.[24] The basic reason for this seems to have been the conscious and selective nature of terrorist operational scenarios and targeting. As Brian Jenkins has stated, "terrorists want a lot of people watching, not a lot of people dead."[25] The confirmation of this observation lies primarily in the fact that most terrorism to date has been claimed to be altruistically motivated and ideologically explained and has had as its goals recognition for the terrorists as well as the creation of political leverage for terrorist groups. Because of the intrinsic value of human life and the psychological stress when lives are jeopardized, the terrorist target almost invariably remains a human one. The specific types of people targeted are usually those at the top of industrial, governmental, or military/ police hierarchies (judges, politicians, military/police personnel, corporate executives). Attacks against such persons are easily rationalized and justified in that they are perceived as symbols of "exploitive imperialist elements" or as part of the "repressive organs" of the state.

In general terms then, we have not come all that far from the assassination of Alexander II to the murders of Admiral Carrero Blanco and British Ambassador Ewart-Biggs, other than in the technology employed. The point is that terrorists, with minor exceptions such as transnational operations, have not been "terribly" creative to date. The potential, yet untapped, for this operational creativity lies in modern technology. It is this same technology, when coupled with the increasingly fragile, exposed, and interdependent automated systems so essential in our modern society, that appears to offer a drastic change in terrorist targeting from selected individuals to larger and less definable groups. In this context and in light of the improved operational potential afforded terrorist groups, the advance in terrorist weaponry from the rifle to the SA-7 is still only an evolutionary one. In view of technology's potential for a contribution to future quantum leaps in terrorist capabilities—and considering the fact that terrorist operations are predicated on the high value society places on human life—one can only speculate where and how terrorists of the future may escalate their operations. It is this primary question that the traditional analytical approach of the intelligence craft cannot answer adequately and ignores. It is here that the speculative method has its merits and can function usefully, when complemented by the ongoing efforts of traditional analysis. In short, it is in this regard that we must try to out-invent the terrorist.

Out-Inventing the Terrorist: Some Thoughts on the Speculative Approach

Terrorist Targets

The recent past has illustrated that almost invariably the targets of terrorist activity are people, both individuals and groups. Many of the groups have been basically of coincidental composition, such as airline passengers, visitors to facilities, and so forth.[26] Individual targets usually have been selected for their symbolic value—for what they represent. No doubt this type of targeting will remain a significant aspect of terrorist target selection and operational endeavor in the foreseeable future. The "terrorism as theater" notion[27] (that terrorists are actors, that their activities are performed as an operational drama with the world as an audience) is very useful in this context. Within this analogy lies a key element in terrorist motivation: to instill fear or intimidate the spectator by pointing up his own vulnerabilities as illustrated in attacks on selected persons or groups. If these spectators, in turn, become increasingly conditioned to unreflected acceptance of a certain level of terrorism (many societies already have become numbed to growing criminal and fictionalized violence), then the desired transfer of impact from the terrorist target (the direct victim) to the indirect victims (the mass of nonparticipating spectators) will suffer. This phenomenon would appear to be growing, if it is not already in an advanced stage of development.[28] In this context, one might ask, for example, whether those few deaths resulting from aircraft hijacking are so shocking to a world that, in 1977, witnessed over five hundred persons die in a single accidental aircraft disaster on Tenerife, Canary Islands. One must ask whether the nonparticipating spectators differentiate between intentional and accidental killings; and if not, why not? Accidental catastrophes, coupled with the continued increase of criminal violence within our society, would appear to be reducing the impact of calculated terrorism upon the spectators.

Assuming familiarity breeds contempt, repetition conditions, and a degree of one-upmanship exists between and among terrorist groups, they then, it would seem, have two basic alternatives.[29] They can lower the threshhold of violence and redirect their operations at those aspects of society upon which the entire populace depends— utilities, energy, food and water, transportation, communications, monetary and financial systems, and similar essential services. Or, conversely, they may attempt to increase the number and range of casualties (human targets) by mustering greater resources and proceed to mass destruction. For the sake of the following discussion, we shall label the two preceding target alternatives *mass disruption terrorism* and *mass destruction terrorism*.

Mass Disruption Terrorism

In seeking to identify potential targets of disruptive terrorism, one must assume the status of a pseudoterrorist and identify targets on a scale of relative attractiveness. The determining factors in such target selection will include optimum potential impact, the identity and size of the intended victim group, and the type of desired impact. While publicity and recognition remain characteristics of the terrorists' aims, the very nature of disruptive operations will decrease the need for exploitation of media coverage to broaden public awareness of a given operation. The news media will continue to inform the world of specific incidents, but the vastly larger body of actual (through presumably noncasualty) victims will obviate the need for localized publicity. Clearly, media reports to the U.S. east coast that terrorists had succeeded in causing a massive electrical blackout there would be both unnecessary and perhaps impossible. The electronic media could not operate in such an event and electrically powered presses would also cease to function. Absorption of the publicity phase into the disruptive operation itself would have been realized. The recognition or credit-claiming phase would be delayed but no less effective. Credit claimed for such disruption and a threat to repeat it offer untold coercive potential.

In view of the above, terrorists (or pseudoterrorists) must ask what existing targets, or those in the research and/or development phase, could be attacked to bring about the desired degree of disruption, chaos, inconvenience, and frustration. On one level, the terrorist would consider systems in terms of criticalness of impact. Quite simply, what are the aspects of life which, if disrupted, would most quickly and demonstrably affect many human lives? Food, water, means of communication, modes of transportation, sources of energy, management of the flow of goods and services, financial systems, health and emergency services all immediately spring to mind. While a temporary disruption of such services will not of necessity cause a great number of casualties, it would generate considerable concern (to understate the case) among those directly affected, among those responsible for insuring the integrity of the affected systems, and among those who otherwise also could have been victims. In a well-orchestrated campaign of such disruptive acts, democratic states most likely would be unable to deal effectively with these developments by using methods that are acceptable to the voting public. Forcing governmental overreaction (resort to martial law or other methods of controlling both the populace and the phenomenon) will continue to be a primary terrorist objective.[30] This disruptive mode, because of its effect on a large number of victims, has considerably greater potential for energizing and polarizing an audience that previously was watching and now is helplessly involved. The frequent terrorist réclame, "There are no innocent victims, only allies and enemies," will then be no longer merely a rhetorical device. It assumes the greater proportions of a polarizing catalyst.

Having selected a system as his target, the terrorist must then determine the most vulnerable points within that system, that is, identify the weak link or the key element upon which the entire system depends. Obviously, the optimum or ideal case would be for those two target characteristics to coincide at the same locus. Additional considerations for the terrorist include: system redundancy; available inventory of replacement components; time required to respond, to identify the disruption's origin, and to correct or repair it; duration of disruption and permanent effects, if any. Fed by the media, public pressure would increase substantially, the greater the duration and range of disruption. Precipitous government response, however, brings with it room for error, miscalculation, possible overreaction, and failure.

Mass Destruction Terrorism

From the disruptive mode to mass destruction terrorism is indeed a quantum leap with reference to targets and their selection. This type of terrorism does not aim at "a lot of people watching, not a lot of people dead."[31] Instead, destruction is aimed directly at a multitude of people in an escalation toward the creation of maximum fear and perhaps intimidation of the world audience in general. Although this type of terrorism is not specifically systems-oriented in terms of targeting, it would well include as targets any and all materials required by humans that are capable of being destroyed or contaminated rather than merely disrupted. The potential employment of biological, chemical, nuclear, or other highly technological materials or weapons has been discussed at length, and it is not our purpose to review or seek to expand on such discussions.[32]

The mass destructive mode can target materials for acquisition and subsequent use against human targets; it can also target materials in such a way that the initial operation itself yields human victims or, less than that, the threat convincingly coerces governments. For instance, a group could cause release of radioactive materials through some form of sabotage or could first acquire such materials in an initial operation with a logistics objective for subsequent utilization in undertakings against human targets. Thus, there is a need to defend against both the overt attack and clandestine acquisition. Physical protection could become increasingly valueless if it does not secure all available sources of the needed materials. If terrorists possess the requisite resources, the targets and victims become one and the same—people.[33] If a group has already decided upon this terrorist mode, their desired impact is selfevident. Thus, the most attractive and critical target is the greatest concentration of people— densely populated major urban areas. The prospect of a holocaust in terms of the publicity generated is obvious and has already been a favorite subject for the film industry.

Risk Assessment

The counterbalance to the target attractiveness quotient is risk and its assessment in terms of the operation and the target selected. Terrorism has been and will continue to be a tactic of the weak in both a military and political sense. Due to their need to retain a positive, credible image, terrorists who see themselves as representing a constituency cannot afford defeats involving significant personnel or political losses. Thus, regardless of the attractiveness of a target, the group will not launch an operation when the assessed risks significantly outweigh the potential fruits of success. Presuming the current proportion of terrorists with an obvious concern over their mortality endures, one may reasonably also assume the entire notion of assessing operational risks will remain a valid criterion in their target selection processes.

In determining risk and target vulnerability, the terrorist will look at what defensive measures exist. If security is apparent (and with less-seasoned groups this is sufficient to deter) or convincing in its strength and overall capability to protect, the terrorist may assess his risks as relatively high. Even if the protection afforded *appears* to be excellent, a realistic risk assessment process is usually not a simple task to accomplish. The other component is the terrorists' assessment of their own capabilities in a possible confrontation with the security they have actually gauged. Thus, the prevailing attitude that obvious security measures are the best deterrent to preclude selection as a terrorist target remains essentially valid. One might ask what effect publicized efficiency in the physical security sector, as opposed to the emphasis on security weaknesses, might have with respect to terrorist calculations of risks involved. Terrorist successes in an environment that a government has publicly labelled secure may be more devastating in the long run than the absence of such assurances.

In the contemporary mode, the terrorists' risks are established. In the disruptive mode, now and within the foreseeable future, one would have to state that terrorists' risks are probably minimal, particularly in those societies with the greatest technological development and urbanization. At the same time, few cases have yet demonstrated terrorists' intentions or capabilities for deep penetration into industrial targets of the type envisioned. In the third or mass destruction mode, the risks again increase for the terrorist since some segments are gradually becoming energized to the potential damage and loss of life, which a viable employment of this technique could cause. Some measures already have been taken to guard against both attacks on and acquisition of these resources, and security development continues. These measures, however, have been directed primarily against the threat of overt, frontal assault. The potential for an "inside job" should be a very real concern.

People have been and will be terrorist targets and are not able to be fully secured in an open society. Their attractiveness has been based on target symbolism and the inherent value of human life. If technological systems replace people as targets, the security dilemma will not become any easier to solve since the number of potential nonhuman targets and their points of access are so vast that all cannot be completely protected. Their attractiveness will be assessed on the degree and extent of impact that their disruption might cause. In both the disruptive and mass destruction modes, technology provides countless possible targets. Its allure in terms of impact, publicity, and criticalness will be a function of terrorist motivation. A crucial question is whether incidents that inconvenience or disrupt rather than maim and kill can have the same impact. As technology provides targets, it also affords improvements in security, the application of which will continue to lag unless the point of consciously incorporating security into systems as they are being conceived, designed, and constructed is reached. Likewise, technology will provide the means to increase terrorist groups' operational sophistication. The essential balance among advances in security, target attractiveness, and terrorist capabilities may well remain constant, although all on an elevated plane. Technological interdependence among systems that could become targets will further increase system attractiveness to the disruption-minded terrorist, particularly if the possibility exists that the sabotage of one system may lead to problems within others in a domino chain of events.

The proliferation of technology as well as technological expertise places constant pressure on the reliability of physical security as a barrier to terrorist operations. In areas of high technology that are not dependent upon specific physical substances (for example, lasers), optimum physical security would have to include informational security such as constraints on the availability of scientific innovations and their applications. For example, the entire question surrounding genetic engineering (its potential for positive contributions to the sum of human knowledge) touches on this issue and must be recognized as carrying with it the necessity for adequate safeguards against any misappropriation for destructive ends. Another aspect of this particular issue centers on the tolerance of special interest groups, particularly the scientific community, with respect to restricting the free flow of ideas. The specter of state control or management of information looms at the other end of the continuum. In the final analysis, targets will continue to exist due to the impracticability of total security and will be available to terrorists in the future. Both the mode of terrorism and targets selected will reflect the motivation of the terrorist and his group. In terms of human casualties, the mode seemingly could range from "nonviolent" disruptive to mass destruction varieties.

Terrorist Motivation

Terrorism has been used when all else fails, and frustration peaks. We have seen the onset of a withering process in motivation based on systematic ideological schools of thought. Terrorist proponents articulating an adherence to Marxist, anarchist, or other defined ideologies are becoming fewer in number. At the same time, the number of terrorist "true believers"[34] remains fairly constant due to the community of those who oppose the same or similar things in many countries throughout the world. These purely negative motivations tend toward nihilism per se. They are grounded in an existentialism[35] that places emphasis on act(s) seemingly without attention to their "whatness" or nature. Terrorist violence is an act of the will. It is this same characteristic, of course, that always has separated terrorists from the orthodox Marxists who insist on orderly progression toward eventual proletarian revolution. One of the primary tenets of *most* mass movements is that the activists (usually intellectuals) are the vanguard of a constituency for whom they act. As motivation tends away from a positive ideology toward a nihilistic attitude, certain constraints normally characteristic of popularly oriented and ideologically based movements also will fade in importance. The concern of the nonideologically motivated focuses on the requirement for immediate action to alter existing conditions and not upon the creation of an ultimate utopia or the form it should take. While one previously fought for a constituency, the tendency is now basically just to fight. The successors to the Baader-Meinhof gang exhibit this trend more and more.[36]

With a constituency, either actual or perceived, nonselective or random terrorism can be counterproductive, leading to mass alienation and revulsion. In the contemporary mode, where such constituencies are presumed to exist or appear sought-after, this awareness was demonstrated well in the calculated orchestration of Black September terrorism between 1971 and 1973. Having forced the world to ask "Why the violence?"—the campaign (presumably undertaken for Palestinians) was halted in favor of letting international politics run its course. Other groups, however, attempt to use terrorism in order to win popular support for their aims. Thus, the Baader-Meinhof gang, which (as revealed in the writings of Ulrike Meinhof and Horst Mahler) realized it did not have popular support, tried to obtain such support by selective targeting and a cautious avoidance of harm to potential supporters and the common man. These illustrations point up the fact that moderating constraints have been imposed by the group itself, mindful of the need to avoid active popular assistance to the countering forces of governments. Accordingly, it is this idea of constituency that is crucial in weighing a group's motivation for escalation into mass disruptive or destructive terrorism. Neither appears likely to foster, or even retain, a significant level of support among people who heretofore have been unaffected, that is, who are in a spectator status. This loss or abandonment of a constituency can be one of the most important indicators that the group is willing to escalate its operations qualitatively into mass disruption or even perhaps mass destruction. In those few examples of would-be mass destruction operations or such declared intentions, it is significant that the perpetrators thus far have been sociopaths, pranksters, mentally disturbed persons, or others with no claim to either ideology or constituency.[37] With regard to group-based terrorism, an unanswered question remains: Why as yet have no catastrophic incidents occurred?

The basic allure of terrorism is one that we recognize, yet are extremely reluctant to admit openly. Terrorism works, in the short term at least. It is efficient and cost effective. Were it not working or inherently doomed to failure, the resources and urgency devoted to this problem could be more productively employed elsewhere. Other evidence of the realization that terrorism works can be found in increased hostage-taking (perhaps considered terrorism in ultimo in the minds of many laymen), by individuals with various personal grievances or mental problems. This "monkey see, monkey do" development would seem to indicate that a portion of the population,[38] which is not politically motivated or inveterately criminal, has turned to pseudoterrorism as a way out of frustrations brought on by various causes.

As the attitudes of various groups toward critical issues in society harden in terms of their resolve to defend a given point of view, terrorism probably will be considered more frequently as an alternative to merely surrendering to an opposing view or force. For example, when Concorde landing rights were granted in New York over the protests of area residents, some opponents probably gave at least passing thought to doing something to the object of their dismay: the aircraft itself. If such thinking were to culminate in an attack on the Concorde aircraft, the move from citizen concern to terrorist assault would have occurred over an issue that, for homeowners, is essentially apolitical. A similar "terrorist" gambit, if not solution, occurred in Washington D.C., in the Hanafi Muslim hostage-taking operation in March 1977.

Many issues and conflicts in the United States today have the potential for developing opposing views so resolutely held that terrorism appears a thinkable tactic in their furtherance. These include such areas as energy and its nuclear sector, the environment, ethnic conflicts and minority rights, labor disputes, inflation, and various types of shortages, to name a few. Again, consistent with the activist bent away from absolute rights and wrongs, the decision to engage in terrorism becomes one of weighing relative values. Is it more acceptable to endure the foreseen destruction of the ecological balance, for example, than to terrorize one segment of society in order to draw attention to a more costly possibility (morally and possibly financially)? In short, will ends that are essentially apolitical justify violent means?

Examination of the use or misuse of the term *terrorist organization* may be useful in this context. The word *organization* implies that individuals band together exclusively or primarily in order to practice terrorism. If terrorism is a tactical means subordinate to a primary, previously existing political objective, the primacy of the political objective(s) remains intact. Thus, the coinage *terrorist organization* and its usefulness are subject to serious question. It would appear that most, if not all, so-called terrorists espouse political objectives. With any increasing tendency toward nihilism as the primary motivation for the adoption of terrorist tactics, perhaps the term *terrorist organization* and its tactics versus strategic connotations will take on new shades of meaning. The likelihood is that terrorism will become both a pseudoideology for some groups with nihilist aims while other political groups will consider resorting to terrorism occasionally for its "attention getting" qualities. Terrorists in industrialized states appear to be so far from achieving their perceived political goals that they may well be losing sight of them entirely.

As with the present mode of terrorism, in disruptive or destructive terrorism, one basic aim will remain consistent—to cause a government or its agencies to overreact so as to alienate the populace that democratic governments exist to serve. While the terrorist trend toward nihilism grows, an inversely proportional disregard of the need for a constituency on the part of terrorists takes place. However, democratic governments themselves feel the need to act, aware of the needs and desires of their constituencies. Lacking the inducement of

governmental overreaction, the terrorist alternately seeks to prove
the establishment's inability to cope. Again, the future terrorist may
show little regard for his own constituency, if any. Instead, he may
concentrate on showing the government that its attempts are hopeless
and incapable of stemming the tide of a disruptive or destructive
campaign of terrorism.

The government is faced with the apparent dilemma of choosing
between nonselective retaliation, which will be the overreaction
sought by the terrorists, or flexible response, which may be doomed
to failure in its inadequacy. Obviously, the discriminate, reasoned
response is the ideal. But there may even be problems in convincing
the citizenry and the media that such is in fact the proper course,
given persistent, irritating disruption of systems and services due to
terrorist operations. Indeed, the quandary would be worsened if
officials are faced with the total elimination or contamination of a
residential area, town, or city. In this context, an effort devoted to
speculative analyses to aid in planning for both security precautions
and crisis management could be very useful.

Terrorist Capabilities

The gap between a terrorist group's desired capabilities and its
actual skills and resources is a crucial one. Having proposed some
operational possibilities under both the mass disruption and mass
destruction target alternatives, we turn our attention to the capabilities that would be necessary to carry out such acts. One point in these
considerations is very significant: even qualitative changes in terrorism do not necessarily require notable advances in acquiring or
developing new skills or resources. The inherent attractiveness of
terrorism lies in its simplicity. Tremendous expertise and large
amounts of material or manpower are not required. Noted earlier was
the qualitative change into transnational terrorism. This move by the
PFLP was without any particular increase in skills or resources. It
centered on exploitation of certain otherwise criminal practices
(kidnap for ransom, extortion). These techniques were employed
against the enemy (Israel) at its weakest points ("third country operations" and against "nonneutral" targets). They were carried out with
reliance on the standard clandestine tradecraft of the espionage agent.
The fact is that with these exceptions terrorists have not been particularly creative or inventive.

The potential for operational creativity among terrorists is afforded by our technological advances and increasing reliance on
sophisticated systems. To take advantage of technology targets,

terrorists will need some technological knowledge in order to locate and disrupt systems. Various possible sources of such information exist. Terrorists can include persons with the requisite academic training or vocational experience. Turkish and Iranian terrorist groups were cited earlier as having a considerable number of such people already in their ranks. Other avenues include recruiting persons with the necessary knowledge, obtaining witting or unwitting cooperation of experts,[39] coercing persons to aid the terrorists in their endeavor, or even obtaining training or knowledge with specific operations already in mind. The potential for coercive, monetary, or ideological recruitments and the idea of "terrorists-in-place" are worthy of separate study as spin-offs from the worlds of intelligence, counterintelligence, and espionage.

Before ascribing any real limitations to terrorists' potential in the area of learning about technologies, one should recall that most of those seen thus far have university training and are worldly-wise. Their resourcefulness and willingness to commit themselves to study is evidenced in the dispersion of terrorist literature such as the *Anarchist Cookbook* and the works of Carlos Marighella, Abraham Guillen, Regis Debray, and others.[40] Exploitation of existing military training publications in the use of weapons, explosives, and partisan warfare tactics is commonplace. The so-called underground press focuses on and is a vehicle for dissemination of much of this information. In his prison-circular correspondence, Andreas Baader referred his colleagues on the outside to a multivolume East German work on explosives fabrication.[41] Irish terrorists have long extracted sufficient chemicals from fertilizers to circumvent legal prohibitions on explosive substances and build their own devices. Why should this type of ingenuity somehow decrease in the targeting of more advanced technologies? While overestimating terrorist capabilities has its faults, some of which already may have cost millions of dollars in the security sector, the real dangers lie in underestimating their ingenuity and resourcefulness. The same applies in the area of the terrorists' own emphasis on outflanking counterterrorist methods and advances. Once again, the Baader-Meinhof group is an excellent example of incarcerated and other terrorists routinely studying professional law enforcement journals where much of the countermeasures discussion is carried on.[42] The vast amount of open academic discussion in this area presumably is of interest to terrorists as well. We will return to this dilemma in our observations.

In the area of weapons and resources potentially available to future terrorists, one can envision a spectrum from carpenters' tools to the most sophisticated man-portable missiles. While concerns center on the SA-7, the Redeye, its second generation (the Stinger), and others, disruptive organizations will doubtless be most dependent upon excellent intelligence and target access. If a group can locate target vulnerability in a system (be it a power grid, relay point, or whatever), then its problem is to gain access through ruse or force. Thus far, success in such penetration has not been plentiful. Once a penetration has been made, if one is indeed necessary, then wire cutters, a small charge, or even foreign matter may trigger the desired disruption. In mass destruction terrorism, the necessary resources are those discussed above and others like them.

Another resource available to terrorists, and already in increasing use, is cooperation. They learn from each other around the world, directly through training and exchange of personnel or indirectly through the media, handbooks, and, of course, the entertainment industry. Terrorist "technology transfer" has been documented continually. Letter bombs, used by the Cubans in the 1960s, were adopted by Palestinians and the IRA in 1972-1973; the technique was not even original with the Cubans. Other examples of technology transfer include the IRA duplication of the Carrero-Blanco operation in Dublin, the use of people's prisons, and so on. The basic types of operations are not endless and variations on proven, successful techniques are the rule in terrorism at present.

We will doubtless see the creation of at least a limited division of labor, especially where certain groups or individuals perform a specific operational or support task very well. This may become a necessity in cases where resources or manpower shrink, such as occurred following the Baader-Meinhof demise in June 1972 and may be underway in Argentina, Iran, and Japan. Refinements in false documentation, clandestine communications, and other tradecraft will occur as necessity proves to be the mother of invention. Experience remains the best teacher. The dry-run operation, practice session, and test explosion presumably will continue, even in disruptive or mass destruction terrorism to some extent, and may be communicated to use more frequently by the terrorists in order to prove their credibility and to extort concessions lest the "real" operation be launched.

Terrorist Groups

Having sketched two qualitatively new terrorist target alternatives and some of the attending motivations and resources for such operations, we will now focus on terrorist groups. We must ask ourselves if and how terrorist groups in the future will differ from those we see today. Of equal interest are some preliminary judgments as to which types of current groups appear most likely and capable of escalation into mass disruption or destruction terrorism.

It appears likely that fewer tightly structured groups with the longevity of the IRA or PFLP will emerge. Assuming ideological motivation will yield more to a nihilist attitude, larger numbers of smaller, perhaps fleeting, groups might be expected to appear and try their hands at the terrorist approach. In addition, other groups not primarily of a preconceived political persuasion will resort to its use on a selected basis. The complexity of intergroup links will grow as single operators change their affiliations, are exchanged, or seek new contacts. The already difficult task of intelligence collection against terrorists will be complicated even more by such developments. Groups showing the greatest innovation and resolve in the operational arena will attain a level of prestige, as did the PFLP with its transnational acts, and be able to select from a pool of willing recruits or transfers from other groups. Solution of the Palestine question, which Rejection Front elements doubtless will find unacceptable, will not eliminate certain trends toward cohesion and cooperation. Success becomes its own reward and terrorists, both actual and potential, will continue to seek ties with "winners." In fact, ad hoc competition among groups for media attention and recognition could well be one external stimulus for escalation into mass disruption or mass destruction operations.

Group configurations may be altered in the sense that terrorists who do not, in fact, participate in operations may no longer be acceptable in leadership ranks. People like Shigenobu Fusako, Abu Daoud, and the like may be forced to accept commando risks in order to claim leadership rights. As mentioned above, while the number of groups may grow, they will presumably be smaller and could conceivably consist of single cells of only several individuals. Such a pool of operatives floating among "revolutionary cells" may be the current state of affairs in West Germany. Women, who have increasingly entered the operational sphere—particularly among German and IRA groups—will more often participate in operations and be group leaders. The precedents have long been established for including women as well as for lowering the entry age for terrorist involvement. Teenage terrorists already have appeared within IRA and Palestinian ranks in more than isolated instances.

Multinational groups, such as we already have witnessed around Carlos and most recently in the arrests in April 1977 in Sweden, may very well be quite common in the coming years. Expansion in the geographic breadth and general accessibility of support networks can be expected with organizations such as the Fourth International playing a larger role. Aside from a tendency toward younger terrorists and a larger percentage of women, the characteristics of the terrorist sociological profile of today will remain the same. One alteration could be indicated by a trend underway in Italy to draw increasingly on the participation of professional criminals in terrorist undertakings. The combination of political activists and criminals is already evident in the Armed Proletarian Nuclei and Ordine Nuovo. Other groups, such as the now defunct Symbionese Liberation Army in the United States, have sought to recruit fellow inmates while in prison. This is also true of German groups and was evident in the JRA request for release of non-JRA criminals in the October 1977 hijacking.

Terrorist bases of operation will continue to be largely in urban areas, aside from safe locations in sympathetic sponsor states. The possibility of some groups operating against cities from more rural areas exists (Baader suggested it and Latin American groups in countries with uninhabited hinterlands do so now), but the urban environment lends itself to good cover if security is practiced judiciously. It appears obvious that elimination of external safe havens will not solve the terrorist problem in its entirety.

If such developments as we have extrapolated indeed occur, the role of intelligence will be increasingly significant. At the same time, its functions will be much more complicated. If speculative approaches are pursued with reference to optimum terrorist targeting possibilities, it will fall to conventional intelligence activities to determine the status of any and all groups with respect to the skills and resources needed to escalate operationally. Intelligence analysis coupled with speculative models will be called on to verify the convergence between presumed terrorist objectives and estimated capabilities and to postulate credible intentions. Intelligence collectors and analyzers will have to be watchful for qualitative (revolutionary) changes in capabilities while seeking to anticipate short-term intentions. While cogent speculation can add new insights and vastly aid planning, traditional analysis will retain its premier position in the day-to-day confrontation with terrorism.

Among terrorist groups currently operating, entities whose constituencies are vague or nonexistent and whose motivation is basically nihilist offer the most likely candidates for escalation into disruptive terrorism. These could include the JRA, West German groups, and even fledgling American groups (such as the New World Liberation Front and Weather Underground), whose ideological underpinnings are essentially anarchist. These groups emerged from so-called socialist student federations in the late 1960s. German groups, for instance, have destroyed mass transit automated ticket venders and issued counterfeit tickets. Palestinian groups could opt for such a qualitative change, but this decision would no doubt be based on a significant setback in the international political arena. Preceding the 1973-1974 energy crisis, Black September targeted the petroleum industry more than most observers realize. Transnational operations have served the Palestinians reasonably well and continue to be efficient and manageable. Other national groups that have, or had, the resourcefulness to engage in large-scale disruption operations include the Revolutionary People's Army and Montoneros in Argentina and the now inactive Uruguayan Tupamaros.

No extant groups appear on the verge of using mass destruction operations. Despite the lack of present indicators, crisis planning should proceed on the basis that such a potentiality does exist, at least in the minds of some terrorist groups. Perhaps the most severe test for us in the entire spectrum of mass destruction terrorism will be the response to what will have been determined to be a technically credible threat to kill thousands.

Crisis Management: Nontechnical Threat Assessment

The previous discussion ends with the observation that dealing with threats of either massive disruption or destruction, which scientific experts have determined to be technically credible, may well be our most difficult task. Accordingly, let us for argument's sake postulate that a government has received a technically credible threat. Those making it threaten to perpetrate massive disruption or destruction with so many casualties that the government involved must weigh seriously full or partial fulfillment of the terrorist demands. The question of technical credibility has been answered. What the terrorist says he can and/or will do is credible. At the same time, the act has not been perpetrated. Perhaps only a demonstration attack of the type alluded to earlier has been carried out. The extortion dilemma remains. This constitutes a hostage-taking in which the government is both the hostage and would-be negotiator.

One German commentator has captured well the essence of this key dilemma with these words:

> it stands to reason that a state which, in pursuing small terrorist groups, is forced to permanently make use of a seemingly excessive police force and numerous other related preventive and defensive measures will not win many friends, even if one disregards the enormous cost for which the citizen has to foot the bill. . . . This is particularly true in cases of false alarms which fit perfectly into the concept of the urban guerrilla. The fact that a determined group can force the state apparatus to follow up every imaginable clue, to implement every conceivable preventive measure—regardless of how disrupting and costly it might be—all this demonstrates the strength of the guerrilla concept. A telephone call suffices to stop an express train, to evacuate a skyscraper or a stadium, or to switch off the electrical supply. *The actions and above all the feigned actions of the guerrilla force the state to overreact. The guerrilla can thus force the state to react to pinpricks or even mere threats in a manner which must eventually discredit it in the eyes of the citizens whom it is trying to protect.*[43]

Extortion of the type for which we have greatest concern relies on threats of massive disruption or destruction. The terrorists will seek to maximize the fear, coercion, and intimidation they can create. At the same time, threat credibility will be a primary consideration—both technical and personal. If the threat is carelessly overstated or implausible for any reason, its credibility will be called into question. The government or other recipient of the threat will not readily submit to coercion. How are we to determine whether the threat communicator will in fact execute the feared act?

This entire area of nontechnical assessment of the group or individual communicating the coercive threat is one deserving a great deal of research. How do we assess whether a group that presumably has a high-order operational capability or mass disruptive potential will, in fact, resort to its use? What characteristics of individual terrorists and groups exist or can be determined to aid us in assessing probability of execution, hoax potential, level of resolve, willingness to negotiate, motivation, and so on? In general, how do we know when to call the terrorists' bluff and when to negotiate or consider entering some other relationship with them rather than suffering the *possible* consequences of a mass disruption or destructive act?

Throughout this discussion we have stressed the obvious, yet crucial, notion that intentions generally remain unknown to us as we seek to cope with terrorist groups and their operations. Despite hypnosis, extrasensory perception, palmistry, and other forms of "seeing," we have yet to be able to read men's minds. It is not until ideas, desires, intentions, and fears are articulated that they become known. So it is with extortion threats. Once uttered in whatever form, they obtain the status of a communication using language. In many incidents we may only have the contents of the threat communication itself from which to work.[44] Its authorship may not be claimed by a person or group at all; the professed communicator may remain unknown or may blame the threat on another person or group. In such an instance, one must question the text itself as well as relate it to a data base of previous threats.[45] Key roles in dealing with this model or case type would go to psycholinguists, sociologists, voice analysts, graphologists, forensic and behavioral psychologists, criminologists, and perhaps anthropologists.

Working primarily with the text, and using known terrorist writings as well as other threat communications, those involved will need to answer a multitude of difficult questions: the nature of the threat itself in all its components, what the threat reveals about its perpetrators (regardless of any previous reporting on them), and the motivation for the threat.[46] Also of concern are the mental and sociological characteristics of the terrorists; their attitudes toward communication and negotiation; and their operational history, modus operandi, sophistication, and leadership. Equally critical are questions concerning their dedication and ideas about death, their grievances, and even the future course of their efforts. Are they desperate, doomed, or even intent on martyrdom? Keeping in mind the time constraints in crisis situations, one must make a maximum effort to pursue all lines of questioning until each response is properly evaluated. Some of the smallest aspects of grammar or word choice may reveal key traits to aid identification of those communicating the threat. Support to the crisis manager must include determination of any tactical opportunities for buying time as well as intelligence adequate and timely enough to favorably resolve the entire incident.

With only the text of the threat available and no prior data on the threat communicator, the assessment maker must focus on the form and content of the communication itself. By their very nature, human language and linguistics (its "science") are unique. Language alone among the subjects of science can prevaricate. No other phenomenon in nature can reveal itself in one form but actually mean another. Were this not the case, the whole question of assessing threats from the standpoint of questioning likelihood of execution would be moot. In such a case, any threat to act always would be executed. Webster's definition of "threat" reads: "A statement or expression of intention to hurt, destroy, punish, etc."

In instances where the identity, background, group affiliation, and motivation of terrorist threat communicators is known, we can call upon intelligence data and analytical assessments to aid in answering some questions. It is the proper function of intelligence to be preemptive and to monitor group activities and capabilities as they occur. Composite analyses of groups can and must be drawn up on a continuing basis to support decision making in crises. Incident or crisis management, on the other hand, is reactive in approach and focuses on a single instance. While using intelligence assessments of the group(s) involved, the crisis manager must not rely solely on such group-oriented assessments. The individual terrorists may indeed not act in accord with the group's dictates or established patterns.[47] We must not be deluded into assuming that the lack of precedent in some way constitutes an argument against probable execution. Just because the German remnants of the Baader-Meinhof had not used mass destruction thus far, it was not considered prudent to dismiss the questionable relationship between the terrorist Hans-Joachim Klein and nuclear physicist Dr. Klaus Traube, as noted previously. The Black September terrorists who, in December 1972, opted in favor of what has become known as the "Bangkok solution"[48] certainly defied group policy in doing so.

While this discussion has centered on incident management questions, terrorist threat data obviously emanates from intelligence analysis of patterns and trends in operations, targeting, and modus operandi. Threats, therefore, can exist short of some form of overt communication. A known capability, for intelligence analysts, constitutes a threat, communicated or not. However, as in the context of strategic military deterrence, an adversary cannot be intimidated by something of which he is totally unaware. The fear that arises from knowing only part of what one would hope to know about an adversary is central. Terrorists recognize this and intimidate via articulated threats.

In seeking to assess the credibility of a threat in terms of the terrorists' resolve to execute it, we must turn again a priori to group analysis focusing on motivation. We said earlier that constituencies moderate terrorist operations. Most ideologies proceed on the basis of larger constituencies whose lot is to be bettered. The stronger the perceived bond with a constituency, the less likely a group is to engage in mass destruction simply because it may affect that constituency, either physically, morally, or otherwise. However, temporary mass disruption is still thinkable in the context of a constituency. Accordingly, let us consider briefly four tentative group models with respect to motivation and constituency, make-up, leadership, size, and outside cooperation.

The first is the nationalist/ethnic separatist group whose motivation lies in creating an autonomous nation state for members of an ethnic minority (its constituency). Such terrorist groups (for example, the IRA, ETA, Palestinians, Bretons, and so on) are led by political figures who could be expected to head eventual states. Examples include Yasir Arafat, Ben Bella, Menachem Begin, and George Grivas. These groups vary in size depending on the size of the minority itself, the presence of ideologues and foreign allies in their midst, and the level of friction between the minority and the superimposed power. On the surface, such groups would appear willing to kill thousands for their purposes. They can rely on assistance from international apparats that aid "national liberation" struggles.

A second group type is ideological (Marxist, Maoist, fascist, and so on) and may or may not include hardened criminals. The Italian Armed Proletarian Nuclei and Ordine Nuovo have been examples of such a mixture. As ideological true believers, they seemingly would avoid harming the "little man" via disruption and mass destruction, unless either operational alternative could have a predominantly upper-class or industrial target. Leadership in this group type still resides with the articulate ideologues and standout operational performers. The group is composed of highly intelligent, well-educated middle-class men and women who correspond well with the sociological profile sketched earlier. Again, international procommunist or revolutionary apparats and sympathetic states will assist to some extent.

A third group type, and for our purposes the most enigmatic, is the nihilist group. Some of its members may be criminals, as in the Symbionese Liberation Army in the United States. They are bent on destruction along the lines of the once-heard call by black militants in the United States: "Burn, baby, burn!" While moral qualms at killing masses of people may exist, the necessity for a constituency and some eventual political reckoning is generally absent. Destruction is seen as good because it rids the world of what ails it. This type of rationale was seen in 1970 and 1971 in the first contemporary German terrorist group to emerge—the Socialist Patients' Collective (SPK). The SPK was composed of mental patients in Heidelberg, led by the psychiatrist Dr. Wolfgang Huber.[49] Huber and his wife convinced some of his patients that society made them ill and to cure themselves they must in essence destroy the cause— society. This nihilist thrust also garnered some sympathetic student recruits. Although the group met an early demise, many of its cadre floated smoothly into the Baader-Meinhof group where a thin veil of Marxism supplied by Ulrike Meinhof and Horst Mahler cloaked an otherwise nihilist group. For the nihilist, terrorism becomes the object of his true belief—an ideology of sorts. Apparats such as the Fourth International may lend support.

A fourth possible group type is that of the occasional users of terrorism, most of whom may well be issue-oriented interest groups. Their resort to terrorism is incumbent upon certain segments becoming overly frustrated with peaceful methods "within the system" and engaging in a calculated application of terrorism to regain political momentum, recognition, or leverage. A constituency is always present and weighs against execution of high-order actions. Whether achieved or not, the intention generally is to abandon terrorism as soon as certain limited tactical goals have been achieved. In terms of probability, this type of short-term terrorist involvement is least likely to perpetrate high-order disruption or destruction. It also is less likely to make and exploit contacts with other terrorist groups and support apparats due to its presumably fleeting affair with terrorist tactics.

Examination of the phenomenon of terrorism from both the analytical and speculative points of view and sketches of four tentative models of future terrorist groups are logically followed by questions of practical application and prognosis. Without claiming to exhaust the possibilities or even touch on all key points, let us consider some indicators—outside the technical sphere—that may be harbingers of escalation into either mass disruptive or mass destructive terrorist operations. As pointed out earlier, the latter may be actual or threatened.

In monitoring group motivations, we must be mindful of trends away from constituency relationships toward nihilism. Is the group that claims to be Marxist or nationalist, for example, based really on ideology or simply on shared negative attitudes, failures, rejections, frustrations, and so on? In its writings, communiques, or statements, is the group increasingly disdainful of the people, class, or ethnic group for which they earlier claimed to be fighting? Is ego gratification, hunger for power, or financial aggrandizement more and more the center of their activities, targeting, and demands? Can one assume that motivations such as money and muscle-flexing per se are indicators that a group is less likely to execute a threat due to the lack of overriding political motives? Or is it likely that, lacking constituencies, they may indeed escalate and execute?

Group size is an important indicator to watch. With the proliferation of smaller groups, competition for prestige and media attention may force such groups to escalate or fade. If such small groups have been reduced through police or military counteroffensives, they may be forced to seek greater impact from each operation due to severely limited resources or loss of self-esteem. Alliances with other groups, international apparats, and support states are avenues for depleted cadres to increase group vitality. Are surrogate relationships developing where one or more groups act for a sponsor state or even perform operations that another group may desire but would need to disclaim? Are police or right-wing counterterrorists so oppressive that the resolve and desire for retribution within a group grow rather than decline.

Despite the complexity of the task, we must look at individuals as well as groups. Who composes a group? Does a group of both sexes and various nationalities have less emotional stability than a more homogeneous one? With the influx of women into operational roles we may see more fanaticism and emotionally driven activists.[50] The younger the membership, the less selective the targeting becomes. As emotional maturity decreases, the "responsible" terrorist tends to vanish. Operations increase quantitatively; leadership is less able to control operational personnel. Generally, the tempered approach to operations appears to be likely to fade as maturity decreases.

We must follow closely any moves to coopt or recruit exploitable scientists and technicians. Can we let go unnoticed any unusual attempts to obtain information on systems or substances that are essential to the national order? At the same time the availability of such data, particularly in the United States, is tremendous. Obviously, attempts to buy, steal, or create sophisticated weaponry or highly lethal substances are of great concern. A tactical change to attacks on hardened targets warrants close scrutiny. The same is true of any series of unclaimed or anonymous acts. What about strange incidents of a few unexplained deaths from unknown but suspicious causes or even very short periods of disruption of essential systems? Occurrences similar to Legionnaires' disease and the New York blackouts are most often cited as models. Could these be dry-run high-order operations? Moves out of densely populated areas, which coincide with other indicators, may be a sign that terrorists are clearing a target area. The presence of target sketches, gas masks, or other paraphernalia may be telltale signs of pending escalation. Are intelligence analysts aware of and tracking fictional treatments of terrorism along with the literatures of terrorism and the extremist

press? Are terrorists duplicating fictional scenarios? Are they dis-
cussing counterterrorist literature and methods? In short, do they
read our discussions about them?

One of the most disturbing potential developments could be the
appearance of a series of presumed terrorist incidents to which no
one lays claim. How can we label an act as terrorist in origin if no
perpetrator claims credit or can be tied to the incident? At the same
time, a nihilist group has no political need to seek recognition for
its activities. It has no constituency and destruction/disruption are,
for it, strategic objectives, not intermediate goals. In a sense, claims
made for an incident tend to violate operational security. Can we be
content with less than totally acceptable explanations of such incidents if possible terrorist motivation has been discounted? Nihilists,
it would seem, find ample satisfaction in the success of destruction
itself.

These are some of the indicators that bear watching. Chief among
them remain motivation and constituency; group size and make-up;
the effects of countering efforts and techniques; and attempts to
acquire technical expertise via recruitment, coercion, or education.
An ordered approach to this crucial area of research will revolve
around the gaming of well-considered operational scenarios using
group models and speculatively derived optimal targets. The post-
mortem on such "terrorist games" should reveal answers to some of
our concerns as well as many more valid questions for intelligence,
security, and crisis management to contemplate. The role of the
pseudoterrorists and social scientists in this endeavor is both vital and
full of promise.

In seeking to determine the likelihood that a mass disruptive or
destructive threat will be executed, we must ask ourselves what the
terrorists hope to achieve. Will such an act, once executed, aid that
objective? Is goal attainment more likely, or solely possible, through
successful extortion rather than operational execution? We must find
out as much as possible about the threat communicators, their backgrounds, known affiliates, and above all their motivations. The
latter may in fact change or multiply. Pessimists could argue that
the pool of potential terrorists includes all of mankind. Use of refined
analytical models of group/motivation types seems to be worth our
attention. There is no room for error in this regard. Indeed, the
social sciences and their practitioners may find a new significance,
unforeseen needs, and practical applications for their body of knowledge and abilities. The policymakers will have to call upon and
depend upon the skill of social scientists once the technical credibility

of a threat has been established. How likely are responsible officials to accept such assessments from experts outside the world of the so-called hard, empirical, or quantitative sciences? Do linguists and sociologists have a place on terrorism crisis management staffs? Are there potential profiles or models that can help us sort out the suicidal or nihilist terrorists from those more likely to accept negotiation or even compromise? All of these questions demand close examination and study if we are to remove the guesswork from decision making in the face of technically credible, high-order terrorist threats. In this area of threat perpetration, the terrorist retains the offensive. Inventiveness and success in creating fear—the fear inherent in the awesome responsibility of decision makers faced with an extortion threat involving the fate of thousands—is his or her primary avenue of access to political power.

In the beginning of this discussion we consciously included the aspect of threatened violence as a large part of our definition of terrorism. Assuming technical credibility to accomplish a specific act is established or at least cannot be discounted, its threatened use is probably terrorism's greatest tool. Extortion and intimidation maximize the pressures on the fragile institution of democratic government. This results from terrorist recognition that our weakest area of information and analysis centers on true motivation and intentions. The paradox of mass disruptive or destructive extortion revolves around our having been told specifically what a group's intentions are. In this case, where intentions are reported overtly by the terrorist himself rather than clandestinely via intelligence collection, the assessment or judgment required is one that we otherwise consider impossible to make: Will the terrorists do what they can and say they will do? The time to consider approaches to this ever-present quandary is now—prior to the actual moment of truth for the crisis manager and his team. If we are to out-invent the terrorist, we must defuse the virtually unlimited coercive potential of threatened mass disruption or destruction now available. We must develop models for inquiry, working intelligence composites of groups and their motivations, and the research mechanisms to anticipate cultural, sociological, and psychological changes among present and future terrorist groups.

Observations

As pointed out, we see the likelihood of terrorism increasingly becoming an end in itself. This would result from a nihilist attitude that already appears to be quite prevalent over other actually ideological motivations. As terrorism loses its tactic status in favor of a strategic and/or philosophical one, it tends toward elevation to an "ism" among existing ideologies. This same trend is fed by the prestige inherent in success and the recognition that inventive terrorist operations may be expected to reap. Such recognition will be both notoriety and fame, depending upon the observer's status.

In the area of creativity and ingenuity, the terrorists' potential hardly has been scratched. Aside from mass destruction, which although worrisome still appears less likely, the potential havoc to be wrought with reasonably simple disruptive operations is virtually unlimited. It is also nearly untapped thus far. Terrorists who either lose or drop a primarily political objective and are willing to endure alienation and even disgust will resort to disruptive operations and consider small-scale destruction operations using high-technology or bacteriological resources. In the latter instance, they may either seek to demonstrate their capabilities in a limited way in order to coerce victims and governments to meet demands or may simply want to prove their power through perpetrating vast destruction. They may even be well-thinking persons who have sought to change what they view as incorrect and unwise decisions or policies, but were ignored or overruled. Most current terrorists rationalize their acts as justifiable, whether they believe so morally or not. The notion of a terrorist group composed of disgruntled scientists who seek to demonstrate how vulnerable to terrorism we all are by simulating their own terrorist acts is not unthinkable by any means.

One of the areas where our preparation is weakest is that of assessing the likelihood that a technically credible threat to inflict devastating disruption or mass casualties will actually be executed. We must devote our attention and resources to analyses and model construction of terrorist motivational, behavioral, and psychological typologies. The purpose of such an endeavor is to improve the analytical methodology in an area where technical expertise and quantitative approaches may never be of any avail. The social scientist, whose exactitude has occasionally been adversely compared with that of the natural and physical scientists, has a large role to play in crisis management. Decision makers will rely on their expertise while recognizing the inherent limits of sciences whose object of study is man, his mind, his language, and his social behavior.

Having provided some thoughts using a speculative approach, we have one misgiving. We have illustrated in several contexts the resourcefulness of terrorists in studying what is written about them and how best to deal with them. They obviously do not lack their own "good" ideas. If a speculative approach is to be of benefit to those of us outside the terrorist camp, then its conduct as well as its output must be handled with discretion similar to that used for traditional intelligence analysis. We will not succeed in "out-inventing" the terrorist if we disclose each card (or conclusion) as it is drawn.

Notes

1. Robert H. Kupperman and Harvey A. Smith, "What To Do Until The Terrorist Comes," 5 April 1977, p. 10.

2. Beyond this abstract definition, limitations that exclude both civil disorders and military confrontations need to be added. "Political" is understood in this usage to connote the entire range of social, economic, religious, ethnic, and governmental factors impacting on a body politic, stressing the notions of power and influence. The ideal definition is one that both the adherents and abhorrers of terrorism could agree upon.

3. In May 1972, the "national" Baader-Meinhof nucleus bombed U.S. Army buildings in Frankfurt and Heidelberg, resulting in the deaths of four U.S. Army members. In June and December 1976, a group or groups calling themselves the Revolutionary Cell again bombed two U.S. military officers' clubs in West Germany, completely destroying a million dollar facility at Rhein-Main Air Base. Since 1972, four high-ranking U.S. officers have been attacked in Teheran by Iranian terrorists. Three were killed and a general officer was seriously injured. These same "national" terrorists assassinated three American business officials of Rockwell International on 28 August 1976. The Latin American context yields an even greater pool of examples showing the foreign impact that such groups have had.

4. An example of the basic disagreement was reported by the Foreign Broadcast Information Service (FBIS) from *Izvestiya*, 30 March 1977, p. 1: "Expounding the USSR's principled position to the [UN Special Commission on Terrorism], the Soviet representative emphasized that the Soviet Union is opposed to acts of terrorism which disrupt the diplomatic activities of states and their representatives, transport communications between them and the normal course of international contacts and meetings. *It is quite inadmissible, he pointed out, to extend the concept of 'international terrorism' to the national liberation struggle, to actions offering*

resistance to an aggressor on territories occupied by him and to working people's demonstrations for their rights against oppression by exploiters." [Emphasis added.] This position was reiterated by a number of communist powers during the October/November 1977 Belgrade review of the Helsinki agreement. FBIS quoted the 28 October 1977 TANJUG report citing the Polish statement that Poland "is opposed to double standards in the struggle against terrorism, since some forms of this violence are occasionally explained with political motives."

5. The Japanese Red Army is perhaps the best example of the variance in modus operandi. In six operations to date, it has executed two hijackings, one explosives attack, one automatic weapons attack, and three hostage seizures, the latter spawning one secondary operation. Their targets have included Israel, Japan, the United States, France, Sweden, and Lebanon. Operations sites have ranged from India, Bangladesh, Malaysia, and Singapore to Sweden, France, West Germany, Israel, and Kuwait. While one might like to identify hostage-taking as a key JRA technique, one must also note that each hostage operation has included freeing JRA terrorists as part of its motivation. For an excellent summary article on the JRA, see "Terror: Behind the Red Army," *Asiaweek*, 26 November 1976, pp. 26-31.

6. The flight, a 707 jet carrying thirty-one passengers and a crew of ten, was diverted to Algeria by the hijackers who demanded release of Palestinian guerrillas held in Israel in return for the plane and its passengers.

7. "Action cadre" refers to the innermost circle of a terrorist group, those persons who actually perpetrate the terrorist act, such as bombers, hijackers, assassins, and so on.

8. Charles A. Russell, "Transnational Terrorism," *Air University Review*, January/February 1976, pp. 31-32.

9. Ibid., pp. 28-29.

10. Ibid., pp. 29-32.

11. Israeli Defense Forces press release, "The Terrorists' Connections in Foreign Underground Organizations," 16 November 1976.

12. This profile is based on information concerning some 350 known terrorists from eighteen different groups involving eleven nationalities. The data was drawn largely from foreign press reporting 1968 to 1976 and is discussed in Charles A. Russell and Bowman H. Miller, "Profile of a Terrorist," *Terrorism: An International Journal*, Vol. 1, No. 1 (November 1977).

13. For purposes of this discussion, "nihilism" is used in a non-

doctrinaire sense and connotes the desire for violence and destruction as ends in themselves.

14. The October 1977 Arab seizure of a Lufthansa jet departing Mallorca, designed to increase the pressures engendered through the kidnapping of Hanns-Martin Schleyer and ending in the Mogadishu commando success, marked the first purely Arab terrorist act on behalf of a non-Palestinian counterpart.

15. See "Ich bin der beruehmte Carlos," *Der Spiegel*, 2 August 1976, and Israeli Defense Forces press release, op. cit.

16. Hans Josef Horchem, *Extremisten in einer selbstbewussten Demokratie*, Herderbuecherei, Freiburg, 1975, p. 29.

17. See also John Barron, *KGB: The Secret Work of Soviet Secret Agents*, Reader's Digest Press, New York, 1974, pp. 239-246.

18. "The State Department has accused Libya, Iraq, South Yemen, and Somalia of actively supporting terrorist groups, according to congressional correspondence made public yesterday." (*The Washington Post*, 9 May 1977, p. A10).

19. See "ETA va a clase en Argelia," *Dia* 32, 24 December 1976; "Argelia no tiene vinculación con el Grapo, segun un portavoz de la Embajada en Madrid," *Ya*, 1 February 1977, p. 12.

20. *Milliyet Halk Gazetesi* (Istanbul), 12 August 1976, pp. 1-3; and "Istanbul Governor: Hijackers Received Instructions in Libya," *FBIS*, reporting Ankara Radio, 12 August 1976, p. T-6.

21. Israeli Defense Forces press release, op. cit.

22. See "Le patron des réseaux d'aide aux terroristes," *Le Point* (Paris), 21 June 1976.

23. See Walter Laqueur, *Terrorism*, Little, Brown and Co., Boston, 1977, pp. 49-53.

24. This observation was the focus of Dr. Ted R. Gurr's presentation at the Conference on International Terrorism hosted by the Department of State on 25-26 March 1976. Dr. Gurr's research, based on data concerning terrorism in eighty-seven nations from 1961 to 1970, indicated approximately 4,600 total deaths, fewer than 2,000 from the four most violent campaigns. No single incident has thus far claimed as many as 100 lives.

25. Brian M. Jenkins, *International Terrorism: A New Kind of Warfare*, RAND Publication P-5261, June 1974, p. 4.

26. This nonparticularized target composition was an important aspect in the 23 July 1968 PFLP hijacking previously mentioned. Dr. Habbash later articulated the PFLP's "two camp" proposition that there are no neutrals; everyone is either part of the solution or part of the problem. This notion too attends the quantum leap

character of the transnational "third country operation" concept.

27. Jenkins, op. cit.

28. A poll of German citizens taken by the Emnid-Institute following the Schleyer murder revealed 61 percent feel helpless against terrorism since total protection is inconceivable. (*Die Welt*, 31 October 1977, p. 2)

29. An interesting comparison and contrast might be made between the PFLP and BSO in this context. The former was first in transnational operations, the latter second. The PFLP was skyjacking-oriented; the BSO tended toward assassination. While both received international press attention and their activities were seen as furthering "the cause," we are left with the question of whether their campaigns were (are) essentially a vying for leadership within the Palestinian "constituency."

30. One of the statements to this effect by terrorists themselves is in a Basque ETA training manual quoted in *Blanco y Negro*, 29 June–5 July 1977, p. 27: "The enemy, altogether, is a thousand times stronger than we are. But each time we attack, at that very moment and place, we are stronger than he is. The enemy, as a massive animal, stung by many bees, is infuriated to the point of uncontrollable rage, and strikes out blindly to the left and right—on every side. At this point we have achieved one of our major objectives; forcing him to commit a thousand atrocities and brutal acts. The majority of his victims are innocent. Then the people, to this point more or less passive and waiting, become indignant and in reaction turn to us. We could not hope for a better outcome." (Translation by C. A. Russell.)

31. Jenkins, op. cit.

32. See also R. W. Mengel, "Terrorism and New Technologies of Destruction: An Overview of the Potential Risk," in *Disorders and Terrorism: Report of the Task Force on Disorders and Terrorism* (Appendix 2), U.S. Government Printing Office, 1977, pp. 443-473; Brian M. Jenkins, "Will Terrorists Go Nuclear?" California Seminar on Foreign Policy and Arms Control, January 1976, and "The Potential For Nuclear Terrorism," RAND Publication P-5876, May 1977; and Martha C. Hutchinson, "Defining Future Threats: Terrorist and Nuclear Proliferation" and "Terrorism and the Diffusion of Nuclear Power," papers delivered during 1976.

33. In countries where governments are not freely elected, the decision-making process in the face of coercion and intimidation would presumably end up with differing value considerations than with democratic/representative forms of government.

34. The term is drawn from Eric Hoffer's excellent treatise, *The True Believer*, Harper, New York, 1951.

35. One of today's foremost existentialist philosophers, Jean-Paul Sartre, took great pains to visit Andreas Baader during the latter's imprisonment.

36. "The less clear the political purposes in terrorism, the greater its appeal to unbalanced persons. The motives of men fighting a cruel tyranny are quite different from those rebels against a democratically elected government. Idealism, a social conscience or hatred of foreign oppression are powerful impulses, but so are free floating aggression, boredom and mental confusion. Activism can give meaning to otherwise empty lives." Laqueur, op. cit., p. 128.

37. For an interesting typology of terrorist personalities, see Frederick Hacker, *Crusaders, Criminals and Crazies*, Norton, New York, Norton, 1976.

38. The recent incident in the Philippines in which a felon was overcome and killed by his hostages is one of a growing number of such cases.

39. The West German interior minister recently was convinced that such a possibility existed with reference to a German nuclear expert and terrorists affiliated with the Carlos apparatus. For background on the incident surrounding Dr. Klaus Traube and the questionable audio surveillance of his residence, see "A Scientist's Terror Link Worries Bonn," *The Washington Post*, 1 March 1977, p. A8; "Bugging of scientist's home puts Minister in awkward spot," *The German Tribune*, 3 March 1977, p. 4; and "Man muss mit allem rechnen," *Neue Rhein-Zeitung*, 3 March 1977, among others.

40. The drawings published in William Powell's *The Anarchist Cookbook* (Lyle Stuart, New York, 1971) originally appeared in Cuban documents that surfaced in the 1960s in Puerto Rico. They have been used in the German version published in 1974 and others.

41. "There is a standard work about explosives from the DDR [German Democratic Republic]; two volumes in which there is really everything (all explosives since their invention, fabrication, etc.)— one of us stole it from a library in Frankfurt." *Dokumentation über Aktivitäten anarchistischer Gewalttäter in der Bundesrepublik Deutschland*, Federal Interior Ministry [1974], p. 66.

42. Ibid., p. 10ff.

43. Bernd Guggenberger, "What motivates the urban guerrilla?" (from *Die politische Meinung*, No. 166, 1976) in *The German Tribune—Political Affairs Review*, No. 28, 3 October 1976, p. 16.

44. Our experience with the telephonic bomb threat should be of

some assistance in this regard.

45. Among others, Murray Miron, a Syracuse University psycholinguist, using a computerized data base, has done considerable work in linguistic text analysis of threat communications. In an address to the 1976 Seminar on Clandestine Tactics and Technologies of the International Association of Chiefs of Police, Washington, D. C., Professor Miron stated his computerized threat dictionary consisted of 140,000 entries in some 300 contruct categories which were of use in assessing demographic and psychological traits and disputed authorship of threat communications. He proposed an analytical model of terrorist communications needs with three axes: impotence denial ("the weak pretending to be strong"), affiliative needs traits, and destructive reaction.

46. For example, despite the wealth of reporting, does anyone really know Patty Hearst's motivation?

47. A case in point is the recent series of assassinations/kidnappings carried out by German terrorists. While calling themselves the Red Army Faction, their personnel and modus operandi are not those of the original RAF or Baader-Meinhof group, as Baader himself stated to authorities shortly before his suicide.

48. The term refers to incident resolution wherein terrorists release hostages in exchange for their own freedom. Its coinage resulted from the BSO takeover of the Israeli embassy in Bangkok.

49. See Horchem, op. cit., p. 22; *Betrifft: Verfassungsschutz '72,* Federal Ministry of the Interior, Bonn, 1973, p. 61; *Dokumentation,* op. cit., pp. 6-7; and *Innere Sicherheit: Informationen des Bundesministeriums des Innern,* Bonn, No. 28, 2 June 1975, p. 1.

50. See, for example, "Why Women Turn to Terrorism," *San Francisco Chronicle World Magazine,* 6 August 1978, p. 31.

Part 2

The Causes

2
Social Scientific Theory and Civil Violence

Paul Wilkinson

We really understand very little about the origins and causes of human violence in all its daunting variety. One is haunted by the dire warning in Alexander Pope's *An Essay on Man*:

Trace Science then, with Modesty thy guide;
First strip off all her equipage of Pride;
Deduct what is but Vanity or Dress,
Or Learning's Luxury or Idleness;
Or tricks to show the stretch of human brain,
Mere curious pleasure, or ingenious pain;
Expunge the whole, or lop th' excrescent parts
Of all our Vices have created Arts;
Then see how little the remaining sum,
Which served the past, and must the times to come!

Almost every scientific discipline has produced some discovery or hypothesis relevant to an understanding of human violence and aggression. It is a truly Olympian polymath who can claim to have untangled and mastered them all, and those who do so, almost inevitably invite accusations of folly or charlatanism. And no modern social scientist can fail to be aware of the serious Popperian objections against grand theories of human behavior:[1] they are inescapably reductionist, unfalsifiable, historicist, and covertly ideological.

There is no substantial theoretical literature in social science concerned specifically with terrorist phenomena. It can be shown, however, that some general theories of violence have yielded hypotheses about terrorism which, though hotly disputed, are of considerable academic interest. Some of the more influential of these theories, and their underlying assumptions, are the subject of the initial discussion in this essay. We shall then proceed to examine

45

some of the more suggestive hypotheses relating to the causation of civil violence and terrorism.

Some of these attempts at theory turn out to be, on closer investigation, no more than crude models positing a possible general relationship between human violence and certain arbitrarily defined variables. Others turn out to be merely statements of statistical correlates of various kinds of violence, while others only provide useful checklists of possible preconditions and precipitating causes of violence.[2] Such approaches do not provide any purchase on the really big questions about human violence. Why is man the only species that indulges in intraspecific violence on a really massive and disruptive scale? Why does man alone among all creatures commit acts of mass murder and promiscuous cruelty and sadism? Under what conditions and for what reasons do men resort to one form of violence rather than another? And why is it that, faced with similar threats, conditions, circumstances, or pressures, some individuals react violently when others do not? It may well be that such broad questions are inherently unanswerable.[3] Certainly the most that can be claimed for any of the scientific theories discussed here is that they have added some fresh insights and concepts to the body of knowledge about human violence.

Evolutionary theory and social Darwinism, it is widely agreed, exerted a seminal influence on late nineteenth and early twentieth century social thought.[4] Darwinist ideas were developed and diffused not only by authoritative scientific writers such as Sir Julian Huxley and Sir Arthur Keith, but also by social Darwinists such as Benjamin Kidd and Karl Pearson,[5] who popularized much cruder and more extreme social Darwinist and eugenicist doctrines. The basic assumptions of the social Darwinists and the social imperialists who readily exploited their ideas were: (1) the evolutionary processes of natural selection and the survival of the fittest applied to the development of races, nations, and empires; (2) war and violence constituted necessary tests or proving grounds of a nation's fitness to survive; and (3) on these assumptions, social Darwinists prescribed the inculcation of warriorlike virtues, physical fitness, and war-readiness as vital conditions for national, racial, or imperial survival.

Social Darwinist influence was also a development of ominous significance in the social thought of Wilhelmine Germany. Among the most popular exponents of crude social Darwinism in Germany were Ernst Haeckel and Wilhelm Boelsche.[6] Haeckel, author of the best-selling *Die Welträtsel*, was actually a very competent biologist who prostituted his talents by sensationalism and journalistic excess.

Even his fellow social Darwinists were embarrassed by the exposure of Haeckel's crude tricks of charlatanism, for example, his substitution of shark embryos to represent human embryos. However, what is important and interesting in the long term is that these authors not only provided ready-made source books for Nazi race "theory," but also exerted a deep and lasting appeal for a whole generation of German and Austrian biologists and zoologists, of whom the best known survivor is Konrad Lorenz. Lorenz has himself admitted his own indebtedness to the writings of earlier German social Darwinists and eugenicists,[7] and his own very influential modern version of instinctivist theory is perhaps best understood as a direct successor to the "high" social Darwinism of Haeckel and Boelsche subtly adapted for the needs of a contemporary public, yet nevertheless informed by some extraordinarily illuminating and original research into animal behavior.

Lorenz's most influential exposition of his instinctivist theory, *On Aggression* (1966), argues that human aggression is a basic organic drive or instinct as vital for man's basic physiological needs as the drives of hunger and sex. Aggression is, according to this theory, phylogenetically programed in man as part of our equipment for survival. Lorenz is interested primarily in intraspecific aggression (i.e., aggression against members of one's own species) rather than in interspecific or predatory violence. What are the vital social functions served by intraspecific aggression according to Lorenz? Clearly, the anthropological and paleontological evidence does not support the notion that man has indulged in large scale intraspecific aggression simply for the purposes of obtaining mates or for cannibalism. Lorenz argues that man's aggressive instinct performs at least eight basic functions in the struggle for survival: (1) to defeat his rivals and enemies; (2) to protect his mate; (3) to protect his young; (4) to protect his community (why this should be seen by the individual to be necessary for his personal or family survival is not satisfactorily explained by Lorenz; his references to group loyalties are so vague as to render them indistinguishable from any other feelings of altruism); (5) to space out individuals of the species over the available habitat; (6) to protect his territory; (7) to ensure the success and leadership of the best (i.e., strongest) of the species through the mechanisms of natural selection; and (8) to assist thereby in establishing a social rank order, which in turn strengthens social stability, solidarity, and efficiency. Furthermore, Lorenz claims, man's aggressive instinct is such a powerful basic drive that it must inevitably find an outlet even under conditions where survival is in no way endangered. Lorenz's model has hence been dubbed "hydraulic" by his critics because it envisages a bottled up flow of aggression constantly welling up within the individual or group, demanding expression, and spilling over into aggressive behavior. Moreover, he suggests that it is extremely unhealthy for human development if attempts are made to suppress or sublimate this aggressive instinct, for to do so would be to destroy the wellsprings of human creativity and competitive progress (the price for eliminating or reducing conflict).

In *On Aggression*, Lorenz implies that man was an aggressive creature even in the primitive foodgathering, hunting, and nomadic phases of human evolution. More recently, he has revised this account to suggest that it was in the Neolithic Revolution, between about 9000 and 7000 B.C., when permanent settlements based on agriculture were first established, that man became dangerously aggressive. But, according to neoinstinctivist theory, it was the invention, diffusion, and use of deadly weapons that finally broke down the inhibitions that had previously tended to contain or limit intraspecific aggression. Rifles and guns made it possible for individuals to kill each other at great distances and hence the killer was unable to see suffering in the eyes or faces of his victims. Moreover, when man became able to manufacture deadly weapons, he was no longer constrained by the physical self-restraints or inhibitions, which Lorenz suggests are inherent in bodily struggle with an opponent. Lorenz does not seriously consider, however, the far more tangible sources of culturally imposed inhibition against intraspecific aggression. Clearly uncontrolled intraspecific killing or maiming in even the most primitive agriculturalist settlements could be self-destructive as a result of depleting the available manpower for production of food and necessities and for communal defense. Also, on the eugenicists' own assumptions, unrestrained intraspecific violence would "program" the breeding of the fiercest humans and hence ultimately endanger the survival of the species through fratricidal strife.

It is because Lorenz believes that intraspecific human aggression has "gone wild" and become a danger to man's survival that he lays great stress on the need to channel aggression into what William James termed "moral equivalents for war." As human aggression demands an outlet, it must be released or expressed in adventure, sport, or contests or diverted into ritualized or symbolic aggression, which will not harm or disrupt the species. Despite frequent references to the ritualization of aggression occurring in animal behavior, Lorenz finds no reassuring evidence that it will provide a solution to the problem of human aggression. The gloomy diagnosis of neo-instinctivism is that man may be irreparably warped or wild: we may be on a suicide course, but there is nothing that we can do about it.

Robert Ardrey has, in several recent works,[8] presented his own variant of neoinstinctivist theory, drawing heavily on social Darwinist ideas and Lorenz's ethological studies. He argues that human aggression is partly rooted in struggles for identity, security, and stimulation, but that the dominant source of all human aggression is what he terms the "territorial imperative," the human instinct to defend one's territory. This emphasis is considerably at variance with Lorenz's theory, but as Ardrey's work has been so widely publicized and discussed, his variant of neoinstinctivism will be briefly covered in the critical discussion of instinctivism that follows.

We must begin by questioning the utility of the concept of aggression, for in Lorenz's usage it is so vague and ambiguous that it invites even more confusion than the difficult concept of violence that we discussed earlier. Much aggression in both animal and human behavior is shown by warning signals, combatant postures, fierce expressions, and cries. In many cases, the show of aggression does not give rise to physical attack on the opponent: in Lorenz's terms it remains at the symbolic or ritual level. But how is one to distinguish aggression from mere expressions of anger, annoyance, or frustration? Does verbal conflict count as a manifestation of human aggression? Lorenz appears to interpret the term so broadly that even a baby's exploration of its mother or a businessman's thrusting style of competition could be counted as aggressive. Surely we need to make a basic distinction between displays of aggressive feeling or intent and the actual infliction of violence. But how are we to deal with the case of violence in self-defense against an act of violent aggression? Surely there is an important sense in the discourse of politics, law, and diplomacy, in which the term "aggressor" is reserved for he who strikes the first blow. Hence, in the context of collective human violence, Erich Fromm's concept of benign aggression[9] appears to be a contradiction in terms. A victim of aggression *may* respond by a display of aggression or by counterattack, but such aggression is hardly benign in its intentions or its possible effects upon the opponent. Much instinctivist and psychopathological discussion of violence is seriously skewed by its neglect of acts of pure self-defense, which may indeed have an instinctual basis (for example, the use of one's limbs or a convenient object to ward off an attacker's blows) and which it would be patently absurd to term "aggressive."

Fromm is surely right to draw attention to the instinctivists' failure to distinguish between aggression committed in the course of individual, family, or communal protection, or for the purposes of defeating rivals or gaining territory, from purely destructive acts of violence lacking any apparent instrumental motivation. Fromm designates this form of purely destructive human violence "malignant aggression" and, in his fascinating clinical case studies of the psychopathology of sadism and necrophilia,[10] he makes an extremely convincing case that promiscuous acts of cruelty and sadism have their roots not in instinct but in personality disorders.

The instinctivists' neglect of the differences between animals and humans—their willful dismissal of the human psyche, personality, passions, and character traits—naturally renders their approach incapable of dealing adequately with pathological violence. More damagingly, however, it also accounts for the crude reductionism of neoinstinctivism's "ethological" approach to explaining normal human violence and aggression. Lorenz admits that man is one of the least instinct-dominated creatures, that man is peculiarly "open" or malleable to the influences of acquired behavior. Yet the instinctivists neglect the rich and growing research literature on child development, learning, and socialization. Instead, Lorenz and his followers depend almost exclusively on analogies with animal behavior (in particular the behavior of geese and apes). It is one thing to hypothesize about the importance in animal behavior of the right stimulus arising at the appropriate time to provoke the requisite innate response; it is close to charlatanism to apply such hypotheses in crude reductionist fashion to all the complex and subtle variations of human behavior.

Neoinstinctivism has been powerfully challenged, even on its own terrain, as a theory of animal behavior. Recent research findings in the neurological sciences indicate that animal and human brains have built-in neural mechanisms which, in response to attacks threatening individual survival, may trigger responses of *either* self-defense *or* flight from the attacker.[11] It is therefore quite arbitrary of the instinctivists to focus on man's "aggressive instinct"; as Fromm has pointed out, one might as well propound a theory based on man's instinct to flee. Moreover, Lorenz's hydraulic theory of dammed-up aggression demanding outlet is falsified by the field studies of animal behavior generally. Even the fiercest predators do not exhibit such continual and intense aggression either in the wild or in captivity.

And, so far as primitive human societies are concerned, there is abundant evidence in the studies of Benedict, Mead, Murdock, and

Turnbull[12] to show that many tribal communities (such as the Arapesh of New Guinea, the Lepochas of Sikkim, and the Zuni Indians of the southwest United States) have established entirely peaceful and cooperative modes of life in which intraspecific violence is almost unknown. There is no anthropological evidence to support the Hobbesian and instinctivist assumption that for man the state of nature must inevitably be the state of war.

Ardrey's theory that human conflict stems mainly from an instinct to acquire and hold territory is also falsified by the sociological evidence. Man is an intensely gregarious creature and does not apparently require or seek (as some birds and mammals appear to do) a minimal ratio of individuals to land area or a designated territory in order to survive. Indeed, the processes of industrialization and modernization have been accompanied universally by a tendency towards larger urban conglomerations. Nor is life in the densely populated cities of, for example, Holland, Belgium, or Britain necessarily characterized by increased aggression and violence among the general population. It is not crowding or population density per se that appears to be correlated with high levels of violence. Rather it is pressure on scarce resources, the intensification of relative deprivation, or sudden crises bringing economic or political disruption. The territorial imperative theory is also falsified in terms of its own instinctivist premises. If human behavior is to be understood as merely another species of animal behavior, then the territorial instinct must be common to both. But among many species there is, in fact, great flexibility exercised in regard to territorial boundaries and access. And, in any case, the more rigid observance of territory by certain species tends to have the function of avoiding or reducing conflict rather than of increasing it. Perhaps the most damaging evidence against Ardrey's theory, however, is the research finding that the binding of a male to its own territory is not instinctual, but *learned.*[13]

All of the above criticisms seem to me to constitute an overwhelming argument against instinctivist and neoinstinctivist "theory." It is my contention that Lorenz's account of aggression is fatally flawed and that it has nothing to tell us about the nature, origins, or implications of the large-scale human violence that has been employed by man since the beginnings of recorded history as an instrument for achieving political ends. It yields neither insights nor hypotheses to aid us in our studies of the violence of conquest, repression, emancipation struggles, rebellion, or revolution. Why, then, does it continue to be influential in the popular culture? The most likely reasons for its success are, first, its aura of scientific authority, and, second, the fact that neoinstinctivism provides a comforting soporific against the problems of modern life and the fear that humanity might destroy itself. For if man's inhibitions against intraspecific aggression really have irreparably broken down, as Lorenz suggests, then the hope that this aggression may be diverted into harmless channels is clearly in vain. Where is the deus ex machina that will bring about the diversion? The message of neoinstinctivist theory is one of hopeless resignation: eat, aggress, and be merry, for tomorrow we die.

Behaviorist theory approaches the phenomenon of human aggression from an entirely different viewpoint. This powerful movement in modern psychology developed from the work of J. B. Watson, I. Pavlov, and B. F. Skinner and has two main features in common with instinctivism: the claim to the absolute certainty, authority, and predictive power of science and the application of a crude positivist reductionism to the study of human behavior. It is important to clarify at the outset the rather special meaning it gives to "behavior." Behaviorism's sole interest is in observable *physical* behavior and not in the subjective feelings or mental life of the individual. Concepts such as "personality" and "mind" are redundant in behaviorist language. The human brain is conceived as being a mechanism that has the function of triggering and coordinating learned or acquired behavioral responses to specific stimuli. Behaviorism does not concern itself with the social or biological *origins* of particular traits or features of human behavior beyond simply taking for granted the variability of individual genetic endowment. Its model or doctrine of man is therefore absurdly simple: man is basically a hedonistic machine attempting to adapt itself to a hostile environment. Because the individual will inevitably seek to maximize pleasure (rewards) and minimize pain (punishments), it is possible to condition or train him to adopt particular desired behavior patterns through manipulating the contingencies or environmental influences that determine them.

There are three main kinds of conditioning discussed in the psychological literature, though each has been frequently misunderstood or confused by critics of behaviorism. Classical conditioning occurs when an animal links a response to a specific stimulus with which it had not previously been "connected." This happens when an animal recurrently experiences a stimulus followed a sufficient number of times by the stimulus that evokes a specific response. An example of this is the well-known work of the Russian psychologist, Pavlov, who "trained" or conditioned the salivary reflex response in dogs to the stimulus of a ringing bell. This was done by systematically training the dog to associate the ringing of a bell with the presentation of food. After a lengthy period of training the dog, Pavlov discovered that the ringing of the bell evoked the conditioned response of salivation even when the additional stimulus of the appearance of food was omitted from the sequence.

American behaviorist psychology has contributed the major work in the field of instrumental conditioning.[14] This form of conditioning is accomplished by systematically compelling an animal to choose or perform a desired action among a limited number of alternatives by the use of rewards and punishments. The most recent and sophisticated American research on conditioning has been conducted by B. F. Skinner. He has developed and refined the third type, operant conditioning, which involves the use of a more permissive, but nevertheless highly structured, laboratory environment. Here the animal is left to "accidentally" perform an action (e.g., pushing a button), which is then rewarded by the experimenter. Skinner and his colleagues discovered that by increasingly discriminating use of positive and negative reinforcement, animals could "teach themselves" to perform quite complex sequences of behavior, for example, the simulation of table tennis by pigeons. A crucial part of the operant conditioning process developed by Skinner is the successive rewarding of the animal's *partial* performances of the desired response until, finally, the action is perfectly performed.

Behaviorist work on conditioning has extremely interesting applications and implications concerning the problem of human aggression. Skinner and his school are quite certain that operant conditioning techniques are just as valid and practicable for humans as they are for animals.

> Behavior which operates upon the environment to produce consequences ("operant" behavior) can be studied by arranging environments in which specific consequences are contingent upon it. The contingencies under investigation have become steadily more complex, and one by one they are taking over the explanatory functions previously assigned to personalities, states of mind, feelings, traits of character, purposes, and intentions. The second result is practical: the environment can be manipulated. It is true that man's genetic endowment can be changed only very slowly, but changes in the environment of the individual have quick and dramatic effects. A technology of operant behavior is, as we shall see, already well advanced, and it may prove to be commensurate with our problems.[15]

Skinner envisages that human violence and aggression, like other forms of disruptive or socially damaging behavior, can be ultimately controlled, reduced, or even eliminated by the correct use of a technology of operant behavior. He would retain an important role for traditional forms of punishment.

> Punishable behavior can be minimized by creating circumstances in which it is not likely to occur. . . . Aggressive behavior which is otherwise uncontrollable is suppressed by putting a person in solitary confinement, where there is no one to aggress against.[16]

(This implies an extraordinarily naive view of the functioning of the penal system and the potentialities for aggressive behavior and violence within the prison system. Perhaps Skinner has not read George Jackson's *Soledad Brother?*) However, traditional forms of punishment need to be augmented by operant technology to "break up the contingencies under which punished behavior is reinforced . . . aggressive behavior is attenuated by making sure that nothing is gained by it."[17] Skinner prescribes several techniques for suppressing punishable (undesirable) behavior. For example, one may arrange circumstances under which the undesired behavior may occur without being punished—presumably in some place where it can do no harm to society (an interesting echo of the instinctivists' ideas for alternate safety valves for the release of aggressive behavior). "Punishable behavior can also be suppressed by strongly reinforcing any behavior which displaces it."[18] Suppose these techniques fail? Then Skinner is prepared to countenance, if all else fails, "changing physiological conditions," for example, using surgery (lobotomy) to "control" violence and drugs to control aggression.

In his concern for the scientific design of a "better culture for man, Skinner fuses the utopian fantasy of his *Walden Two* (1948) with the aggressive superconfident positivism of behaviorist technology. He apparently believes that the "intentional design" of a human culture is both practicable and desirable and that human communities can be made into vast benevolent laboratories for domesticating the human animal. To be fair, he does seem to recognize that his theory implies despotic power for the culture designer or experimenter, and that there is no guarantee that the "science and technology of behavior" would be used for the good of man. But Skinner does not allow that this is a sufficient reason for abandoning the theory. What most concerns him is the possibility that the whole venture of a behaviorist-designed culture might be sabotaged by the persistent and dangerously subversive literature of freedom, "which may inspire a sufficiently fanatical opposition to controlling practices to generate a neurotic if not psychotic response. There are signs of emotional instability in those who have been deeply affected by the literature."[19]

In *Beyond Freedom and Dignity*, Skinner candidly declares his belief that the ideas of human freedom, free will, and moral responsibility are obsolete. They are "prescientific." It is impossible, according to Skinner, to have *rational* objections or arguments against the "controlling practices" (a euphemism for repression) of a behaviorist-controlled society. There is the authentic ring of totalitarianism in his insistence that participation in the opposition would stem solely from psychosis or instability and that the literature of freedom is inherently subversive.

There are a number of serious objections, in my view quite fundamental, against the underlying assumptions, principles, and methods of the behaviorist approach to the problem of aggressive and violence. First, behaviorism fails to give an adequate account of the sources and nature of aggression and violence because its terms of reference limit it, in the realm of aggressive behavior, to the investigation of aggressive or violent responses to external stimuli and "contingencies." Thus, behaviorist theory entirely neglects those manifestations of aggression that are self-induced rather than learned and that seem to stem from some inner malaise or passion. Second, the behaviorists' analogy from the controlled and simplified environment of the animal laboratory is entirely specious and flies in the face of all the evidence from human history, sociology, and literature. Man's social life is not a tabula rasa which the behaviorist can redesign from scratch. The facts of human conflict, oppression, greed, exploitation, envy, and suffering mock Skinner's simplistic utopianism. Can behaviorism offer any insights into the large-scale problems of political violence and terror? Ironically, as scientific theory, it is of no avail.

And what of the philosophical difficulties raised by the ultra-determinism of the behaviorists? As a form of grand theory it is, like Marxist dialectical materialism, inherently nonfalsifiable. For its explanations of human action are always ex post facto and, faced with its apparent failure to predict numerous political and cultural changes and innovations, behaviorism falls back on familiar special pleading: the behavioral processes and the laws that determine them are only just beginning to be understood, and furthermore, they (the experimenters) are having to struggle to develop the new science against the strong rearguard action of unreasoning opposition, superstition, and prejudice. Yet despite behaviorists' claims to scientific purity and value-freedom, their model of man and their blueprints for a scientifically designed culture, complete with "control mechanisms" and techniques of conditioning, have a dangerously close resemblance to the black science of totalitarian state control. There is clearly no guarantee whatsoever that attempts to harness such a technology of behavioral control to political practice would take those forms of benevolent despotism implicitly favored by Skinner. Indeed, one horrifying potentiality of ultrabehaviorist science is that in malevolent hands it could develop antihuman techniques to add to Skinner's repertoire of control mechanisms: technologies of persecution, terrorization, and liquidation. The history of Nazi and Stalinist totalitarianism, the refinements of their terror apparats, and recent developments in Soviet psychiatry indicate that a black science of behaviorism is already with us. The liberal theorist can therefore clearly recognize in behaviorism, the Janus-headed nature of scientific positivism. It is true that the literature of American behaviorism, as it stands, exudes a kind of cozy hedonism. It assumes a comfortable, relatively anxiety-free, hygienic, and orderly existence safe in the cocoon of an environment designed and controlled by behavioral technology. It has little to tell us about the origins or nature of collective human violence and terror. Yet once science is prepared to dispense with the classical liberal doctrine of man as an autonomous, morally responsible person, once one is prepared to believe that all human actions are determined and therefore potentially manipulable, once the very ideas of freedom and dignity are held to be subversive, society no longer has any means of self-defense against tyranny. The literature of behaviorism is a sharp reminder to the liberal that those who profess to be developing a "value-free" science of human behavior are actually engaged in an enterprise potentially inimical to human freedom. There is a worm in the bud of behaviorism.

The early behaviorists did not primarily concern themselves with developing a general theory of the causes of aggression. However, in 1939, J. Dollard and co-workers presented what came to be known as the frustration-aggression theory. This theory soon became accepted by a majority of social psychologists and was later taken up by other social scientists who used its basic assumptions in the development of the influential deprivation theory of violence and aggression.[20] Dollard's frustration-aggression hypotheses were devastatingly simple: (1) "aggressive behavior always presupposes the existence of frustration," and (2) "the existence of frustration always leads to some form of aggression." Miller, one of Dollard's co-authors, later retracted[21] the second part of the theory on the grounds that aggression was only one of a whole range of alternative responses that could be triggered by frustration. However, there are other possible objections to the initial hypothesis. Acts of promiscuous cruelty and sadism, or what Fromm terms "malignant aggression," are by no means always instigated by frustration. And many of the more spontaneous aggressive acts may be responses to noxious stimuli rather than to frustration. Frustration is a confusing and ambiguous term. It can mean simply denial or deprivation of some "good" desired by an individual or group; but this usage is misleading because it implies that there is some psychological state in common between those who are deprived of or denied different kinds of desired "good." But there is clearly a world of difference between the feelings of, say, a nationalist who finds the demand for national independence rejected and those of a motorist who is deprived of gasoline by a tanker-drivers' strike. It is not clear what there is to be gained by the use of such undiscriminating terms in theory building. Dollard's frustration-aggression syndrome may be more relevant to the somewhat rarer type of frustration experienced when an on-going goal-directed activity is interrupted. But, even among members of the same family or community, responses to denials or deprivations of the same desired good vary enormously in nature and intensity. As Fromm argues,[22] the kind of frustration an individual experiences, and the likelihood and nature of any aggressive behavior induced thereby, will depend considerably on individual personality differences. In a crude way, when we recognize wide differences in individual capacities for patience and tolerance, we are admitting the empirical variability of individual thresholds for aggressive responses.

A further basic objection against frustration-aggression theory is its imprecision in the use of the concept of aggression, criticized earlier in relation to instinctivist theory. Even if we accept that aggressive behavior is frequently preceded by frustration (without for a minute conceding that frustration *always* leads to aggression), surely it is important to known what *forms* and *intensities* of frustration are linked to what *forms* and *intensities* of aggression. In the context of political violence, we need to know what particular forms and intensities of collectively perceived deprivation lead to riot, rebellion, terrorism, revolution, and civil war. And why is it that large-scale collective deprivations (e.g., those of famine, economic collapse, or defeat in war) sometimes lead to massive acts of political violence, yet sometimes fail to do so? Frustration-aggression theory as such has not seriously grappled with these problems. However, relative deprivation theory, which derives some of its basic assumptions from frustration-aggression theorists such as Dolland and Berkowitz, does appear to offer concepts and insights of more direct applicability to political violence.

The insights that popular satisfactions and discontents are of a *relative* nature, and that feelings of injustice can be intensified by a revolution of rising expectations or exacerbated by a sudden crisis, were familiar to earlier generations of social analysts. Marx notes: "Our desires and pleasures spring from society; we measure them, therefore, by society and not by the objects which serve for their satisfaction. Because they are of a social nature, they are of a relative nature."[23] And there is a vivid perception in Durkheim of the extent to which the hierarchic distribution of rewards of society is sanctioned and legitimated by moral beliefs.

> At every moment of history there is a dim perception, in the moral consciousness of societies, of the respective value of different social services, the relative reward due to each, and the consequent degree of comfort appropriate on the average to workers in each occupation. The different functions are graded in public opinion and a certain coefficient of well-being assigned to each, according to its place in the hierarchy.[24]

Clearly, it is an important truth that low levels of poverty or deprivation do not automatically breed responses of aggression and violence. Hence, the poorest masses of the Third World are unavailable and unprepared for revolutionary mobilization or indeed any political participation: they are simply engaged in a daily struggle to keep alive. They lack both energy and resources to organize political parties or movements of their own. Envy, on the other hand, is universal, though its sociology has been almost totally neglected. Hence, even in an affluent community in which all the population share to some degree in the prosperity, there will be those who covet their neighbors' goods or who envy others for their knowledge, skills, status, or political power.

Modern theorists of the relative deprivation school of aggression have been preoccupied with exploring the implications of frustration-aggression theory for the analysis of civil violence. According to this theory, at the individual level, perception of frustration arouses anger, which then functions as a drive.[25] Gurr argues that the implication of this theory is

> that civil violence almost always has a strong appetitive sensational base and that the magnitude of its effects on the social system is substantially dependent on how widespread and intense anger is among those it mobilizes. . . . If anger implies the presence of frustration, there is compelling evidence that frustration is all but universally characteristic of participants in civil strife.[26]

Gurr's basic premise is that the necessary precondition for violent civil conflict is relative deprivation (RD), defined as the actors' perception of discrepancy between their value expectations and their environment's value capabilities. In *Why Men Rebel* (1970), Gurr defines RD as the perceived discrepancy between men's value expectations and their value capabilities. "Value expectations are the goods and conditions of life to which people believe they are rightfully entitled. Value capabilities are the goods and conditions they think they are capable of getting and keeping."[27] He uses a threefold classification of types of values: welfare, power, and interpersonal. Interpersonal values are further subdivided into status, communality, and ideational coherence, but this does not help us very much because Gurr does not adequately explain these terms. Gurr's axioms are interesting but rather too loosely drawn to offer any theoretical purchase on the problem of political violence. For example: "the more intensely people are motivated toward a goal or committed to an attained level of values, the more sharply is interference resented and the greater the consequent instigation to aggression."[28] The term "instigation" is itself unsatisfactory because it is not clear whether Gurr means the goal-seeker will simply be further *incited* to civil violence or whether violence will actually be brought about. Moreover, surely the nature of the goals and values involved is crucially important. What if the goal-seekers are religious or pacifistic? May they not interpret the interference as an incitement to turn the other cheek? Moreover, this "axiom" illustrates another grave flaw in Gurr's relative deprivation theory of *Why Men Rebel*. Gurr constantly generalizes about intensities of motivation, anger, and resentment and about *likelihoods* and *magnitudes* of civil violence; yet nowhere does he explain how these things can be scientifically measured.

Some of Gurr's generalizations have a surface appearance of common sense until one begins to test them against historical realities. For example: "The likelihood and magnitude of civil violence tend to vary inversely with the availability of institutional mechanisms that permit the expression of nonviolent hostility."[29] How can that assertion stand up in the light of the American Civil War, or the endemic civil violence in postcolonial India, or the intensity of violence in Northern Ireland? We should note, also, that Gurr does not explain how or why some aggression is mediated into actual violence. For this reason, *Why Men Rebel* can be more accurately described as the presentation of a model rather than a theory.

Finally, and perhaps most damaging of all, Gurr's theory does not allow for the phenomena of elite-initiated and elite-directed violence in which mass participants are under authoritarian, military or paramilitary control. In such circumstances, by no means unfamiliar in internal wars, mass participants' perceptions of relative depriva- tion are utterly irrelevant to explaining the causes of the violence. Gurr's point that elite groups themselves sometimes resort to aggres- sion as a consequence of the frustration-aggression syndrome is a fair one. However, it would be a distorted view of history that saw all aggressive wars as being induced by elite frustration and omitted all consideration of wars as acts of policy or as expressions of dynastic or national self-assertion!

In this analysis, criticisms of relative deprivation theory of violence have thus far been directed at the work of Gurr. This is to some extent justified by the fact that he is the most prolific and widely known exponent of this theoretical approach. His trenchant remarks on everything from revolution and riot to the crime rate are avidly noted by commissions and experts. Nevertheless, there are other influential contributors to this school who have explored more fully than Gurr the political implications of four basic models of relative deprivation of social groups, classes, or societies:[30] (1) the revolution of rising expectations in which social expectations and aspirations rise at a much faster rate than capabilities, (2) the so-called J-curve situation when capabilities increase and keep pace with rising expectations for a short period and then suddenly suffer a sharp decline, (3) the serious crisis or malaise that causes a reduction in capabilities while expecta- tions remain constant, and (4) situations in which expectations and aspirations increase while value capabilities remain constant.

It is, of course, true that none of these models was invented by con- temporary relative deprivation theorists. All are deployed and dis- cussed in the somewhat more elegant literature of nineteenth century social theory. For example, Alexis de Tocqueville delineated situa- tions (1) and (2) as contributory causes of the French Revolution. He brilliantly discerned the crucial role of changing expectations in the prerevolutionary period.

> The evils which were endured with patience so long as they were in- evitable seem intolerable as soon as a hope can be entertained of escaping from them. The abuses which are removed seem to lay bare those which remain, and to render the sense of them more acute; the evil has decreased, it is true, but the perception of the evil is more keen. Feudalism in all its strength had not inspired as much aversion in the French as it did on the eve of its disappearance.[31]

De Tocqueville, however, was careful not to elevate his insights into a monocausal theory of revolution. In comparison, the confident generalizations of James C. Davies, the contemporary exponent of J-curve theory of relative deprivation, are based on a narrow and dogmatic reductionism.

> Revolution is most likely to take place when a prolonged period of rising expectations and rising gratifications is followed by a short period of sharp reversal, during which the gap between expectations and gratifications quickly widens and becomes intolerable. The frustration becomes focussed on the government, the violence becomes coherent and directional. If the frustration is sufficiently widespread, intense, and focussed on the government, the violence will become a revolution . . .[32]

Marx and Engels made the most influential classic contribution to exploring the implications of model (3) in their theory of the roles of major economic crises and the gradual immiserization of the proletariat as contributory causes of revolution and civil conflict. But again their theories of revolution are infinitely more subtle and complex than the so-called empirical theories of the modern relative deprivation school. Marx and Engels went beyond the evidence when they claimed that differences in their ideologies, beliefs, and expectations of the various social classes are invariably a reflection of their relationship to the means of production. Nevertheless, Marxist theory of revolution does possess a historical sweep and a wealth of insights that modern relative deprivation theory cannot begin to match. Marxist theory does take into account the phenomenon of the unawakened exploited class that has not yet recognized either the injustice of its situation or its revolutionary potential. Marxist theory therefore lays great emphasis on the revolutionary movement's responsibility for equipping the proletariat with revolutionary consciousness, leadership, and the correct revolutionary theory. It can be argued that although Marx made somewhat crude and unsupported assumptions about the nature of bourgeois rationality, he did not make the mistake of assuming that the working-class masses were all efficient rational maximizers who would be able, unaided as it were, to arrive at an adequate understanding of the nature and causes of their oppression and the means of their emancipation. In the last resort, Marx's revolutionary theory does not rely on spontaneity or the natural evolution of revolutionary consciousness. Marx and Engels were among the first social theorists to recognize the importance of popular ideologies and beliefs in legitimating, explaining, supporting, criticizing, or denouncing specific social orders and their various distributions of wealth, status, and power: they were thus saved, almost in spite of themselves, from falling into the trap of their own materialism.

In *Why Men Rebel*, Gurr disparages the notion that ideologies "cause" violence. Yet although ideologies qua abstract doctrine do not in themselves directly cause violence, ideological *movements*, which define enemies and incite to combat, do frequently instigate political violence, wars, and "crusades," with or without benefit of widely perceived relative deprivation. The work of Gurr and his colleagues reveals a failure to appreciate the influence of certain ideologies in *creating* and legitimating aspirations and expectations and equipping militant minorities to act in the name of the masses. Ideologies both define and articulate the sense of deprivation and claims of injustice and oppression. Most important of all, for our purposes, they bring powerful influence to bear in determining the kind of response made to frustration and anger by key groups or social strata. If an ideology tends to sanction violence or even to encourage and glory in it, then this inevitably strongly influences the nature of its adherents' collective response to anger, rejection, or opposition.

Relative deprivation theory, then, seriously underrates and misunderstands the role of ideology in inducing discontent, aggression, and conflict. In searching for alternative general causes of civil violence, certain relative deprivation theorists have plumped heavily for socioeconomic modernization. I. K. and R. L. Feierabend and B. A. Nesvold argue that the modernization process tends to simultaneously intensify modernizing groups' aspirations while challenging the entrenched positions of traditional groups. Hence, the probability of conflicts between "modernizers" and "conservatives" is enhanced as socioeconomic development accelerates. The faster the rate of modernization, they conclude, the greater the degree of disruption and the conduciveness to civil violence.[33] The Feierabend and Nesvold hypothesis is strongly reinforced by the work of Samuel Huntington[34] on political violence in what he terms "transitional" societies, societies that are in the midprocess of modernization. Huntington does not question the assumption that increased relative deprivation renders civil violence more probable. His analysis suggests that rapid modernization always involves intensified relative deprivation because it widens the gap between the changing aspirations and capabilities of the groups involved: social mobilization, education, and increased opportunities of political participation enhance aspirations while the already inadequate levels of production, employment opportunities, and governmental and administrative resources cannot keep pace with fresh expectations and needs. For some groups, capabilities actually decline (for example, peasants who are made landless by agricultural modernization programs and who cannot find work in the cities). Huntington observes that deprivation of political capabilities (such as the basic civil liberties and the right to vote) is more likely to lead to civil violence than purely economic deprivation.

> By broadening the range of political participation, political modernization increases the *scope* of civil violence, unless broader institutional channels for peaceful participation also come into being. The combined effect of both social-economic and political modernization, however, is to undermine traditional political institutions and to make it most difficult to create broad-based political party systems and other forms of political institutions. The idea of "peaceful change" or "development without violence" thus becomes almost wholly unreal.[35]

The whole tone of Huntington's discussion is heavy with gloomy realism. He argues that the modernization process even stimulates and intensifies traditionally-rooted communal conflicts and that most of the forms of political violence likely to ensue from development—praetorian violence, political repression, and communal conflict—are of a destructive and debilitating character. The case studies and comparative analyses deployed by Huntington are grounded on an impressive knowledge of contemporary history and of developing states. Unfortunately, space does not permit a more detailed consideration of Huntington's hypotheses concerning the links between modernization and civil violence. But enough has been quoted to enable the reader to learn something of its wide range, authority, and interest.

There are, however, some leading questions and difficulties to be raised about the modernization version of relative deprivation theory. None of the four general models of relative deprivation discussed by Huntington allows for the possibility of declining expectations and aspirations. Why should this be considered empirically impossible? Is it so exceptional for individuals and groups to actually lower their expectations or throw aside long-term aspirations—especially in conditions of acute crisis such as those caused by natural disaster or war? Humanity in extremis tends to adapt by concentrating on the immediate problems of survival, clutching hold of families and possessions, and riding out the storm. The mass of the world's poor suffer in passive resignation. Most are resigned to the fact that their conditions are more likely to worsen than to improve. When mass despair and fatalism are omitted from the academic theorist's model of the world, one suspects that the theorist has himself fallen prey to one or other of the powerful ideologies of modernization championed by Western aid experts, nationalist elites, and communist revolutionaries, all of whom have their own versions of the gospel. It is a cardinal error to confuse elite ideologies of modernization with the actual ideologies, beliefs, hopes, and fears of the masses.

It should be stressed that Huntington's modernization theory only purports to explain why transitional societies undergoing rapid modernization experience high levels of civil violence. He does not attempt to explain the widespread (and since the late 1960s) growing incidence of civil violence in the advanced industrial societies. As Huntington observes, "There may be violence without development, but there cannot be development without violence."[36] Can the modernization hypothesis conceivably be extended to cover the violence of the Black Panthers and the Weathermen in the United States? Can it explain the violence in Northern Ireland or on the streets in Watts, Newark, or Tokyo? Do terrorist and other violent groups active in liberal democratic societies really represent the rearguard of reaction and traditionalism in industrialized societies? It seems unlikely. And, like all the other attempts at social scientific theory included in our brief critical survey, this approach offers no explanation as to how the supposedly civilized industrial states of Germany and Italy came to descend into the barbarism of fascist violence and terror between the world wars or for their current waves of terrorism. An adequate liberal theory of political violence and terror must come to terms with the historical facts of murder and massacre within the West.

Psychopathological and Freudian theory, the final approaches to be included in this survey, do claim to illuminate the dark areas of what Fromm terms "malignant aggression," the promiscuous forms of cruelty and sadism, which, for example, characterized the behavior of many leading Nazis. But what do these theories contribute to our understanding of the sources of malignant aggression and of acts of psychopathic violence? And what do they tell us about "normal" collective or individual acts of violence?

Freud, the founder of modern psychoanalysis and still the most dominant single influence upon it, emphasized the role of personality development as the crucial determinant of individual behavior. Personality, according to Freud, is formed by the interaction between instincts or impulses and environment, each personality being a unique product of this process of individual development. Freud's major discovery was the role of the unconscious impulses and processes in human behavior. In his early works, in particular *The Interpretation of Dreams* (1900), he attempted to demonstrate the significance of the unconscious by means of carefully documented clinical case studies. Freudian theory has obviously significant implications for theory of human aggression and violence, for it suggests that within even the most apparently "rational" and "normal" individual, there lurk powerful hitherto unknown unconscious urges or impulses to kill.

Freud is perhaps best known for his theory that differences and changes in individual character traits are derived from the energy of the libido. The concepts of Freud's libido theory, such as the Oedipus complex, penis envy, incestuous wishes, and castration fear, have become the stock-in-trade of modern psychoanalysis. It is clearly quite possible to deploy Freud's theory of sexuality in attempts to explain individual aggression and violence. In certain cases, aggression could be attributed to a manifestation of the oedipus complex (love for one parent and jealous hostility or hatred toward the other). Freud's later theory of narcissism, which postulates the condition in which the libido has been withdrawn from the external world and has been directed at the ego, may also be utilized to explain individual aggressive acts. Narcissistic individuals may respond with intense aggression or desire for vengeance if they feel their narcissism has been wounded or gravely threatened.[37] Fromm has developed and deepened Freudian theory of narcissism by extending it to groups.[38] Work based on classic Freudian theory of sexuality suggests that the damaging or suppression of sexuality may cause childhood trauma and serious personality disorders, which may, under certain conditions, manifest themselves in forms of violent behavior. Nevertheless, this work remains entirely in the realm of speculative individual psychopathology and cannot be said to provide any theoretical insights or leverage in explaining collective and political violence. Research into the psychopathology of violent killers appears to lend strong support to the Freudian interpretation that such individuals frequently exhibit schizophrenic or sadistic characteristics. But it also confirms the view that the truly psychopathic violent killers, those who see all other persons as objects exploitable or expendable for their own ends, constitute only a tiny proportion of the population.[39]

It was in 1919-1920, however, in the wake of the vast collective destruction of World War I, that Freud began to develop his theory of the death instinct. His biographer speculates that he might have been to some degree influenced by Fleiss's law of inevitable periodicity and Neitzsche's notion of the "eternal recurrence of the same." Ernest Jones explains:

> Freud came to the conclusion that the fundamental aim of all instincts is to revert to an earlier state, a regression. And if instincts aimed at the past, why should they stop before reducing a living organism to a pre-vital state, that of inorganic matter? So the ultimate aim of life must be death. In this way rose Freud's celebrated concept of the *Death Instinct*.[40]

Freud left himself with the awkward task of accommodating the phenomena of sexuality within his new theory. He did so by suggesting that Eros, the life instinct, had the effect of counteracting or indefinitely postponing the goal of the death instinct. Thus, the two basic opposing forces in the mind might temporarily achieve an uneasy balance, even though, he believed, the death instinct was more powerful and was ultimately inevitably victorious. Sexual instincts, Freud now claimed, could help to postpone death "by diverting the self-destructive tendency outwards against other people."[41] These ideas were presented more confidently and systematically in *The Ego and the Id* (1923). Nevertheless, as Freud's biographer frankly admits, Freud's theory was not supported by a body of physiological and clinical evidence comparable to that which he had previously deployed in his studies of sexuality. This lack, combined with the unwillingness of disciples of his earlier theories to follow the master in his radical departures of 1919-1920, helps to explain the comparative neglect of Freud's death instinct theory by analysts and neo-Freudian writers.

The most recent major attempt to develop Freud's death instinct theory has been by Fromm. *The Anatomy of Human Destructiveness* (1974) contains a valuable summary of his ideas on what he terms "malignant aggression." He argues that there are three major kinds of response to human alienation (awareness of separateness from others) that tend to result in malignant acts of violence and destruction: (1) sadism, by which he means the craving to control others; (2) masochism, which is the urge to be controlled by others and which is often to be found in combination with (1) in the sado-masochistic character; and (3) necrophilia, which has been defined as "the passionate attraction to all that is dead, decayed, putrid, sickly; it is the passion to transform that which is alive into something unalive; to destroy for the sake of destruction; the exclusive interest in all that is purely mechanical. It is the passion to tear apart living structures."[42]

Before proceeding to a fascinating but highly speculative diagnosis and etiology of sadism and necrophilia, Fromm gives a tantalizingly brief but brilliant analysis of revenge. This discussion is of interest to the student of political violence and terror because vengeance is such a universal and deep-seated passion underlying so many individual and collective acts of violence committed by the apparently normal. Fromm argues that vengeful destruction is a form of spontaneous violence in response to "intense and unjustified suffering inflicted upon a person or the members of the group with whom he is identified."[43] It is not to be confused with simple punishment because it is often of much greater intensity that the injury it is supposed to avenge. Vengeance is almost invariably "cruel, lustful and insatiable," and in many traditional societies it is regarded as a sacred duty. Fromm frankly admits that desire for vengeance is a character trait of extremely variable incidence and intensity. He offers a number of interesting hypotheses that could account for the intense and deep-rooted nature of the passion for vengeance: it may be seen as a form of magical reparation, to "wipe the sheet clean by denying, magically, that the damage was ever done"[44]; perhaps through revenge, man is playing the role of an avenging God; it is possible that some acts of revenge may be triggered by the conscience; finally Fromm asks whether vengeful destructiveness could be a kind of projecting device for deflecting awareness of one's own capacity for destructiveness on to others.

Fromm's diagnoses of sadism and necrophilia provide a glittering array of neo-Freudian speculations, but it is extraordinarily difficult to know what weight either Fromm himself, or his highly critical scientific colleagues, can attach to his hypotheses. They certainly do not conform to the canons of scientific theory because they are based on assumptions about unconscious processes that are inherently unfalsifiable. Furthermore, it is not clear whether or to what degree, Fromm means to apply his diagnosis of necrophilia. Does he believe that large groups of necrophiliacs exist in all contemporary societies? It is one thing to suggest, in sweeping terms, that modern technical-bureaucratic societies are developing increasingly necrophilous characteristics and hence becoming more destructive; it is rather more difficult to verify such claims. It is not insignificant that Fromm chooses two notoriously perverted subjects, Himmler and Hitler, for his clinical case studies of sadism and necrophilia respectively. It is of vital importance to distinguish clearly between necrophilous tendencies or potentialities and those whose characters have become necrophiliac in the clinical sense. Common experience even in most highly "technotronic" societies would suggest that the incidence of clinical necrophilia is extremely rare.

Fromm stumbles into this problem but does not, in my view, confront it squarely. He admits:

> it is important to be aware how easily purely defensive aggression is blended with (nondefensive) destructiveness and with the sadistic wish to reverse the situation by controlling others instead of being controlled.[45]

And again he remarks:

> But destructive actions are not necessarily manifestations of a destructive, necrophilous character. Was Napoleon a necrophile because he never hesitated to sacrifice his soldiers' lives for his personal ambition and vanity?[46]

The problem raised for the theorist of political violence by these questions is that if one is primarily concerned with the violence committed by the "normal" and the collectivity, one ought not to overemphasize the importance of the psychopathic minority. The political scientists' main concerns are precisely with those acts of violence that blend Fromm's neat categories of benign and malignant aggression. It is these very manifestations of violence and their perpetrators that are allowed to slip through the net of Fromm's learned and brilliant speculations.

I have suggested that much psychoanalytic theory, including Fromm's highly original contribution, does not really satisfy the canons of scientific theory. However, I make no apology for its inclusion: the approach inevitably holds extraordinary interest for the student of political violence because of its immanent critique of other theories. It has one feature in common with all the other approaches surveyed here: like them it is ultimately determinist. The Freudians and neo-Freudians basically view violence as the product of disordered or diseased personality. This view implies that the etiology of the disease is predetermined by specific patterns of interaction between instinct and environment. If we assume that Hitler, Himmler, and their entourages developed into monsters through some inescapable chemistry of psychopathology, then the corollary must be that there was never any possibility that they could have avoided becoming the perpetrators of crimes against humanity if they had made different choices or moral decisions about their actions. Hitler, according to this theory, was not evil; he was severely mentally ill. Like all other forms of determinism, psychoanalysis denies meaning to the notions of moral goodness, wickedness, and moral responsibility. This view is clearly irreconcilable with the liberal doctrine of man as a free-willing autonomous moral agent, and consequently it is antagonistic to liberal theory of politics and violence.

Notes

1. Karl Popper, *The Logic of Scientific Discovery* (London, 1959), *The Open Society and its Enemies* (London, 1945), *The Poverty of Historicism* (London, 1957), and *Conjectures and Refutations: the Growth of Scientific Knowledge* (London, 1963).

2. See, for example, I. K. Feierabend, R. L. Feierabend, and B. Nesvold, "The Comparative Study of Revolution and Violence," *Comparative Politics* 5, 3 (April 1973):393-424.

3. Anatol Rapoport, *Conflict in Man-Made Environment* (Harmondsworth, 1974), p. 8.

4. V. Gordon Childe, *Man Makes Himself*, 4th ed. (London, 1965) and *Social Evolution* (New York, 1951); Ernest Gellner, *Thought and Change* (London, 1965); and Ashley Montagu, *Culture and the Evolution of Man* (New York, 1962).

5. See Benjamin Kidd, *Social Evolution* (London, 1894), *The Principles of Western Civilization* (London, 1902), and *The Science of Power* (London, 1918); Karl Pearson, *The Chances of Death and Other Studies in Evolution* (New York, 1897), *The Life of Francis Galton* (Cambridge, 1914) (4 vols.), *On the Relation of Health to the Psychical and Physical Characteristics of School Children* (Cambridge, 1923).

6. See Ernst Haeckel, *Anthropogenie oder Entwickelungsgeschichte des Menschen* (Leipzig, 1874), *The riddle of the universe, at the close of the 19th century . . .*, trans. Joseph McCabe (London, 1904), and *Welträtsel* (Leipzig, 1909); also, Wilhelm Boelsche, *Haeckel: his life and work*, trans. Joseph McCabe (London, 1906) and *Die Abstammung des Menschen* (Stuttgart, 1922).

7. Bruce Chatwin, "Man the Aggressor" (a report of conversations with Lorenz), *Sunday Times Magazine*, December 1, 1974.

8. Robert Ardrey, *The Territorial Imperative* (London, 1967) and *The Social Contract* (London, 1970).

9. Erich Fromm, *The Anatomy of Human Destructiveness* (London, 1974), p. 198.

10. Ibid., p. 330.

11. V. H. Mark and F. R. Ervin, *Violence and the Brain* (New York, 1970).

12. R. Benedict, *Patterns of Culture* (New York, 1959), "The Natural History of War," in *An American Anthropologist at Work*, ed. M. Mead (Boston, 1959); M. Mead, *Co-operation and Competition Among Primitive Peoples*, rev. ed. (Boston, 1961); G. P. Burdock, *Our Primitive Contemporaries* (New York, 1934); C. M. Turnbull, *Wayward Servants, or The Two Worlds of the African Pygmies* (London, 1965).

13. N. Tinberger, *Social Behavior in Animals* (New York, 1953).

14. See Abram Amsel, "Frustrative Nonreward in Partial Reinforcement and Discrimination Learning: Some Recent History and Theoretical Extension," *Psychological Review* 69:306-328; Harry F. Harlow, "The Formation of Learning Sets," *Psychological Review* 56:51-65; B. F. Skinner, *The Behavior of Organisms: An Experimental Analysis* (New York, 1938) and *Science and Human Behavior* (New York, 1953).

15. B. F. Skinner, *Beyond Freedom and Dignity* (New York, 1972), pp. 18-19.

16. Ibid, pp. 64-65.

17. Ibid, pp. 65.

18. Ibid.

19. Ibid, p. 165.

20. J. Dollard, N. E. Miller, O. H. Mowrer, G. H. Sears, and R. R. Sears, *Frustration and Aggression* (New Haven, 1939). Dollard was a product of the American Purposive Psychology School led by McDougall and Lloyd Morgan. For explicit acknowledgement of Dollard's influence on Gurr's relative deprivation theory of violence, see T. R. Gurr, *Why Men Rebel* (Princeton, 1970), p. 33. It is noteworthy that although Gurr there defines frustration, in Dollard's terms (that is, as an interference with goal directed behavior), his own theory discards this usage and generally equates frustration with the nonachievement of any desired good or condition to which one believes oneself to be entitled.

21. N. E. Miller, "Frustration-Aggression Hypothesis," *Psychological Review* 48:337-342.

22. Fromm, op. cit., p. 68.

23. Karl Marx, "Wage Labour and Capital" (1847), in Marx and Engels, *Selected Works in 2 Vols.*, 1:94.

24. Emile Durkheim, *Suicide: A Study in Sociology*, trans. John A. Spaulding and George Simpson (London, 1952), p. 249.

25. L. Berkowitz, "The Concept of Aggressive Drive," in *Advances*

in Experimental Psychology, ed. L. Berkowitz (New York, 1965), 2: 307-322.

26. T. R. Gurr, "Psychological Factors in Civil Violence," *World Politics* 20 (January 1968):250.

27. Gurr, *Why Men Rebel*, p. 24.

28. Gurr, "Psychological Factors in Civil Violence," op. cit., p. 257.

29. For Gurr's evasion of the problems of "measuring" the intensity and scope of relative deprivation, see Gurr, *Why Men Rebel*, pp. 59-91. Gurr fails to acknowledge the hazards of inference from the crude aggregative data of cross-national studies. Gurr's generalization about the "availability of institutional mechanisms" appears in Gurr, "Psychological Factors in Civil Violence," op. cit., p. 257.

30. See James C. Davies, "Toward a Theory of Revolution," *American Sociological Review* 27 (February 1962):5-19; James C. Davies, "The J-Curve of Rising and Declining Satisfactions as a Cause of some Great Revolutions and a Contained Rebellion," in *Violence in America: Historical and Comparative Perspectives*, H. D. Graham and T. R. Gurr, eds. (New York, 1969), chap. 19; I. K. Feierabend and L. Feierabend, "Aggressive Behavior within Polities, 1948-1962: A Cross-National Study," *Journal of Conflict Resolution* 10 (September 1966):249-271; and I. K. Feierabend, R. L. Feierabend, and B. A. Nesvold, "Social Change and Political Violence: Cross-National Comparisons," in Graham and Gurr, eds., chap. 18; also I. K. Feierabend, R. L. Feierabend, and B. Nesvold, "The Comparative Study of Revolution and Violence," *Comparative Politics* 5, 3 (April 1973): 393-424.

31. Alexis de Tocqueville, *On the State of Society in France Before the Revolution of 1789* (L'Ancien Régime et la Révolution), trans. Henry Reeve (London, 1856), p. 323.

32. James C. Davies, "The J-Curve," op. cit., p. 547.

33. Feierabend, Feierabend, and Nesvold, "Social Change and Political Violence," op. cit.

34. Samuel P. Huntington, *Political Order in Changing Societies* (New Haven, 1968) and "Civil Violence and the Process of Development," in Adelphi Paper No. 83 (London, 1971), pp. 1-15.

35. Huntington, "Civil Violence," op. cit., p. 3.

36. Ibid.

37. See Fromm, op. cit, pp. 200-205.

38. Ibid, pp. 203-205.

39. See Hans Toch, *Violent Men: An Inquiry into the Psychology of Violence* (Harmondsworth, 1972).

40. Ernest Jones, *The Life and Work of Sigmund Freud* (Harmondsworth, 1964), pp. 508-509.

41. Ibid.

42. H. von Hentig, *Der Kekrotope Mensch* (Stuttgart, 1964).

43. Fromm, op. cit., p. 271.

44. Ibid., p. 273.

45. Ibid., p. 200.

46. Ibid., p. 395.

3
The Transnational Flow of Information as a Cause of Terrorism

Amy Sands Redlick

Introduction

Developments in transportation and communications have made cultural interactions of communities an important dimension of international relations. Because technological improvements tend to augment the speed, scope, and range of contacts between societies, they have affected significantly the global flow of information. Today, a continuous stream of information is dispersed by radio, television, newspapers, literature, and journals on an international scale, enabling societies to observe and imitate other groups.

The impact of this type of transnational[1] link on a domestic controversy, such as ethnic strife, may be profound. The worldwide structure of informational flows may cause attitudinal changes, such as changes in frame of reference, perceptions, and mood. For example, external information may shape the strategy, tactics, and ideology of the groups involved in a conflict; it also may foster an atmosphere that is not conducive to the settlement of difficulties. A type of demonstration effect also may result from the international flow of information. As Nye and Keohane explain:

> By facilitating the flow of ideas, modern communications have also increased intersocietal sensitivity. Certainly, there have been indirect "contagions" of ideas in early periods such as the European revolutions of 1848 or Latin American university reforms in 1917.[2]

In particular, transnational interactions, by providing tactical, strategic, and inspirational information to dissidents, may link turbulent situations, such as the one in Quebec in the sixties or Northern Ireland today, to other unstable situations. Thus, the transnational flow of information is a process that facilitates the penetration of the outside world into many domestic social, economic, and political problems.

The significance of transnational factors to any one situation differs according to the accessibility, vulnerability, and sensitivity of one society to another. Because improved technology and modernization have hindered the separation of societies and increased the characteristics shared by societies, the sensitivity and vulnerability of most modern communities have increased in recent years;[3] consequently, the degree and scope of transnational influences have tended to increase.

Analysts have not examined carefully the interaction of the non-institutional, interstate flow of information and stability. One reason for the lack of research is the difficulty of formulating indices to locate and measure this type of societal penetration. In addition, research concerning transnationalism and instability normally has examined the problems of less developed states, especially during their pre- and post-independence stage, rather than similar interactions within the context of a developed, Western state. This chapter will attempt to fill in part the vacuum in the research on international interdependencies by analyzing the interaction that can occur in destabilized situations between violence and the transnational flow of information. We hypothesize that the transnational flow of information can affect significantly a crisis or an event in an open, ethnically divided society and, more specifically, that external information may be a catalyst to the outbreak and development of terrorism in tense situations.

The Catalytic Role of the Transnational Flow of Information

The causes of violence in a society tend to be varied, complex, and deeply rooted in a community's historical, political, and cultural development. No one has developed a comprehensive theory that can explain fully the outbreak of violence or, more specifically, political violence.[4] Most of the theories concerning violence stress one or more of the following factors: the unstable individual; the social, economic, and political atmosphere; the historical and cultural legitimacy of violence; the international situation and current events; and the psychic need for violence by individuals. Often, because more than one of these factors is involved in the cause of violence, models that try to explain why men rebel may be lists of interconnecting and interdependent variables that may add to or diminish the likelihood of violence. Although these models are usually very intricate, they provide a framework for further hypotheses and exploration concerning the reaction of groups and individuals to certain stimuli and situations.

Modernization, accompanied by urbanization, secularization, and industrialization, may lead to societal violence as groups compete for the same opportunities and resources within a changing and often disrupted social and economic structure. According to Mancur Olson, Jr., rapid socioeconomic growth is a destabilizing force because it

> must involve fast and deep changes in the ways that things are done, in the places that things are done, and in the distribution of power and prestige.[5]

Although the aggregate community's standard of living may improve, individuals and groups may suffer losses in absolute and/or relative levels of prestige, power, and income. Moreover, even upward shifts in an individual or group's economic or social status may be disruptive because of the unsettling changes in living styles, aspirations, and values. Thus, negative and positive changes caused by socioeconomic growth may result in societal instability and uncertainty until the community and all of its components have adapted to recent developments.[6]

Collective political violence may occur when a group becomes mobilized for action because of frustrations and deprivations it has experienced in the tense competition for socioeconomic gain. Ethnic groups in some societies have become focal points for such mobilization because the pressures of industrialization and mass society have increased the ethnic awareness and identification of individuals. Once an individual in an ethnic group realizes or perceives a link between his ethnicity and his relative deprivation, he may become dissatisfied and frustrated with the political system responsible for the inequality and his deprivation. When the political system in a divided society does not respond fairly or appropriately in the eyes of one group, it may lose its legitimacy and viability for that group. Given the proper catalyst, violence aimed at the group or institutions apparently responsible for causing the frustrating experience may occur at this point.

The transnational flow of information can be a catalyst in destabilized, and especially ethnically divided, situations. For example, an ethnic cleavage that exists within a population may be aggravated if one ethnic group looks to one foreign group for information while the other ethnic group looks to another. Such a divergence in model seeking will serve only to highlight differences, since the information received from these external sources may vary significantly.

In addition, technological progress in the field of communications has facilitated and exacerbated the growing awareness of, interest in, and contact between revolutionary and nationalist groups. When the international communication system transmits information concerning revolutionary struggles or ethnic terrorism, it provides information easily utilized by disgruntled groups elsewhere. Communication received via mass media, international travel, or intellectual exchanges can supply normative and utilitarian justifications for political violence as well as detailed explanations of revolutionary or terrorist tactics and strategy. Thus, the transnational flow of information can activate and then reinforce violent tendencies within an individual or community.

The catalytic role of transnational factors stems from the interdependent nature of the international system, the easy penetration of most states, and the global range of modern communications. However, the type of influence that foreign events and ideas have differs from context to context according to the effect that industrialization, urbanization, and secularization have on a society and to the type, source, and timing of the external communication. Thus, while internal pressures and external influences combined to cause French-Canadian separatists and Moluccan radicals to utilize terrorism in their quest for national independence, other types of political violence, such as coups in Latin America, result from different internal and external factors.

Since the colonial liberation struggles of the fifties, certain modes of violence have become acceptable methods for correcting perceived social injustice and have permeated the international milieu. The penetration of society by the thoughts and acts of radicals has given the use of violence and the resort to revolution an "aura of legitimacy"[7] that has not existed for decades. Although an international flow of revolutionary ideas is not a new phenomenon, its extent, degree, and speed have been increased significantly as a result of modern communications and technology. Throughout the world, revolutionary groups utilize and extol the same ideas and strategies because they are taken from the same radicals. For example, a wide variety of militants justify their struggles and attempt to win more support by referring to Frantz Fanon, Fidel Castro, Carlos Marighella, and Mao Tse-tung, all of whom condoned political violence and expressed a need for an international brotherhood of revolutionaries to overthrow imperialism. Although many of these groups utilize similar antiimperialist or nationalist rhetoric, their goals are rooted in their local situations. Moluccan, Basque, Croatian, and Puerto Rican terrorists have little in common despite the similarity in their tactics and rhetoric. Thus, by making the revolutions, liberation struggles, and terrorist attacks so widely known and honored, the transnational flow of information has contributed to the creation of an atmosphere in which violence, especially terrorism, appears justifiable and acceptable.

The Causes and Consequences of the Penetration of a Society by Volatile Information

A critical factor in the development first of discontent and then of political violence is information. Information may be transmitted via international travel and conferences; the import of books, films, journals, and so on; and the transfer of relevant technology. Because changes in the transportation and communication of information have increased the speed and ease of such communications, information that once influenced only a limited area may now affect societies throughout the world. The repercussions of one event or idea now spread across the globe so quickly as to make it difficult to respond to the proliferation of reactions. As a consequence,

> Modern change is noted for its rapidity, due to faster communication and tighter functional interdependence. Modern change is international, hard to confine within geographical limits. These qualities make it difficult to deal with an issue or group in a vacuum or for its own sake.[8]

In addition, increased information can broaden perspectives, create an awareness of similarities and dissimilarities between groups, and bring in new models for action and thought.

By broadening the outlook of a group, one also broadens its desires and interests. Once aware of what other groups have, a group may demand the same things for itself. Also, a group, expecting to attain goals that others already have, may be frustrated when its own development does not provide it with the desired rewards. For example, during the fifties, *Cité Libre*, a progressive French-Canadian review, drew similarities between Quebec's situation and the colonial struggle. When the colonial struggles succeeded, the comparisons increased until many French-Canadians wanted for their nation what "scores of other previously occupied nations had achieved in the last twenty years in Asia and Africa."[9] As the 1960s passed, some French-Canadians became frustrated when Quebec's Quiet Revolution failed to fulfill their expectations, and they resorted to terrorism in order to attain their goals. Thus,

> human expectations are significantly influenced by events taking place in larger and larger segments of the world. And the level of inter-dependence within the system goes up as these perceptions and expectations are translated into political actions [for example, terrorist attacks].[10]

Furthermore, as societies modernize and break out of their parochial shells, their interest and connections will broaden so that more information will be able to penetrate them. There is little doubt that "through international communication, world culture impinges upon the developing country, frequently shaping or reducing its options."[11] The growing exchange of ideas and skills in the form of

> the transmission of intellectual movement, . . . the exchange of technical skills and know-how, the communication of management techniques, the contagion of fashions and patterns of consumption, . . . the impact of tourism on human perception and expectations,[12]

and the proliferation of techniques for violence has increased and strengthened the interdependence and interpenetrations existing between societies.

In a society disrupted by the process of modernization, societal cohesion can disintegrate. Traditional ideology and institutions may yield to new government agencies and patterns of family life as old values and norms become irrelevant or archaic. During this transitional period, economic changes caused by industrialization may precede social ones and increase the society's instability and vulnerability.[13] If conflict should arise as a result of two or more groups (ethnic, class, or interest) competing for limited opportunities or resources, one group might begin to identify with and imitate the strategies and ideologies of external groups. Not only may one group's resurgence spark another's, but it may also provide the rhetorical and tactical framework for another group's nationalism and violence. As Ted R. Gurr observed:

> A community may have a nonviolent tradition itself, but if its members see similar groups elsewhere making gains through political violence, they are likely to see utilitarian justifications for violent tactics themselves. In the modern world this demonstration effect of one group's successful use of violence can have almost simultaneous, worldwide consequences.[14]

Although such foreign involvement often is committed unconsciously and may play a small role in an internal struggle, it can become a significant factor in terms of the type of tactics employed and the outlook of the groups involved. Therefore, the process of modernization and communication causes a society to become vulnerable to externalities and, thus, may expose it to information whose influence on the community may be destabilizing.

Because technological progress has facilitated the flow of information into and within a society, it has increased the penetrability of a society. One expert in the field of communications observed:

> Recent technological developments in communication make it increasingly possible for people everywhere to focus their attention on the same issues and to engage in an exchange of ideas about them. Satellite broadcasting, in particular, has led to the expectation of closer international contacts.[15]

Information released about events, groups, and ideas in one area of the world may have an important effect on the course of events in another, unrelated area of the globe. For example, the student demonstrations in Europe may have sparked similar demonstrations in Berkeley and elsewhere in the United States; the American student riots, in turn, may have contributed to problems with students in other parts of the world.[16] Furthermore, as a result of improvements in transportation, it is easier to travel, and the number of student and cultural exchanges has increased, providing another relatively easy means of attaining information about other places or events. Literature also may be a source of new information and may increase a society's knowledge about another group's progress, difficulties, or norms.

Returning from a foreign country with tales of strange and wondrous

things, the traveler can sometimes influence the culture of his home-
land. Even stay-at-homes such as Franz Kafka, Karl May, Giacomo
Puccini, and Bertolt Brecht could produce works of art about countries
and peoples they had never seen—works that could subsequently condition their own countrymen's views about these faraway lands.[17]

Two factors seem to determine a society's sensitivity to external
information. First, the nature of a society, its structure and stability,
is critical because it determines its accessibility and vulnerability.
Accessibility, which refers to the quality of being available and
approachable, is dependent upon the ease of getting access to a
country's population and of providing access for the population to
outside sources; thus, an accessible society is an open one in which
information may flow uncensored and unfettered.[18]

The degree of openness of a society has an impact on the extent
and depth of penetration by external information. Both mental and
physical accessibility contribute to a society's sensitivity and vulnerability to outside events and influences. Ethnic groups in the
Soviet Union, for example, have been unable to react to the worldwide resurgence of nationalism because of the closed nature of their
society. Political and military repression limits access to objective
information about current events and ideologies and ethnic and
political dissent. External information can have little effect on the
average Russian citizen who has few chances to interact with or read
about outsiders without government involvement. Hedrick Smith
comments:

> The tragedy is not that communication is impossible, but that so much
> effort is expended to prevent it, for these are often precisely the
> unplanned, uncontrolled contacts the Soviet authorities seem deter-
> mined to obstruct—not the friendships and emotion, but the revela-
> tions that go with them.[19]

Moreover, information about events such as fires, deaths, plane
crashes, much less terrorist bombings or dissident protests, is not
provided to the public. Because the Soviet Union, like other closed
societies, is an "information vacuum," the government can better
control the population and its activities than an open society.[20] Thus,
the restrictions and suppression of a closed society make the society
inaccessible to external communication and any potential effects.

Vulnerability in this context refers to the state of being weak and
exposed in an unstable society. This condition often occurs as a result
of modernization, during which a society's foundations may be

challenged or, at least, threatened in such a way that individuals lose faith in the society's values and norms. As described earlier, such instability and uncertainty may produce tensions within the society. If changes are not forthcoming or fail to resolve the problems, the political system may lose its legitimacy as internal and external forces threaten the survival of the traditional society. The effect of this process is to expose the society to the influence of foreign models, norms, and ideology.

Because the basis of its society was in tremendous flux after World War II, Japan was vulnerable to penetration by Western economic, political, and, eventually, cultural ideas. As its society became part of the mass consumer community of the West, Japan's political system was also westernized and democratized. However, all of these changes were superimposed upon Japan's culture so that personal interrelationships remained virtually unchanged. In his instance, information in the form of new ideas about government and its relationship with its society probably had a stabilizing and calming effect.

But external forces can often have a different effect on society. In Quebec, for example, external influences provided models of action and frameworks of thought that led to radical action, destabilization, and violence. The economic changes that had taken place in Quebec since World War II disrupted the traditionally conservative pattern of life and thought in Quebec. The exposure that resulted from economic transformation and later sociopolitical changes destabilized the Québécois community; thus, Quebec proved quite vulnerable to penetration and influence by external information. As one commentator observed:

> It is hard to resist, especially when you are a small human group like the Québécois, appropriating other peoples' searchings and solutions when in search of yourself.[21]

Initially, the radicals of Quebec, including the terrorists, found intellectual nourishment and spiritual identification with the colonial struggle as described by Frantz Fanon, Albert Memmi, and Jacques Berque; later, the antiimperialist writings of Marx, Lenin, and present-day European communists, such as André Gorz, provided them with ideological and tactical information. In their search for help and models, the radicals made some direct and indirect contacts with foreign groups; for the most part, these links resulted in increased awareness of other groups' struggles, hardships, and ideolo-

gies, but not significant interaction. Many of the international operations, conferences, or rallies undertaken by Québécois radicals were
failures or temporary symbols of international cooperation between
revolutionaries.[22]

However, the transnational flow of ideas, strategies, and tactics
did critically affect the Quebec terrorists and, subsequently, the
Quebec society.[23] External information concerning terrorist events,
revolutionary tactics, and radical ideologies sparked some radical
separatists to terrorism. The continued transnational flow of information supporting terrorism, liberation, and radicalism dominated
the milieu and mood of the terrorists and prompted them to action.
One analyst has commented that mass communication can often
"affect the mood of individuals or large groups. A steady diet of
stories about disaster, corruption, and stupidity can stimulate a
mood of anger, pessimism, or despair . . ."[24] Thus, the socioeconomic
changes and instability caused by World War II and modernization
had exposed Quebec to ideas that further aggravated the situation
by creating a climate in which violence appeared justified and
necessary, disseminating information about terrorism to a radical
fringe, and influencing the philosophical orientation of the terrorists.

A society's sensitivity to external influences can also stem from
its identification with the outside force. Identification refers to the
perception by one society of being similar in some way (for example,
culturally, economically, or politically) to another society. Such an
attitude may be the result of some historical, economic, military, or
geographic relationship, such as Algeria might have with France. It
should facilitate communication between such groups since the
transmitter and receiver will have something in common.[25] Furthermore, because much of the world shares the same fears and aspirations,

> those populations that are at roughly the same psychological phase
> of development share somewhat the same pattern of concerns, and
> therefore may find it simpler to enter into communication with each
> other than with populations that are at different phases.[26]

Cultural and linguistic similarity also can ease communication flow
and contribute to its penetration of a society. For example, many
of the French-Canadian elite who went to Paris for their education
were influenced by Parisian thought and life-style. Moreover, French-
Canadian separatists began to take "pride in the achievements of
contemporary France"[27] after World War II because they saw it as an

alternative to North America's English-speaking society. Views put forth in French radical intellectual circles as well as events occurring in French-speaking colonies influenced the newly attentive and proud French-Canadian separatists. Consequently, some of these French-Canadians began to rely on Paris for guidance in their intellectual and political thought and, eventually, for new ways of perceiving situations and reacting to them.

While such a link tends to sensitize the thinking and actions of elite French-Canadians to events in French-speaking or French-controlled areas, it also may cause some Québécois to apply inappropriate French concepts or perspectives to Canadian situations. The potential for the misuse of foreign information is great because of the differences in societal values, historical experiences, and cultural perspectives. The use of terrorism in Quebec is indicative of the problems that can result from imitating other societies. First, the Québécois terrorists never gained mass support for their cause or tactics because the masses never perceived terrorism as an acceptable means to change their society. The difference in perspectives between the terrorists and the majority was the result of differences in education, role models, and communication links. The average Québécois was part of the North American cultural framework while the terrorists were operating within a much more radical French milieu. Second, when they kidnapped two officials in 1970, the terrorists expected the government to imitate the appeasement response of the Latin American government. They were completely unprepared for the intransigent position that the Canadian government took and the months in hiding that they faced. The terrorists had failed again to perceive cultural differences that might affect the decisions, actions, and opinions of Canadians. Thus, because the meaning and salience of communication can vary from group to group and from individual to individual, its utility and relevance also may vary; indeed, the potential for the misuse of information is extremely high and possibly harmful.

The increase in kidnappings and hijackings since the mid-sixties is another example of the volatile influence of informational flows. The upsurge in terrorist attacks must be linked partially to the international flow of information because it not only provided events and the involved groups with enormous publicity and perhaps even sympathy, but also inspired other groups to try similar acts.[28] The Quebec terrorists, imitating the Tupamaros, kidnapped two officials while the Croatians and Moluccans copied the hijackings of the Palestinians. Hence, the desire of certain societies to permit freedom of movement and accessibility to information leaves them vulnerable to penetration by potentially harmful information and groups.

The scope and degree of penetration by external communication depends on the stability of the society, the cultural and linguistic similarities between the transmitting and receiving societies, and the availability of information within the transmitting or receiving society. Specifically, communication with, about, or from extra-societal sources can provide a new ideological frame of reference as well as new strategic and tactical considerations for groups. New ways of approaching old problems may become apparent when societies copy what other groups have done. Another effect of the transnational flow of information stems from the success and publicity given an international event or ideology. Seeing or reading about the successful use of a method via some type of mass media may lead to a contagion of this method's use even in inappropriate situations. Finally, international information flows may contribute to a global atmosphere that is more open to conservatism (such as after the Napoleonic wars) or to revolutions (such as those of the late eighteenth century).[29] The cumulative consequence of all of these different aspects of the transnational flow of information is that open societies are more sensitive to the sways and pulls of external events or ideas than closed ones, especially if such a society is in the midst of a destabilizing and/or modernizing experience. Thus, the accessibility, vulnerability, and sensitivity of a society determine the extent of influence that transnational communications will have on a society. Thus, officials of open, unstable societies may have trouble retaining control over a situation because of the pressure and challenges brought on by the international flow of information.

Terrorism and the Transnational Flow of Information

There are two basic motivations for the use of terrorism as a strategy or tactic, although other factors may influence a group. First, the overwhelming balance of forces between the rebels and their opposition may offer the dissidents no other option. According to this view, terrorism is the weapon of last resort and is used by

> militant minorities who feel themselves driven at last to have recourse to violence in service of their cause, where the inequality of forces as between themselves and the government they seek to overthrow or constrain to different policies is such that victory for themselves in open warfare is out of the question.[30]

Second, the transnational flow of information may provide dissidents with the inspirational and material spark that will cause them to resort to terrorism. For example, a variety of external factors, such as the writings of Frantz Fanon, had subtle and extensive influence on the Quebec and Palestinian terrorist movements. The information obtained from external sources provided the terrorists with tactical, strategic, and ideological knowledge about the art of bomb-making, hostage-taking, and kidnapping. Moreover, information concerning the Algerians, Palestinians, and Tupamaros permeated the intellectual milieu of Quebec and contributed to the creation of a climate in which the use of violence appeared justifiable and necessary to a small group of Québécois. Inspired by militant anticolonial rhetoric, this radical fringe of the separatist movement quickly became committed to terrorism as utilized elsewhere in its pursuit of Quebec's independence. Thus, when some radicals resorted to terrorism, they were taking into account not only their limited capabilities, but also the successful examples of the Algerians, Cubans, and later the Palestinians and Tupamaros.

While external forces did not create the environment where the necessary frustration and disorientation existed, they did affect the outbreak and evolution of terrorism in Quebec. Without the example of colonial liberation movements and the expertise of two immigrants,[31] the violence in Quebec might have been of a different type—mass demonstrations, for example—and might have occurred at a later date. Furthermore, once the terrorists had resorted to violence, their selection of tactics and ideology was critically influenced by the transnational flow of information that publicized, sensationalized, and justified certain terrorist activities and movements. The Quebec Liberation Front imitated the Algerian bombings and cell organization and the Tupamaro kidnappings. Their rhetoric was borrowed from Fanon, Memmi, and Berque in the early years, and Marx and Lenin, and Antonio Gramsci in the later ones. The Quebec terrorists shifted their ideological emphasis from anticolonial to anti-imperialist and later changed their tactics from bombings to kidnappings as a result of external information concerning radical ideologies and movements. Thus, transnational factors played a critical role in sparking the outbreak of terrorism in 1963 and, subsequently, inspiring more terrorism in Quebec until after 1970.

Dissidents also may utilize terrorism in order to gain publicity for their cause and increase the interest and support of their own community and international society. The range of communication has enabled terrorists to accomplish this goal as their activities and their demands are quickly and easily dispersed via international communications. Terrorists, cognizant of the power of international communications, will attempt dramatic and often vicious acts of terrorism in order to get extensive international publicity and exposure for their grievances. Undoubtedly, the plight of the Palestinians would have received less attention in recent years had members of the Palestinian militant faction not resorted to hijackings, kidnappings, and murder.

The world today offers an attractive setting for terrorist acts. As J. Bowyer Bell observed:

> we live in times where technology has made possible both the magnification of violence and also created complex and vulnerable targets for that violence. It has become far more alluring for the frantic few to appear on the world stage of television than remain obscure guerrillas of the bush.[32]

In addition, terrorism is a form of political violence that requires few people and resources to be successful. The modern and highly interdependent nature of society has created many new, vulnerable, and potentially disruptive targets for a terrorist attack. Thus, terrorists could hold a city hostage by threatening to pollute its water supply or bring one to a standstill by bombing the critical electric and gas centers.

The rise in nationalism and ethnicity reflects the frustration and dissatisfaction resulting from the complexity, bigness, and remoteness of the institutions and bureaucracies in an industrial society. Ethnic discontent can become the basis for ethnic terrorism. Moreover, an apparent turn in the overall political environment has given revolutionary acts the appearance of being proper and acceptable. The new revolutionary atmosphere, combined with ethnic dissatisfaction and aggravated by improved telecommunications, has facilitated the transnational contact and cooperation between terrorist groups, increased the ability of terrorists to attract favorable publicity, and hindered attempts by some states to use international measures to prevent terrorism. Consequently, the progressive developments in communications and the destabilizing ones of the modernization process have led to a more accessible, interdependent, and permissive international system that is fertile ground for the occurrence of political violence in the form of terrorism.

The Policy Implications of the Catalytic Role of the Transnational Flow of Information

Given the developments in communications and transportation that facilitate the transnational flow of information and individuals, the vulnerability of open societies to disruptive external influences will increase. If societies are to remain accessible, they must adapt to the problems that the flow of information creates. In terms of news, more accurate, less sensational reporting of events and groups might lessen the inspirational and educational aspects of daily media releases. Less front-page publicity might be given to terrorist attacks and the terrorists themselves who thrive on that type of attention. Finally, delayed releases of information about certain potentially explosive news events might be utilized voluntarily by news groups in order to let the situations defuse and interest wane. This tactic, involving a type of censorship that is voluntary and, thus, self-regulating, is used by the Israeli government. Little news is released about a terrorist attack in Israel until the event is over. Israel has accepted limitations on the media and the access to information because of the high stakes involved in every terrorist attack made within Israel. Although people in open societies already accept certain limitations on airport use in order to deter airplane hijackings, it is questionable whether they would accept substantially increased regulation of their accessibility and mobility to control other types of terrorism. The transmitters of information, perhaps, could forestall the imposition of such limitations by demonstrating a greater awareness of the effects of information, and consequently, a greater sense of civic responsibility.

A society is also exposed to information via fictional television shows. An increasing awareness exists concerning the harmful effects of violence in television programs.[33] Much of the attention has focused on the psychological effects television has on children; however, other groups in society also seem to be influenced by the violence shown on television as these programs often seem to provide discontented persons with methods and strategies by which they can violently express their frustrations. For example, imitating fictional events that were portrayed in a movie broadcast on television, a group of youths in Massachusetts set a person on fire.[34] However, one cannot fault the media entirely for broadcasting programs depicting violence because they are only responding to the large audiences and numerous advertisers these shows attract. A community might re-organize the television industry so that audience size and advertisers do not determine programming, but the likelihood of such a change seems small. Thus, if government and public groups want to lessen violence on television, they will have to exert pressure on the media industry through government regulations, program boycotts, or other methods.

Another way to undercut the significance of informational flows is, of course, to try to resolve some of the problems directly causing the violence. The problems that confront a modern, urban, industrial society are often the ones that also motivate terrorism in the urban setting. As one observer has commented:

> The megalopolis spawns the urban guerrillas; gives them their distinct characteristics; continues injecting the forces which keep them going. . . . It keeps them alert and active by never ceasing to parade before their eyes the reasons for their alienation and the butts for their hatreds.[35]

Ethnic and social inequalities in education, opportunities, or income could be ameliorated; legitimate means of protest expanded; or political freedoms increased. However, we do not mean to imply that the problems resulting from urban crowding and poverty can be readily resolved or that their resolution will eliminate terrorism. Moreover, improvements in socioeconomic areas may spark unrest not only because expectations and desires tend to increase once some positive change occurs, but also because such changes may threaten some individuals and may not affect others. Thus, attempts to lessen tensions in a society may result in the opposite;[36] proponents of progressive or radical programs should consider this potential for societal instability and make preparations to control it if they expect to implement their reforms successfully.

Terrorism confronts both open and closed societies in the world. Terrorists, without being part of a conspiracy or international organization, have succeeded in instigating fear, in receiving international and national publicity, in causing governments to implement reactionary policies, and in increasing community awareness of and sympathy for their struggle. In Quebec, despite their lack of widespread popular support throughout the sixties, the terrorists played an important part in enlarging the polarization and radicalization evident in local politics. The violence of the terrorists did contribute to the development of the Quebec independence movement and, in that sense, did succeed. Moreover, given the climate existing in the international and national spheres, one could reach the same conclusion about other terrorists in other areas of the world, that is, terrorists can use violence to attain certain goals.

Open societies will continue to be vulnerable to disruption because of their accessibility and, hence, vulnerability, to transnational factors, especially the flow of information, materials, and people. Thus, although a specific situation may be a domestic problem, such as in Quebec or Northern Ireland, its worldwide implications will be enlarged because (1) some members of dissident groups see themselves as part of an international revolutionary struggle to destroy imperialism and, thus, change the balance of forces to favor the anti-imperialists; (2) these struggles have relied on and will rely on ideas, tactics, and strategies from abroad; (3) some members of these groups are increasingly trying to establish contact and stronger links with other radical revolutionary groups; (4) these groups have created and are contributing to a revolutionary environment which their revolutionary activities, the media's coverage of them, and international support of their causes have created.[37]

Control and even limitation of societal accessibility and, thus, penetration by external information, may be an increasingly desirable but unlikely solution to the problems created by or influenced by external information. First, the problem resulting from the flow of information pertains not only to external sources, but also to internal communications. For example, the demonstration effect seemed to be in operation during February 1977 in the United States when a number of incidents occurred involving hostages. First, a Vietnam veteran occupied a bank in Silver Spring, Maryland, and refused to leave; after a prolonged siege, he surrendered to the police. Within the week, Anthony Kiritsis kidnapped and held as hostage one of the owners of the mortgage company that had foreclosed on his mortgage. Next, a thirty-three-year-old weightlifter, angered by his suspension from his job in a warehouse, occupied the building and killed five persons.[38] During the next few weeks, a black man, attempting to publicize the deprivations that blacks experience, took a hostage in a suburb near Cleveland, and Hanafi Muslims, attempting to revenge the murders of some of their followers, seized three buildings in Washington, D.C., and held occupants as hostages. The wide publicity and notoriety connected with each incident led other frustrated individuals to utilize the same means to solve their own difficulties despite the high failure rate of many of those who took hostages.[39] The same type of contagion occurred with plane hijackings in the United States until measures were taken to deter future hijackings.[40] Thus, highly publicized coverage by the mass media of domestic, violent events can spark more such events.

Second, and perhaps more important, the ability and right of the communications system, including those aspects in transportation and education, to present external and internal information uncensored is a critical quality of an open society. Societal accessibility and the resulting penetration is perceived as a necessary and positive aspect of a pluralistic society despite the potential for negative effects.

The ability to act, speak, move, and participate freely is one of the basic principles of an open society. Hence, the imposition by the government of some regulations limiting the society's access to certain information would be theoretically unacceptable.[41]

Third, information flows may not be the direct cause of a problem; more likely, a variety of other factors have caused the individual or group to become frustrated, impatient, and radical to the point where certain information will inspire or provide the means for violence. The Quebec Liberation Front, the Irish Republican Army, and the Palestinian Liberation Organization are products of long-endured, ethnically tense, and bitter situations. In terms of the outbreak of terrorism, the significance of the access to information differs in each case. Informational flows were probably less of a factor in Northern Ireland or the Middle East than in Quebec. Nevertheless, the flow of information was important to all of these terrorists because of their desire to gain international and national publicity and recognition and their awareness from past experiences that such exposure was possible.

Another factor that affects the interaction of the transnational flow of information and terrorism is the international milieu itself. The international environment at present seems to accept the use of violence as a means for dissident groups to resolve their problems. An atmosphere tolerating and, at times, supporting revolutionary violence has been created.[42] The effect of this atmosphere has been to convince

> many active revolutionaries that a world revolutionary comradeship exists. It may be a band of quarreling brothers, but it is a band never-theless. Besides the widespread alliance of the lineage of revolutionary ideologists and strategists, rebels everywhere feel a solidarity with others waging armed struggle against colonials or neoimperialists.[43]

Moreover, the revolutionary milieu "permits and encourages the exchange of aid and comfort between parties as diverse as Basques, Turks, Irish, and Arabs."[44] Thus, as long as terrorists receive the kind of moral support from the international environment that they have received in the past, terrorism will continue to threaten the international system and its various subsystems.

However, an increasing awareness of the explosive effects of con-doning revolution and political violence seems evident among many world leaders. For example, because terrorists have found it more difficult to find a safe landing spot for their hijacked planes, they have not resorted to this tactic as frequently as in the past; moreover, some Arab leaders, realizing the internal hardships and dangers of war, have become more interested in resolving the Middle East conflict. Although one cannot expect this type of progress when dealing with other troubled areas in the world, the situations elsewhere can only benefit by a lessening of support for terrorism and a decrease in the news about terrorist activities.

Furthermore, the international milieu is not as revolutionary as all the rhetoric might make it appear. Few truly international revolutionaries are active, although some revolutionary groups may become involved in struggles beyond their own boundaries. In effect, because more modern revolutionary movements are national, bent on seizing the state power that holds the "prime political loyalty of its citizens," these groups have in common only their rhetorical support for a world revolutionary society that would paradoxically come into existence only by destroying the nationalist basis of the movements themselves.[45] Because of the inherent difficulties and contradictions, the appearance of an organized, international revolutionary movement seems extremely unlikely despite the technological advances in communications and transportation that could facilitate such a transnational movement.

Informational flows, thus, seem to benefit militants or discontented individuals or groups in today's international system in four main ways. First, mass media coverage of an event will lead to greater attention, even if momentary, being given to the individuals or groups involved and their reasons for causing such a controversy. In this sense, it is a propaganda tool. Second, the flow of information may expose societies to information that will inspire and justify an individual's or group's use of violence. Third, by providing information concerning specific terrorist tactics and strategies, the international communications system has often supplied discontented groups sufficient technological knowledge and ideological justification to support their use of terrorism. Fourth, the flow of information resulting from a successful terrorist attack may provide the utilitarian inspiration needed to cause a contagion of similar events elsewhere in the world. Although this contagion effect is not a new phenomenon, the improvements in the communication system have accelerated the process and, thereby, increased the problems of controlling the outbreak of low-level violence throughout the world. Thus, the transnational flow of information plays an extremely important role in domestic and international affairs today because of the improvements in the breadth, range, and speed of communications which, in turn, can affect the type, timing, and scope of individual or societal instability.

Notes

1. Transnational interactions relate to "the movement of tangible or intangible items across state boundaries when at least one actor is not an agent of a government or an intergovernmental organization." Joseph S. Nye, Jr., and Robert O. Keohane, eds., *Transnational Relations and World Politics* (Cambridge: Harvard University Press, 1972), p. xii.

2. Ibid., p. 376.

3. Ibid., p. 375.

4. In this study, "political violence" will be used in the same way that Ted R. Gurr used it in *Why Men Rebel*; that is, it will refer to "all collective attacks, within a political community against the political regime, its actors—including competing political groups as well as incumbents—or its policies." Ted R. Gurr, *Why Men Rebel* (Princeton, N.J.: Princeton University Press, 1971), pp. 3-4.

5. Mancur Olson, Jr., "Rapid Growth as a Destabilizing Force," *The Journal of Economic History* 23 (December 1963):551-552.

6. Ibid., pp. 532, 540, 551-552.

7. See Karl W. Deutsch, *Nationalism and Social Communication: An Inquiry into the Foundations of Nationality*, 2d ed. (London and Cambridge, Mass.: The M.I.T. Press, 1966), pp. 87-106; or Richard Merritt, "Transmission of Values," pp. 5, 11-15, and David Bobrow, "Transfer of Meanings Across National Boundaries," pp. 33-61, both in *Communications in International Politics*, ed. Richard Merritt (Urbana: University of Illinois Press, 1972); or Melvin L. DeFleur, *Theories of Mass Communications*, 2d ed. (New York: David McKay Company, Inc., 1970), pp. 76-96, 118-154.

8. Cynthia H. Enloe, *Ethnic Conflict and Political Development* (Boston: Little, Brown, and Company, 1973), p. 6.

9. Claude Ryan, "The French-Canadian Dilemma," *Foreign Affairs* 43 (April 1965):471.

10. Oran R. Young, "Interdependencies in World Politics," *International Journal* 24 (Autumn 1969):737.

11. Frederick W. Fry, "Communication and Development," in *Handbook of Communication*, ed. Ithiel de Sola Pool, et al. (Chicago: Rand McNally College Publishing Company, 1973), p. 388.

12. Young, p. 738.

13. The Kondratieff cycles, "the long waves of economic activity named after the Russian economist who first described them," predict a lag between economic and sociopolitical changes. Kondratieff's cyclical theory, which assumed that there are "regular and predictable relationships among the technological, economic, social, and political systems" of countries, claims that because political systems resist the technological or economic waves of change, a lag of ten years or so occurs during which time dissatisfaction and turbulence increase in the society. Thus, the political system will be "badly out of phase with the times" even once it makes the necessary accommodations to the changes and will still be the cause of uncertainty and instability in the society. This part of the Kondratieff theory of cycles seems to be applicable to the Quebec situation during the fifties and sixties. See Ehud Levy-Pascal, *An Analysis of the Cyclical Dynamics of Industrialized Countries* (Washington, D.C.: Central Intelligence Agency, Office of Political Research, January 1976), passim.

14. Gurr, p. 231.

15. W. Phillips Davison, "International and World Public Opinion," in *Handbook of Communication*, p. 882.

16. W. Phillips Davison, *Mass Communication and Conflict Resolution: The Role of the Information Media in the Advancement of International Understanding* (New York: Praeger Publishers, 1974), p. 30.

17. Ibid.

18. Degrees of openness and, thus, accessibility exist. Brazil is an example of a relatively closed society, yet it receives more information concerning external events and ideas than Cambodia and less than West Germany. The critical qualities of an open society revolve around the governing power's policies towards freedom of speech, press censorship, foreign contacts, and freedom of movement within and outside the state.

19. Hedrick Smith, *The Russians* (New York: Random House, Inc., 1976; Ballantine Books, 1977), p. 25.

20. Ibid., p. 465. See also Richard Pipes, "Reflections on the Nationality Problems in the Soviet Union," in *Ethnicity: Theory and Experience*, ed. Nathan Glazer and Daniel P. Moynihan (Cambridge: Harvard University Press, 1975), pp. 453-465, for more information on non-Russian nationalities and their dissent.

21. Malcolm Reid, *The Shouting Signpainters: A Literary and Political Account of Quebec Revolutionary Nationalism* (Toronto and London: McClelland & Stewart, 1972), p. 236.

22. Ibid., p. 302. See also Sheilagh Hodgins Milner and Henry Milner, *The Decolonization of Quebec: An Analysis of Left-Wing Nationalism* (Toronto: McClelland & Stewart, 1973), chapter 10, passim.

23. For more detail on Quebec terrorism and transnational factors, see Reid, passim; also Marc Laurendeau, *Les Québécois Violents* (Montreal: Les Editions du Boreal Express, 1974); Detective Sergeant Masse, "L'évolution du terrorisme au Québec, 1963-1972," unpublished manuscript; and Amy Sands Redlick, "The Impact of Transnational Interactions on Terrorism: A Case Study of the Quebec Terrorist Movement" (Ph.D. dissertation, The Fletcher School of Law and Diplomacy, 1977), passim.

24. Davison, *Mass Communication and Conflict Resolution*, p. 12.

25. See Deutsch, pp. 87-106; or Merritt, pp. 5, 11-15; or Bobrow, pp. 33-61, for more information on the effect that similarities between transmitting and receiving societies can have on the flow of information between the two.

26. Davison, "International and World Opinion," p. 881.

27. Ramsay Cook, "The French-Canadian Question," *Political Quarterly* 36 (January/March 1965):14.

28. Karl W. Deutsch, "External Involvement in Internal War," in *Internal War*, ed. Harry Eckstein (New York: Free Press, 1964), p. 100; see also David Milbank, *International and Transnational Terrorism: Diagnosis and Prognosis* (Washington, D.C.: Central Intelligence Agency, April 1976), pp. 18-19.

29. See Robert R. Palmer, *The Age of the Democratic Revolutions: A Political History of Europe and America 1760-1800.* (Princeton, N.J.: Princeton University Press, 1959).

30. Edward Hyams, *Terrorists and Terrorism* (London: J. M. Dent, 1975), p. 11.

31. The two immigrants, Georges Schoeters, a Belgian, and François Schirm, a Hungarian, organized the first and third waves of terrorism in Quebec.

32. J. Bowyer Bell, *Transnational Terror*, AEI-Hoover Policy Study 17 (Washington, D.C.: American Enterprise Institute for Public Policy Research, September 1975; Stanford, Calif.: Hoover Institution on War, Revolution, and Peace, September 1975), p. 89.

33. Some recent articles on violence on television include T. F. Hartnagel, et al., "Television Violence and Violent Behavior," *Social Forces* 54 (December 1975):341-351; D. Howitt and R. Denbo, "Subcultural Account of Media Effects," *Human Relations* 27 (January

1974):25-41; and R. Gorney, et al., "Impact of Dramatized Television Entertainment on Adult Males," *American Journal of Psychiatry* 134 (February 1977):170-174.

34. Haynes Johnson, "Everyone Shares in Acts of Violence," *Washington Post*, 10 March 1977, p. 1.

35. John Gellner, *Bayonets in the Streets: Urban Guerrilla at Home and Abroad* (Don Mills, Ontario: Collier-Macmillan of Canada, Ltd., 1974), p. 69.

36. Olson, pp. 551-552.

37. Milbank, pp. 18-20, 28-32.

38. "Crime: Hard Bargains," *The Economist*, 19 February 1977, pp. 47-48.

39. Those people taking hostages in February and March of 1977 were either killed or captured by the police; see Johnson, p. 1. The urban race riots in the sixties in the United States and the coups d'etats in Latin America are examples of internal demonstration effects.

40. The advent of metal detectors and luggage checks has deterred or prevented many terrorist hijackings in the United States. The United States–Cuban Antihijacking Agreement also deterred hijackers since their close, safe haven was eliminated.

41. This is not to imply that such regulation has not or will not occur. Propaganda during wartime, local movie censorship, and curriculum choices are all examples of subtle limitations on the information flow.

42. Bell, pp. 74-75; also Milbank, pp. 18-19.

43. Bell, p. 74.

44. Ibid, p. 75.

45. J. Bowyer Bell, "Contemporary Revolutionary Organizations," in *Transnational Relations and World Politics*, pp. 167-168.

Part 3

The Perpetrators

4
Terrorist Movements
Paul Wilkinson

Introduction

It is a common error to equate terrorism with guerrilla war and violence in general. Terrorism[1] is in fact a special mode of violence, which may be briefly defined as coercive intimidation. It involves the threat of murder, injury, or destruction to terrorize a given target into conceding to the terrorists' will. As a policy or process, terrorism therefore consists of three basic elements: the decision by the perpetrators of violence to use terrorism as a systematic weapon, the threats or acts of extranormal violence themselves, and the effects of this violence upon the immediate victims—the "target" group or "audience"—and the wider national and international opinion that the terrorists may seek to intimidate or influence.

Many have fallen into the error of identifying a single locus, agent, or context of terrorism with terrorism per se. Some equate it with certain criminal and psychopathological manifestations.[2] Many assume it to be purely a mode of urban insurrection and thereby ignore whole aspects of the history of terrorism in rural conflicts in, for example, the Balkans, Indochina, and Ireland.[3]

Commoner still is the attempt to restrict the terrorist designation to acts of movements and individuals. Yet this is to turn one's back on the ghastly facts of the systematic use of repressive terror by states, such as that employed by the revolutionary regime in France 1792-1794,[4] by the Bolsheviks in Russia after 1917,[5] by fascist regimes, and by numerous imperialist and colonialist regimes. Nor should we ignore the growing propensity of states to sponsor, arm, and plan proxy terrorism as a form of coercive diplomacy and subversion against allegedly hostile states. Of course it is true that many acts of state violence have been clothed in the legitimacy of positive law or raison d'état, but many would argue, with Hannah Arendt,[6] that such acts can be shown to violate the more fundamental norms of moral and natural law. I wish to make clear at the outset my agreement with those philosophers who argue that the all-important questions of justification and legitimacy must be posed concerning acts of states as well as acts of individuals and movements. Moreover, although I have been asked to concentrate, in the present discussion, on terrorist movements rather than terrorist states, I do not believe it is possible to adequately understand the former without paying some attention to the effects of the use of force and violence by states. Indeed, the latter often helps to provoke and fuel the violence of terrorist movements. Historically, state and factional violence have repeatedly displayed this symbiotic relationship.

Terrorism is inherently indiscriminate both in its physical and psychological effects. This is partly a consequence of the destructive nature of much modern terrorist weaponry (bombs, landmines, and so on) and partly the result of the human error factor (the terrorist cannot always be certain that he gets the "right" target or that no third party will be harmed); but it is frequently the outcome of deliberate terrorist attacks on public places to cause generalized terror and havoc. The elements of unpredictability and arbitrariness are inherent in the strategy of spreading terror. As Raymond Aron has noted,

> an action of violence is labelled "terrorist" when its psychological effects are out of proportion to its purely physical result . . . the lack of discrimination helps to spread fear, for if no one in particular is a target, no one can be safe.[7]

Even if terrorists claim, as they frequently do, to "select" individual targets with precision, these acts of assassination are inevitably planned in secret. Whatever the terrorists may say about warning certain targets that they are liable for "execution," the fact is that no one can be sure who will be the next victim. Hence, the acts appear arbitrary to the community or group subjected to the terror. One writer has expressed this point very clearly: "no observance of commands—no matter how punctilious—on the part of the prospective victims can ensure their safety."[8]

Another important distinction between terrorism and other forms of violence is that terrorists recognize no ethical or humanitarian limits to their use of violence: any means are permissible and everyone (including civilians, women, children, and neutrals) is expendable in the interests of "revolution," "justice," or "liberation." Thus terrorists neither recognize nor observe any rules or conventions of war. They assume a license to savagery.

Ultimately, it must be faced that terrorism is an evaluative concept.[9] The whole notion of terrorism as something extranormal and intolerable is only meaningful in a society where social peace and order and freedom from fear and the natural expectations. But of course there are extremists of both right and left whose evaluation of terrorism is quite different. Some have seen terroristic violence as positively desirable or even "liberating" or "cathartic." Others have been willing to espouse it as an occasional political expedient, and some have actually developed monstrous regimes based on repression, torture (the extreme form of individualized terror), and mass terror.[10]

Those who place a high value on the sanctity of human life and freedoms recognize terrorism's intrinsic inhumanity, its fundamental denial of, and assault upon, human rights. To assert, as I do, that terrorism, like torture, is incompatible with a humane and civilized society, is to make a value judgment. Hence, to pretend that interpreting or theorizing about terrorism is a "value-free" activity is sheer obfuscation. One of our greatest needs, in this field of social theory as in others, is to develop a conceptual framework and method in which value assumptions are made explicit. In other words, I am arguing that if the study of violence is to be meaningful and fruitful it must come to terms with fundamental ethical and philosophical issues.

The study of terrorist movements is evaluative both in general and in a more specific sense. When a historian designates a specific movement or faction as "terrorist," he is also making a value judgment, presumably in the light of his knowledge of the group's professed motives, its modus operandi and the effects of its violence upon its immediate victims, its "target audience," and its host community. It would clearly be foolish to assume that all those groups labeled as terrorist by regimes are necessarily terrorist in reality. For example, many modern dictatorships find "terrorist" a ready-made pejorative for any opposition group of which they disapprove.[11] The historian, and especially the contemporary historian, therefore has the vital task of carefully examining all the evidence about the activities of specific movements. Very often this evidence will not be fully available, perhaps because of a deliberate coverup by a regime or by the movement leadership or because of fear of retribution on the part of witnesses. Often one of the most intractable problems encountered by the analyst is that of establishing the motivations of perpetrators of violence. What did they aim to achieve? Was there a specific policy of terrorism?[12] Even supposing it is possible to identify the individual bomb-planters or hit men—and this after all often defeats even the best police experts in the world—where does the responsibility for planning and ordering the act of terrorism reside? Generally, the pathetic and frightened creature who actually performs the act of violence, and who stands greatest risk of capture, is at the end of a very long chain of command. One is reminded of Gorky's comment that an act of violence is sometimes "like a stone thrown by an unknown hand. Is the stone therefore guilty?" The historian and the social scientist must therefore constantly strive to establish the truth about events, motivations, organizations, and effects, in relation to each campaign and act of violence. As Feliks Gross has enjoined, they must at very least ask, For what? By whom? Why?[13]

One problem that arises for the student is that there is often no clear and unambivalent policy to which all revolutionary or national liberation movements subscribe concerning terrorism. More often than not, terrorism is pursued by small factions or militant groups that, though operating under the broad ideological umbrella of the movement, act autonomously and without even the official approval of the political leadership. Sometimes, as in the case of the Basques, the liberation movement fragments into warring sects and schisms, each with their own leadership, aims, and tactics.

The Palestine Liberation Organization (PLO) is a good contemporary example of a national liberation-style movement that is, in reality, a congeries of different ideological factions. Recently, Yasir Arafat and the PLO "moderates" have been attempting to shake off the terrorist image and if not to outlaw, at least to restrain, hijacking and other terrorist activities of the kind favored by the Popular Front for the Liberation of Palestine and Black June. Some argue that the new image of respectability and diplomatic responsibility reflected at the Rabat summit and informal recognition at the UN is not very convincing. Nevertheless there is overwhelming evidence of a fundamental split in the PLO over the question of the desirability of further terrorism. It is neither accurate nor helpful to blur these important distinctions.[14] There is certainly a pressing need for further detailed case studies of terrorist movements and campaigns, using the normal canons of scholarly rigor and historical accuracy.

One other preliminary point needs to be made about the general concept of terrorism as a mode of violence. It is vital to recognize the distinction between terrorists who are politically motivated, and who evince some degree of political rationality and idealism, and those who are merely criminal or criminally insane. A major difficulty arises in trying to identify the borderline between these categories.

Increasingly, certainly since the great upsurge of international terrorism in the late 1960s, criminals and psychopaths have tended to borrow the rhetorical clothes and methods of the political terrorist. Was Donald DeFreeze of the Symbionese Liberation Army more criminal than revolutionary or vice versa? It may be relatively straightforward to resolve such a problem in an extreme case, such as that of the Manson family, who claimed, at their trial, that their motivation was political. But in organizations such as the Red Army Faction, the Front de Libération du Québec, or the Provisional Irish Republican Army, revolutionism and criminality are found to be inextricably intertwined. As I have argued elsewhere, there is a special syndrome of revolutionary criminality that characterizes certain revolutionary terrorist movements, especially those of nihilist and anarchist tendencies. Interestingly, it is tiny movements of this kind that have shown the greatest propensity for international and transnational terrorist operations.

Major Types of Terrorist Movement[15]

In the present discussion I shall concentrate upon what might be termed the archetypal "pure terror" movements that explicitly practice terrorism as their primary weapon for certain professed political ends. It is not difficult to find examples of movements whose polemics commend, promote, and justify the systematic use of terror:

> The revolutionary (terrorist) despises all dogmas and all sciences, leaving them for future generations. He knows only one science—the science of destruction . . . the object is perpetually the same: the quickest and surest way of destroying this whole filthy order. . . . For him, there exists only one pleasure, one consolation, one reward, one satisfaction, the success of the terror. Night and day he must have but one thought, one aim, merciless destruction . . .[16]

> Violence is a purifying force. It frees the native from the inferiority complex and from despair and inaction. It makes him fearless and restores his self-respect.[17]

> We have to form groups and settle accounts, once and for all, with the whole gang of those damned, heartless exploiters . . . There is enough dynamite in Quebec to blow up all of them. It will be the turn of the millionaires and militarists to taste blood—their own blood. After all, guns can be used for something else but hunting . . .[18]

One can distinguish at least four main types of terrorist movement currently active: (1) nationalist, autonomist, or ethnic minority movements; (2) ideological sects or secret societies seeking some form of "revolutionary" justice or social liberation; (3) exile or emigre groups with irredentist, separatist, or revolutionary aspirations concerning their country of origin; and (4) transnational gangs deploying terrorists and logistic support from two or more countries, generally in the name of some vague "world revolutionary" goal. Often a number of different factions and movements, often quite tiny, representing several types, coexist uneasily within the same umbrella organization, as in the case of the Algerian FLN or the present-day PLO.

If the "success" of terrorist movements is to be judged by their ability to realize their long-term political objectives, then those in the nationalist category have the best track record. Wherever there is a deeply felt sense of oppression and resentment against alien rule on the part of large sections of the population, the nationalist rallying cry is a grave danger signal for the incumbent regime. For the terrorist movement that proclaims national independence as its major goal can bid to represent a whole ethnic constituency, however dubious the credentials of the terrorist leadership and however undemocratic their internal processes. If a nationalist terror movement is recognized as legitimate by a large proportion of its proclaimed constituency (say a quarter to a third of its members), it will have a more powerful basis on which to challenge the incumbents than any nihilist or utopian revolutionary could hope for. Moreover, if, in addition, the nationalist movement can use terror and agitation to neutralize a further third of the population, that is to say, to withhold positive support and cooperation from the incumbent regime, the way is open for them to exploit any military or political weakness, internal division, or lack of will, on the part of the authorities.

The practical advantages to the terrorists of having a large corps of activists and sympathizers, and a large passive element waiting fearfully to see who wins the struggle, are obvious. Terrorists need, in addition to plentiful recruits and supplies of cash and weapons, reliable lines of communication, safe houses, and a constant flow of intelligence on what the authorities are up to. But there is a still more important advantage in having, to use the Maoist image, a favorable sea in which the terrorist fish can swim: the incumbent security forces will be denied the vital intelligence and cooperation from the public upon which they depend to catch the terrorists. This was one of the winning cards of the Ethniki Organosis Kypriakou Agoniston (EOKA) terrorists in their fight against the British army and police in Cyprus.[19] The British forces found themselves confronted, time and again, by an impenetrable wall of silence which effectively cancelled out the authorities' advantages of numbers and firepower.

These factors certainly help to explain the few solitary successes of movements using terrorism as a primary weapon in the struggle for power, in the modern period. As a weapon against well-established liberal democracies or against indigenous autocracies, terrorism has proved an almost total failure. Only in a small number of armed colonial independence struggles in the 1940s, 1950s, and early 1960s (mainly directed against British and French colonial administrations) did terrorism prove effective in persuading the metropolitan publics and their governments that the costs of maintaining their military presence outweighed the costs of withdrawal. Britain's eventual relinquishments of control in Palestine in 1948 and in Cyprus in 1960 are perhaps the most clearcut instances. Terrorist violence also played a key part in forcing British withdrawal from the Canal Zone base in 1954 and from Aden in 1964, and French withdrawal from Algeria in 1962.[20]

These successes of the terrorist strategy were undoubtedly considerably facilitated by three other key factors. First, the metropolitan governments and their publics were weary of war in general and colonial wars in particular. They wanted to bring their soldiers home, for the public had no real stomach for the conflicts. Both colonialism and imperialism were no longer popular causes: jingoism had long since given way to a guilt-ridden disillusion with any overseas military adventures. Another important factor conducive to withdrawal was the straitened economic circumstances of the mother countries, impoverished by years of world war, preoccupied with the problems of internal reconstruction and economic survival: they simply could not stand the financial costs of prolonged involvements in colonial wars. In Britain's case, there was an additional consideration: a growing popular feeling that there were no vital strategic interests at stake in such distant entanglements. Formally, this new realism was reflected in the official British policy of negotiating independence for one colony after another in the 1950s and 1960s. Indeed it was a bitter irony that it was in situations of internal communal strife, where there was no universally accepted "bargaining agent" for the native population, that Britain found herself swept into the whirlpools of bitter internal war and terrorism (as in Palestine where Arabs fought Jews and in the Graeco-Turkish conflict in Cyprus).

Now the great era of colonial independence struggles has passed. Yet it would be naive to assume that this signifies the end of nationalist and irredentist movements in former colonial states. The intractable problems of struggling to sustain internal cohesion and order have simply been inherited by the successor states, many of which are pathetically ill-equipped—economically, politically, and militarily—to handle them. More often than not the new states inherited frontiers that show scant regard for ethnic, linguistic, and religious divisions. Hence we now have a situation in which there is hardly a single country in the Third World that has not experienced serious internal conflict in the form of separatist struggles or intercommunal strife in the past decade. Movement after movement has resorted to armed struggle: the Kurds, Somalis, Ibos, Bakongos, Khmers, and the Chinese in Malaya are just a few examples of the ethnic groups that have taken up arms against their new masters. As the frontiers of the Third World rigidify in the postcolonial era, we may expect an increasing number of these desperate groups, trapped awkwardly astride the diplomatic frontiers, to resort to the gun and the bomb. No doubt terrorism will not invariably be the primary weapon in the struggles of these new nationalist movements, but all the signs are that this source of terrorism will increase dramatically in Asia, Africa, and the Middle East.

The Soviet Union and other communist regimes have given a high political priority to providing valuable military, economic, political, and diplomatic support to what they term national liberation struggles. True they have occasionally burned their fingers by an injudicious choice of client, and sometimes they have been effectively balked by Western action. But they have recently had dramatic successes in Indochina and Africa, which are likely to tempt them into increasing investments of intervention. It would be naive to assume that Soviet leaders invariably bank on obtaining a totally compliant or satellite regime through these involvements. Undoubtedly, they also regard it as a significant gain if they simply achieve a further exclusion of the Western powers from access to raw materials, markets, base facilities, and political cooperation in the area concerned. Of course, when this has been effected, they will try to use every available economic and military leverage to tie the new Marxist orientated regimes, via closer interdependence collaboration, to the Soviet bloc.

In general terms, the ideological terrorist sects and secret societies constitute nothing like such a serious long-term threat to individual Western states or to Western strategic interests. These movements, whether of the neo-Fascist far right or the neo-Marxist and anarchist far left, are more analogous to tiny gangs of bandits than to serious political movements. Groups like the Red Army Faction, the Japanese Red Army, the Weathermen, the Red Brigades, and the Angry Brigade typically present a bizarre contradiction: Lilliputian membership and negligible popular support coupled with the most pretentious language of people's revolutionary war and struggles against world capitalist imperialism. A more appropriate label, perhaps, for many of these weird cults of violence and hate would be the title adopted by a small group in Heidelberg in 1970, the Socialist Patients' Collective.[21]

Ideological terrorist sects of this kind originate exclusively within the industrialized liberal democracies that they profess to hate so heartily. They like to claim that they are the vanguard of a people's revolution and that their actions will inspire revolutionary consciousness and solidarity with the workers. In practice their tiny memberships are drawn exclusively from the children of affluent and privileged homes. Most tend to be recruited from among extremist political groups in the universities. Far from speaking the language of the working classes, they live in a kind of fantasy world concocted from vulgar neo-Marxist slogans and the half-baked and dangerous ideals of Sartre and Marcuse.

These groups are especially baffling to the outside world because they do not share the same canons of rationality: rather they create their own "transcendental" rationality, which transvalues everything in terms of the revolutionary ideology. The chiliastic utopianism of groups like the Baader-Meinhof gang, the Weathermen, and the Japanese Red Army totally rejects the existing order as being vile and beyond redemption. There is no ground for negotiating any compromise between their ends and those of the rest of society. Ideological terrorists dwell in a Manichean mental world divided into the oppressor-exploiters and their collaborators on the one hand, and themselves as soldiers of revolutionary justice on the other. Instead of viewing the use of terrorism in instrumental-rational terms, involving a realistic calculation of its political effectiveness and the possibilities of success, acts of violence become ends in themselves. In short, for these revolutionary secret societies, terrorism becomes an integral part of their ideology and lifestyle.

In the nineteenth century, the cult of the heroic revolutionary fighter was fostered by the cult of romantic individualism reflected in Goethe, Humboldt, Schiller, and Stefan George. They posited a heroic genius forced into conflict with society or into isolation by the philistinism of the world. Max Stirner elaborated this individualism into a cult of the self-assertive egoist[22] which, in its amorality and antiintellectualism, anticipated certain currents in modern existentialism. The existentialist idea, so powerfully articulated in Heidegger and Sartre, that it is only through our own actions or acts of will that we can escape from despair, has been enormously pervasive. Under certain conditions, such beliefs can become powerfully conducive to acts of terrorism. They can create a kind of politics of will and glorification of action for its own sake of the kind which Marinetti and the Futurists, and later the Fascists, expounded. [23] In an age of mass politics and all-pervasive bureaucracies, extremists of left and right may come to feel that all effective forms of symbolic action are exhausted. They may become convinced that acts of terrorism are the only means of asserting individual will and power. The culmination of this politics of the blood is an utterly amoral aestheticization of politics: *"Qu'importe les victimes, si le geste est beau?"*[24] The fact is that for some terrorists extreme violence is primarily undertaken as an act of self-assertion and self-expression.

It must be remembered that it does not take many people, or indeed large amounts of cash and explosives, to mount a terror campaign. Hence, even if the major guerrilla war never gets off the ground, even if the masses inexplicably fail to rise, the fanatical revolutionary can take some small comfort from the continuation of death and destruction in the name of revolution. Terrorism becomes the fig leaf for their revolutionary virtue and a theatre of revolutionary deeds that can be glamorized and romanticized to help the weak actually *believe* they are strong and that revolution is on the way. Terrorism may become more than a profession: for some it becomes a drug, an addiction to murder, which is in reality a sublimate for the urge to rebel.

In contrast, then, to the movement that has a genuine nationalist legitimacy and popular constituency of support, the ideological sect are outlaws, *francs-tireurs* even in their country of origin. For the nationalist movement, the realities of political power bring their own responsibilities. Nationalists have to concern themselves to a considerable extent with building up their own bases of domestic support and with winning over foreign governments and international opinion to their cause. This inevitably imposes certain restraints on the use of terrorism. They must learn when to play politics, when to exert diplomatic pressure, and how to avoid alienating public opinion. The ideological votaries, on the other hand, are isolated and desperate from start to finish, often hated even more among their own fellow citizens than they are abroad. Constantly hunted and harassed by the police, these tiny groups often have no choice but to operate abroad. Frequently, they resort to acts of international terrorism simply because terrorism at home has become too dangerous and difficult. This trend to greater internationalization of their activities among the terrorist sects, dating from the early 1970s, is one of the most significant trends. Bilateral and multilateral cooperation among such groups has undoubtedly been facilitated by the fact that most of them share a crude neo-Marxist ideology that designates world capitalist imperialism as the common enemy.

Strategies and Tactics of Terrorist Movements

Ideologies and beliefs are not the only important determinants of the characteristics of terrorist movements. Equally important is the broader politicostrategic context of revolutionary struggle, for there are numerous alternative tactical uses of terrorism within the broader revolutionary strategy.[25] Very often the status and influence of the terrorist organization's leadership will depend on the importance of its role in the eyes of the revolutionary directorate.

In a protracted revolutionary guerrilla war, terrorist units may play an important auxiliary role at every phase of the struggle. In Vietnam, for example, terrorism was by no means restricted to the incipient stage of the conflict. Nor was it viewed by the North Vietnamese leadership as merely of propaganda value. It was used with deadly effect to destroy the structure of South Vietnam control in the countryside (through the murder of village headmen and local officials).[26] It was deployed to neutralize the peasant population and to intimidate them into cooperation with the new parallel revolutionary structures providing local control, taxation, and logistic support for the guerrillas. This intensive and prolonged rural terrorism and assassination was carried out by Vietcong guerrilla groups as a routine part of their task in the course of general responsibility for waging guerrilla war against South Vietnamese security forces, and, later on, in the offensive phase, in concerting their operations with those of the North Vietnamese army. In the rural areas, they did not need to create specialized groups for the terrorist function. In the more hostile environment of the South Vietnamese cities, however, they did create special urban terror cells, the Dac Cong units, which concentrated all their efforts on bombings, sabotage, and the murder of police and officials. Nor were these of negligible military value. The North Vietnamese were fully aware of the advantages of diverting considerable enemy forces in the thankless and time-consuming role of urban security and guard duties. But in this kind of protracted guerrilla war, waged on both rural and urban fronts, the terrorist cells, no matter how useful as an auxiliary weapon, can have no decisive voice in determining the overall revolutionary strategy. True, they have to be given a certain autonomy in the conduct of operations, especially in the cities behind enemy lines, but the revolutionary military and political leaders regard them as essentially expendable elements in the overall balance of forces.

The relative importance of the terrorist leadership and organization is, of course, far greater under conditions where there is a prolonged terrorist campaign unsupported by any wider guerrilla war. The leaders of such a prolonged and intensive campaign generally have one of several long-term revolutionary strategies in mind. They may hope to provoke or trigger a wider civil war, perhaps involving some external intervention on behalf of their cause. Or they may adopt what Geoffrey Fairbairn has described as a kind of political jiu-jitsu[27] against the incumbents. Terrorists using this method seek to exploit the moral and political strength of their will to win to compensate for their relative military weakness vis-à-vis the regime. The technique is to maintain a level of ruthless terrorist assaults on the community and the regime, imposing such an attrition rate in life and treasure that it saps the authorities' will to stand firm. Eventually, the terrorists hope, the morale of the regime will break, leading to the government's virtual political surrender. The terrorists, meanwhile, will move in to fill the vacuum and take power for themselves. The leadership of the Provisional IRA probably hope that such a scenario will actually occur in Northern Ireland and bring about British withdrawal and a united "socialist" Ireland. This strategy is better known as the strategy of leverage. Of course, it depends for its success on a number of other variables, such as the influence of international opinion and powerful foreign governments, a lack of willpower and patience upon the part of the incumbent government, and the absence of determined and expert security forces capable of containing or suppressing the violence.

Clearly, the stakes for terrorists who follow such a path are very high indeed. If their gamble comes off, then the terrorists can generally expect to be able to take political power, even if they have to fight it out between themselves to decide who will rule. But if the fulcrum fails to work according to plan, the terrorists stand to lose everything. By staking everything on this strategy they have no other resources to fall back on. The hardcore of terrorist activists will, unless they are lucky enough to flee the country, end up dead or imprisoned for very long periods, and the cause of their revolution may be set back generations.

But these approaches by no means exhaust the possible political uses of terrorism. Terrorist movements can create a general climate of fear and collapse among target communities, governments, or elite groups. Protracted terrorism may persuade large numbers of people that the government can no longer be relied on to uphold the laws or protect life and limb. Public confidence, loyalty, and active cooperation may become gravely undermined. Terrorism is also a useful weapon for inspiring emulation among followers and sympathizers and for heightening revolutionary morale and awareness. Okamoto, one of the captured Japanese Red Army terrorists who gave testimony on the Lod airport massacre of May 1972, in which he participated, stated:

> The incident has been reported worldwide, but it seem to me nobody has grasped the motivation for it. But when a similar operation takes place next time what will the world think? . . . The Arab world lacks spiritual fervour, so we felt that through this attempt we could probably stir the Arab world . . . .[28]

Many terrorist atrocities are designed as "propaganda of the deed."

Perhaps most dangerous of all the possible political uses of terrorism are those designed to provoke and exploit a vicious spiral of violence and counterviolence. It can be used, for instance, in an attempt to polarize intercommunal relations and to destroy the moderates and compromizers of the political center. (This technique was used by the FLN terror squads in Algeria to destroy those groups in the Muslim population in favor of peaceful evolution and cooperation with the French authorities.) Terrorism may also be deployed, as Carlos Marighella proposed, in an effort to "militarize" the political situation.[29] Here the terrorists' aim is to provoke the authorities into a panic and overreaction. If the government can be trapped into ordering its security forces into general repression and harassment of the civilian population and the suspension of civil rights, the terrorists will seek to exploit the position. They will try to get the people to blame the violence and disruption on the government and the security forces and proffer themselves as the party of social justice and the defenders of civil rights.

It has been pointed out earlier that, however plausible and appealing they may be to large numbers of contemporary revolutionary movements, these long-term strategic objectives have very rarely been achieved by the use of terrorism. How, then, does one explain the apparently undiminished appetite of insurgent groups around the world for the use of the weapon of terrorism? There are probably several major factors at work here. First, terrorism is remarkably cheap and easy to mount. Its basic materials can be obtained from any pharmacy or hardware store. Its cruder techniques are explained in dozens of easily obtainable terrorist and military manuals and from very ample media coverage. But perhaps the most crucial attraction of all has been the repeated success of terrorist groups in winning useful tactical objectives at very low risk to their own life and liberty. They have managed to win enormous worldwide publicity, which they so crave. The greater the outrage they commit the larger their headlines. Time and again they have also succeeded in blackmailing the authorities into releasing terrorist prisoners from jails, in winning large ransoms, and in capturing the weaponry and explosives with which to conduct further campaigns. It is these attractions that have, more than any other factor, helped to make terrorism the characteristic mode of conflict in our time. However remote the chances of final revolutionary victory may seem, these practical gains provide the terrorist organization with the lifeblood to sustain campaigns of murder and destruction.

Terrorist Organization

Although individual terrorists very often affiliate to broader mass political movements, their own terrorist organizations are typically very small. The optimum size appears to be between 1,500 and 2,500 operatives, and the minimum for a viable terrorist cell is four or five members. Larger terrorist organizations are generally backed up by a body of dependable political supporters and sympathizers and an outer circle of potentially sympathetic strata who may be prepared to rally in active support of the terrorists under certain conditions. (As we have noted, it is frequently a major aim of terrorist groups to serve as a "foco" or catalyst for popular revolutionary mobilization.) The tiny numbers of the terrorist organization are not necessarily a guarantee of ineffectiveness. In terms of the nature of terrorist strategy and tactics, it makes good sense: it makes it easier to achieve total secrecy and surprise and to evade capture and surveillance by the security forces. It is much simpler for tiny terrorist cells to melt away into the background and take cover or to transfer their theater of operations to a fresh region or country.

In addition, there are significant psychological and practical constraints on recruitment. The professional terrorist requires a particular kind of fanatical dedication and ruthlessness combined with an adequate knowledge of firearms, explosives, and terrorist techniques. Because the job entails a risk to life or liberty for the terrorist, there is an understandable reluctance, even on the part of dedicated political extremists, to become involved. While it is undoubtedly true that some individuals are attracted by excitement, action, and (quite frequently) considerable financial rewards, there is obviously only a limited pool of revolutionary activists in any society who relish the life of the permanent outlaw. It is partly for this reason that the classic exponents of revolutionary terrorism, such as Sergei Nechayev and Johannes Most, have insisted on the need for the individual terrorist to utterly sever his ties of affection with his family and friends. Nechayev, in his notorious *Catechism*,[30] demands not merely that the terrorist be wedded to the revolution but that he should also become its obedient slave. And Frantz Fanon stresses the importance of the first irrevocable act of violence as a means of enmeshing the individual in the terrorist organization. Terrorists seek to make the newcomer an accomplice of terror, safely *hors la loi* in the eyes of the regime.

> The group requires that each individual perform an irrevocable action. In Algeria, for example, where almost all the men who called on the people to join in the national struggle were condemned to death or searched for by the French police, confidence was proportional to the hopelessness of each case. You could be sure of a new recruit when he could no longer go back into the colonial system.[31]

Sergei Nechayev may lay claim to having invented the characteristic cellular structure of the terrorist organization. Despite some regional deviations and refinements, this structure is still being employed by the vast majority of currently active terrorist movements. In this system, terrorists are deployed in small cells or firing groups (to use a Tupamaros term). Only one member of each cell is designated to act as leader and link-man with the higher echelons of the terrorist movement and with other cells. Firing-group members are given the minimum necessary information about the organization. This helps to protect the organization against infiltration by the security forces and ensures that if terrorists are captured little of value will be divulged to their interrogators.

The emphases on secrecy and on thwarting the efforts of police intelligence are obviously obsessional in all such groups. It must be

remembered that the whole conspiratorial ethos of the terrorist movement was developed from the experience of revolutionary secret
societies of the nineteenth century, battling against ruthless autocracies. One manifestation of this is the savage punishment meted
out to informers or spies either within or outside the organization.
Some of the most savage acts of repressive terror are imposed on
the members of the organization in order to impose an iron discipline
of fear on the whole organization.

A constant need of the terrorist movement is a ready supply of
cash, weaponry, and ammunition. To this end, the sponsorship or
collaboration of friendly governments can be invaluable. Groups
such as the Bretons, the Basques, and the Kurds, who have generally
lacked a powerful backer, have not had the necessary resources to
sustain prolonged full-scale internal war. Nevertheless, as the Provisional IRA has proved in Northern Ireland, other sources of
weapons can be tapped even when external aid dries up. In such circumstances, the terrorists can turn to bank robberies, weapons thefts,
and kidnapping for huge ransoms, in order to keep themselves well
supplied. It is known that many of the proceeds from the recent wave
of kidnappings in Western Europe were actually acquired by political terrorist organizations and not solely by purely criminal gangs
as is often assumed. The financial rewards can be huge. In Argentina
it was reported that the Ejercito Revolucionario del Pueblo (ERP)
gained a ransom of 14 million dollars for the release of an oil
executive in June 1974 and 60 million dollars in 1975 for the release of
two Bunge and Born heirs. Another well known fund-raising activity
is protection rackets of the kind run by the provisionals in Northern
Ireland.

These rich hauls completely dwarf the average gain for crimes of
violence. Terrorism in many countries is now big business, and there
is no doubt that many groups around the world have adopted
political slogans and labels as a front for private criminal gain. In
other cases, the terrorists, who may originally have embarked on
revolutionary terrorism from motives of political idealism, begin to
enjoy the unexpected fruits of their way of life and live in a manner
to which they have not been accustomed—in expensive villas or jet
setting in the Arab capitals. There is much evidence that the small
elite of international hit men and professional terrorist organizers
form a privileged "aristocracy" whose affluent lifestyle has little
in common with that of the oppressed humanity they claim to serve.
Not all the proceeds of terrorist blackmail are ploughed back into
arms and equipment. Moreover, the plurality of currencies and

banking systems makes it relatively easy for terrorists to transfer their funds and difficult for the police to identify sources and financial backers.

Trained international terrorists are a scarce and expensive commodity for revolutionary organizations. Their training, expertise, and experience makes them hard to replace. Not that they often need to be replaced. A RAND Corporation study of sixty-three major kidnapping and barricade operations between 1968 and 1974 found that terrorists had a 79 percent chance of evading death or punishment, whether or not they successfully seized the hostages. And less that 10 percent of the 127 terrorist attempts at aircraft hijacking between March 1968 and July 1974 resulted in the death or imprisonment of the terrorists. The RAND study found that even in cases where all concessions to the terrorists' demands were rejected, there was a 67 percent chance of the terrorists being able to escape with their lives either by accepting safe passage in lieu of original demands, or going underground, or by surrendering to a sympathetic government.[32]

Furthermore, the average international terrorist has been conditioned into believing that if he or she is captured it will be only for a short while before the government releases them out of sheer fright or their "brothers and sisters" secure their release by further terrorist blackmail. According to Robert A. Fearey, special assistant to the U.S. Secretary of State and Coordinator for Combating Terrorism, between 1971 and 1975, less than 50 percent of captured international terrorists actually served out their prison sentences; the average sentence awarded to terrorists who stood trial was eighteen months.[33] Hence the terrorists' faith in their own release is grounded on an all too accurate assessment of the weakness and pliability of governments. Release of imprisoned comrades thus becomes a prime motivation for further acts of terrorism. It is a factor that is constantly underrated by academic analysts. And Western liberal states are more vulnerable in this regard than authoritarian regimes. The latter do not hesitate to use capital punishment to dispose of terrorists. The liberal state, with its more lenient penal code, clutches the captured terrorist like an asp to its bosom until he or she is freed by one means or another to reembark on a career of systematic murder.

Notes

1. For fuller discussions of the concept of terrorism, see J.B.S. Hardman, "Terrorism," *Encyclopedia of the Social Sciences,* ed.

E. R. Seligman, 14 (New York, 1937), pp. 575-579; Eugene V. Walter, "Violence and the Process of Terror," *American Sociological Review* 29, 2 (Spring 1964):248-257; and Paul Wilkinson, *Political Terrorism* (London, 1974).

2. For example, D. V. Segre and J. H. Adler, "The Ecology of Terrorism," *Encounter* 40, 2 (February 1973):17-24.

3. For example, Anthony Burton, *Urban Terrorism: Theory, Practice and Response* (New York, 1975).

4. See Donald Greer, *The Incidence of Terror during the French Revolution* (Cambridge, Mass., 1935); and Richard Cobb, *Terreur et Subsistances 1793-95* (Paris, 1964).

5. See Alexander Dallin and George W. Breslauer, *Political Terror in Communist Systems* (Stanford, Calif., 1970); and Robert Conquest, *The Great Terror* (London, 1968).

6. Hanna Arendt, *Eichmann in Jerusalem: A Report on the Banality of Evil* (New York, 1965), p. 253ff.

7. Raymond Aron, *Peace and War* (London, 1966), p. 170.

8. S. Andreski, "Terror" in *A Dictionary of the Social Sciences*, eds. Julius Gould and William L. Kolb (Glencoe, Ill., 1964).

9. On this aspect, see Martha Hutchinson, "The Concept of Revolutionary Terrorism," *The Journal of Conflict Resolution* 16, 3 (September 1972):383-396.

10. For a classic discussion of the system of mass terror, see Hannah Arendt, *The Origins of Totalitarianism*, 3rd ed. (London, 1967).

11. See, for example, numerous official statements by the South African government.

12. For a discussion of the distinction between systematic and epiphenomenal terror, see Paul Wilkinson, *Terrorism and the Liberal State* (London, 1977), pp. 47-64.

13. Feliks Gross, "Political Violence and Terror in Nineteenth and Twentieth Century Russia and Eastern Europe" in Vol. 8 of *A Report to the National Commission on the Causes and Prevention of Violence*, eds. James F. Kirham, Sheldon G. Levy, and William J. Crotty (Washington, D.C., 1969).

14. For informative accounts of the complex of Palestinian groups, see Y. Harkabi, *Fedayeen Action and Arab Strategy*, Adelphi Papers 53 (London, 1968); Edgar O'Ballance, *Arab Guerrilla Power* (London, 1973); John Cooley, *Green March, Black September* (London, 1973); and Christopher Dobson, *Black September* (London, 1974).

15. For typologies of terrorism, see Wilkinson, *Political Terrorism*, pp. 32-34, and *Terrorism and the Liberal State*, pp. 47-64.

16. Sergei Nechayev, "Catechism of the Revolutionist" (1869), reprinted in *Daughter of a Revolutionary*, ed. Michael Confino (London, 1974), pp. 221-230.

17. Frantz Fanon, *The Wretched of the Earth* (Harmondsworth, 1967), p. 74.

18. Pierre Vallières, quoted in Gustave Morf, *Terror in Quebec* (Toronto, 1970).

19. C. Foley and W. Scobie, *The Struggle for Cyprus* (Stanford, 1973); and G. Grivas-Dighenis, *Guerrilla Warfare and "EOKA" Struggle* (London, 1964).

20. For a clear historical assessment of the guerrilla struggle and the role of terror in Algeria, see Alistair Horne, *A Savage War of Peace* (London, 1977).

21. See Jillian Becker, *Hitler's Children* (London, 1977), p. 277ff., for a fascinating account of the SPK's activities.

22. Max Stirner, *The Ego and His Own*, trans. S. T. Byington (London, 1907).

23. See Ernest Nolte, *Theorien über den Faschismus* (Köln, 1967).

24. Words of Laurent Tailhade on hearing that a bomb had been thrown in the Chamber of Deputies. Ironically, Tailhade himself was later injured in a bomb attack.

25. For an excellent general survey of revolutionary guerrilla warfare, see Geoffrey Fairbairn, *Revolutionary Guerrilla Warfare* (Harmondsworth, 1974).

26. See Douglas Pike, *The Viet Cong* (Cambridge, Mass., 1966); Bernard Fall, *Viet-Nam Witness 1953-66* (New York, 1966); and Jay Mallin, *Terror in Vietnam* (Princeton, N.J., 1966).

27. Fairbairn, op. cit., p. 348ff.

28. Cited in Peter Clyne, *An Anatomy of Skyjacking* (London, 1973).

29. Carlos Marighella, "Handbook of Urban Guerrilla Warfare" in *For the Liberation of Brazil* (Harmondsworth, 1971), pp. 61-97.

30. Cited in Confino, op. cit.

31. Fanon, op. cit., 67.

32. U.S., Congress, Senate, Committee on the Judiciary, *Terroristic Activity—International Terrorism: Hearings before the Subcommittee to Investigate the Administration of the Internal Security Act and Other Internal Security Laws of the Committee on the Judiciary*, 94th Cong., 1st sess., 14 May 1975, pt. 4.

33. "Terrorism: 'Growing and Increasingly Dangerous'" (Interview with Robert A. Fearey), *U.S. News and World Report*, 29 September 1975, p. 79.

Part 4

The Issues

5

Northern Ireland, Terrorism, and the British State

Alan O'Day

Irish revolutionaries, like American gangsters, have a romantic image—they are larger-than-life fighters. Violence, death, and executions no doubt have some fascination of their own, but when an Irish brogue is added to this already compelling mixture, the brew is particularly potent. Even Hollywood has done magnificently by Irish revolutionaries. John Ford, the well-known director of Irish birth, gave the film world an acute and sensitive tale set against the background of the Anglo-Irish struggle in his *The Informer*. James Cagney portrayed the revolutionary who did not know when to put down his gun in *Shake Hands with the Devil*, which must remain a classic dramatic interpretation of Ireland's fight for freedom. Irish men and women may have been less than ideal revolutionaries, conspirators, and terrorists (their history is so much one of betrayal and defeat), but even terrible reverses have been lent an aura of romance in the pages of literature. Because the Irish speak and write in English, Ireland's case always has been easily and effectively presented to a wide public. Few such groups have begun with so great an advantage. Then, too, the Irish cause has been abetted by the vast number of people overseas who claim some measure of Hibernian blood, boasted annually on the feast of St. Patrick but remembered in a vague way throughout the year.

As a consequence of the troubles in Northern Ireland, a vast corpus of writings on the politics and violence of the province has appeared. Attention has tended to be focused on the terrorism which Ulster has been experiencing, but a variety of related issues in the Republic of Ireland, in Ulster, and in Great Britain have also been discussed. Violence and terrorism have been prevalent in many parts of the world and, not surprisingly, many writers have been interested in viewing the situation in Northern Ireland in this wider context. Unfortunately, the desirability of seeing a common pattern in all terrorist activities and forms of organization may tempt the contemporary historian to force Irish terrorism into a strait jacket for his own convenience. It is valuable, therefore, to examine the origin and character of Irish terrorism in an attempt to assess the extent to which it is an isolated phenomenon and the degree to which the difficulties there may be relevant to our understanding of movements elsewhere.

Lately, many writers have investigated aspects of terrorism and have attempted to define it. Generally, terrorism has been interpreted to mean the use of threat of violence to intimidate a group of people or government for political ends.[1] That there are forms and acts of terrorism that fall outside the scope of this definition is obvious. Walter Laqueur, for instance, in his recent book, *Terrorism*, has argued that open armed military conflict and even guerrilla activity, although their perpetrators may resort to similar or identical modes of behavior, are a species of violence quite distinct from terrorism.[2] These many, sometimes excellent, attempts to define and categorize terrorism have great value, but overrigorous applications of these principles to the Irish case makes understanding of it impossible. The approach adopted here is that of describing the various strands of the conflict in Northern Ireland in order to assess the relevance of the situation there to a wider pattern. Finally, it will be argued that the breakdown of authority in Northern Ireland is largely a result of the inner failure of British society, which when mixed with local grievances, has created conditions highly suited to extremist activities.

Since late 1968, when the present phase of the age-old Irish question was reopened, the annual number of deaths caused by political disturbances in Ulster has averaged about 200 a year. Relative to population, this is equivalent to 232,668 deaths in the United States and more than 59,010 in Great Britain over the whole period.[3] As a recent observer has put it, "these are truly horrifying figures."[4] Add to them the numbers of people injured or materially affected by the disturbances, and the picture is yet more alarming. Excluding open warfare, no part of Western Europe or North America has suffered such bloodshed for such a prolonged period over the past century. By the norms of Western society, the state of affairs in Northern Ireland is unparalleled. It is only the smallness of Ulster, its comparative remoteness within Britain and Europe, and the extremely low level of outside intervention in the struggle that has kept interest in the problem in a minor key to, say, interest in terrorism in the Middle East. Unlike elsewhere, conflict in Northern

Ireland has not involved crucial international issues or appeared to threaten the overall stability of even Britain or the Republic of Ireland, much less world peace. Given the very high natural interest of Irish issues for so many people in the English-speaking world at least, terrorism in Ulster has not aroused commensurate popular or official interest. This fact has, perhaps, enabled successive British governments to treat the whole matter in a somewhat cursory fashion.

Today's violence in Northern Ireland is part and parcel of the Irish question that has so bedeviled the peace of mind of the British Isles for generations. Received opinion is that Englishmen and Irishmen have fought over who shall rule in Ireland off and on since the twelfth century. At some points, the Irish resorted to open rebellion while at others legal and constitutional avenues were pursued to secure a free Ireland. In the last century, the movements headed by Daniel O'Connell and Charles Stewart Parnell exemplified the non-military, constitutional side of the Irish fight.

History or, more accurately, "myth" about Parnell is highly germane to the current troubles. In his time, the "uncrowned king" of Ireland exercised an apparently complete dominance over Irish nationalism.[5] The magnetism of the man, which was overwhelming in his own time, was further enhanced by the dramatic nature of his political overthrow and death in 1890 and 1891. Afterward, his ideals and policies, though often ambiguous, possessed authority and were sanctified by Irish nationalists. President Kennedy often said that American leaders found it expedient to be "right with Lincoln." In the present crisis, it is not absolutely necessary to be right with Parnell, but it helps. Nationalism without Parnell is rather like socialist revolution minus Marx.

What then is there in Parnellism, an avowedly open parliamentary movement, which endears itself to terrorists? Simply put, Parnell's rise to power, according to legend at least, was on the back of agrarian violence and terrorism in Ireland in the late 1870s and 1880s.[6] Parnell himself always took an ambivalent line on terrorism.[7] But his views in the early 1880s and during 1891 lent impeccable authority to the belief that a united independent Ireland could be won only through armed conflict. Because of Ireland's internal geography and proximity to Britain, armed struggle is likely to be successful only when guerrilla and terrorist techniques are used and open engagements eschewed. Parnell, it is claimed, had no reservations about the use of force for nationalist ends so long as these had the support of the Irish people and there was a prospect of success. Terrorists have also clung to the legacy of Parnell's emphasis upon intimidation—both a moral and a necessarily physical pressure equally used upon opponents and to stiffen the resolve of those who would be useful as supporters. Of course, the Birmingham and Belfast pub bombers have no need of an intellectual justification for their activities, but Parnell's arguments do provide a reasoned justification and do help to attract support from many people who would otherwise be repelled by the thuggish and criminal aspects of terrorism. Such support may be passive but it is, nonetheless, real and important.

The present difficulties may be said to have originated in 1921. The treaty then signed effectively divided Ireland permanently between a twenty-six county south (with an overwhelmingly Catholic population) and a rump, six county northeast (with a decisive Protestant majority). Subsequent transfers of population have tended to increase the level of the majority groups in each sector. A small but affluent and important Protestant community remained in the Republic of Ireland, concentrated mainly in Dublin. This community adapted to the new state quite successfully, helped no doubt by the continued existence of comfortable separate institutions, economic privileges, and the retention of the opportunities and rights of British citizens.[8] All citizens of the republic retain these rights and thus movement between the two islands is entirely free. Those who could not adapt to the new state simply left, leaving Protestants who were prepared to accept their status as a privileged minority.

Partition left the Province of Northern Ireland with a proportionately larger minority. In some cases, whole districts remained Catholic and were contiguous with the border of the republic. This minority community tended to be underprivileged and was discriminated against as a potentially hostile element in provincial life by the formal and unofficial operations of the Northern Ireland government.

Despite reservations about the precise way in which the border between the republic and the province was drawn and the character of the provincial regime, partition was not in itself an unreasonable or an undesirable solution to the Irish question as it existed in 1921.[9] Though partition struck at the emotional roots of nationalism and was explicitly rejected by nationalist ideology and in practice by antipartitionists, it undoubtedly satisfied the legitimate aspirations of a high proportion of Irishmen both north and south of the border.[10] But however reasonable partition was and is, it is the ostensible target of today's terrorists.

Before the British government was ready to agree to such a treaty in 1921, it had to be persuaded by an intense conflict in which the nationalists perfected the tools of guerrilla warfare and terrorism. During the bloodiest period of the fight, nationalists were inspirationally directed by Michael Collins.[11] Collins's importance to the present story lies in the fact that he expanded on the ideology inherited from Parnell and perfected the techniques of selective assassination. Collins's aim was to make British rule in Ireland impossible by intimidating the police into impotence and by destroying the potential for military counterattack by the strategic elimination of Irish informers and British intelligence personnel. His approach was certainly not intended to be "propaganda by the deed," but rather a firm and practical program to enhance the chances of nationalist success by using guerrilla hit-and-run tactics. The British military authorities engaged in bloody and vicious military reprisals.[12] Historians have long debated the impact of Collins's campaign. On balance, it seems that his methods were probably a good deal more effective than has normally been admitted. Police recruitment fell dramatically and, at times, British advance information about nationalist plans and movements was so poor that the military was forced to rely on reprisals rather than preemptive action. Whether Collins's murder policy was, in fact, decisive is almost irrelevant. Since the 1920s, Irish Republicans have remained convinced of the effectiveness of selective terrorism of the Collins variety. Therefore, terrorism has received the blessing of history. Successive generations of Irish Catholic youth in all parts of Ireland believe that terrorism has been effective in determining the course of Irish history.[13] Thus, the techniques that Collins first employed have remained the mainspring of republican terrorism. Hit-and-run attacks on military installations and murders of police, informers, and intelligence personnel always take priority. Sometimes bombings are indiscriminate, but normally they are directed against specific and strategic targets. Thus, what was novel and fearsome in 1919-1921 now has a rather predictable quality; this is true even when we realize that the means of combatting such terrorist activities have not been noticeably improved recently. Occasionally, terrorists have departed from the Collins pattern, as in the Birmingham bombings in November 1974 or in the London underground explosion in March 1976, but such cases ought properly to be regarded as isolated features of the Irish campaign.

Between 1922 and 1968, republicans engaged in a number of terrorist campaigns in Ulster, in Britain, and in Ireland. As a consequence, a few men have been executed. The Irish Republican Army

(IRA) initiated at least one period of terrorism in each intervening decade. Many of these outbursts had more to do with the needs of members of the IRA itself than with any expectation of success in ending partition. None of the periods of violence was very long or very intense. They were chiefly remarkable for supplying the odd martyr for the old cause and for giving the world the genius of Brendan Behan. Behan's presence is perhaps more important than would seem apparent at first glance. Irish violence has been lauded by poets and writers of prose almost from the beginning. The rising in Dublin in 1916 represented the ultimate fusion of literature and violence.[14] It is sometimes said that, in executing the leaders of the rising, the British military was engaged primarily in killing off a generation of poets. Perhaps this was so. But the martyrdom of the writers of violence and terrorism sanctified Irish terrorist methods for future generations. Behan, similarly, has provided the post-1922 IRA with an enduring appeal that its aims and methods alone could not have won. His personality and adventures, and the notorious amateurishness and ineptitude of the IRA, seen in the frequent personal mishaps with explosives, gave these men a comic, romantic, and idealistic character that successfully disguised their true menace. The best in literature offered a screen for the deadly perpetuation of republican aims and methods. In the mid-1960s, the British press frequently alleged that the IRA was all but dead—a view based on optimism rather than any real understanding of the deep-rooted nature of republicanism.

In the 1960s, Catholics, as has often been noted, enjoyed rising living standards but this material success was always tempered in Northern Ireland by constant reminders of inferior civil status. There had always been a very considerable pool of people in Ulster who were both ideologically and practically prepared to support renewed IRA activity—quite often for reasons quite independent of a desire to join the republic.[15] When the Northern Ireland Civil Rights Movement took to the streets in late 1968 to secure peacefully political and social reforms of the Ulster regime, which would guarantee Catholics equal status, there were yet others in the wings who would welcome the opportunity to resort to traditional methods of intimidation to secure these ends. The revival of the IRA campaign could only have been avoided if the aims of the Civil Rights Movement had been gained immediately and completely. Neither the provincial government nor the British cabinet identified the roots of the crisis quickly enough or had the political will to introduce reforms with sufficient haste to nip the problem in the bud.[16] Popular demonstrations were a part of the scene in the 1960s in many countries, particularly in the United States, where the black movement used them to great effect. These marches were not in themselves objectionable to the Irish, but the tradition of terrorism had more firmly established roots and appealed more to the popular and literary imagination. Hence, for a variety of past and present reasons, violence seemed the most natural and attractive mode of protest. It must be borne in mind that many of the people first drawn to terrorism at this time were hoping to use intimidation for their own ends, which were apt to differ from those of traditional republicanism. The battle was, therefore, not only waged between Orange and Green, but also within the Catholic community itself as to how the future might be shaped after a little timely violence.

Terrorism in Northern Ireland, therefore, has much to do with Irish history and is little inspired by movements elsewhere. It is a largely self-contained effort that reproduces its own heroic past and seeks ends that are entirely insular. The aims of the Irish are not at all like those of other groups engaging in terrorism; should the aims be achieved, other movements are unlikely to benefit from the success, except in the sense that their morale might receive a boost. This is not to deny that Irish terrorists have established foreign contacts, (for example, with Libya, the Bretons, the Basques, and the PFLP). Money has come from the usual source, the United States, where a large community of Irish immigrants and their descendants live and where the impact of the glittering figures of modern Irish literature is profound and little of the horror of their violence experienced. In contrast, arms have come mainly from Eastern Europe, which is motivated by a desire to stir up trouble in Western Europe for its own sake. No Irishman, having learned his terrorist skills in Ulster, appears to have been lured into the touring band of terrorists who make their wares available in many locations. Nor have any of the "international stars" of terrorism found a market for their specialties in Northern Ireland or in Great Britain on behalf of Irish interests. Irish terrorism is a very parochial business, which impinges little on the broader spectrum of terrorist movements throughout the world. Irishmen, in contrast to others, have not been able to rely on asylum in other countries and, as a result, have not resorted successfully to the tactics of hijacking and kidnapping. Within limits, Irish terrorism could exist without either moral or military support from outside and is almost totally independent of the existence of similar movements in other countries.

What is the character of Irish terrorism and who are the participants? The presumption so far has been that the terrorists are nationalists. This is only partly true. Terrorist organizations exist within the Protestant community and these groups have been responsible for numerous acts of violence and are especially prominent in engaging in reprisals. The pattern has been to attack Catholic institutions and public houses in retaliation for similar acts against the Protestant community. However, horrible as these deeds certainly are, they are essentially a response to original acts of aggression and might be expected to disappear in the absence of republican terrorism. It is not that the majority in Northern Ireland is naturally pacific and the minority ordinarily troublesome. In point of fact, until the present troubles, both communities in Ulster had, by the standards of most countries, enviable records of law and order. The rate of acts of aggression in the British Isles as a whole has been low when compared with that of many countries, such as the United States. But, even under direct rule from Westminster, the administration in Northern Ireland is essentially in Protestant interests. This is not as sinister as it sounds. In democratic regimes, government is expected to function in accordance with the wishes of majorities, while respecting minority rights. The Protestant community is unquestionably in the majority and no one doubts that a clear majority of the population of Northern Ireland has no wish to become part of a United Ireland, but prefers to remain within the United Kingdom. Republicans do not contest the existence of a hostile majority: they either insist that the entire population of Ireland has to be consulted in order to discover the true majority wish or simply that numbers do not matter in the face of the arguments of history. By the very nature of things, then, the Protestant organizations using terrorist tactics are on the defensive and acting largely in a responsive capacity. For quite logical reasons, the Protestant community looks to the official organs of the state for its protection and for action against republican terrorism. It does not, therefore, seem unfair to concentrate mainly on republican terrorism.

Within the republican movement, there have been competing groups prepared to use terrorism against their opponents inside the movement as readily as against the Protestant community or the state. Internal strife is common in terrorist movements and often provides the bitterest struggles. At the time of the first disturbances in 1968 and 1969, the IRA was in the hands of Marxists who coupled the traditional irredentist quest with that of social revolution for the remaking of all Irish society. There was within the IRA at this stage the potential for attracting worldwide interest and support: Ireland as a whole might have been a fertile ground for a national war of liberation. The IRA, however, was a very small and unrepresentative organization and quickly lost influence to a splinter group known as the Provisional IRA. The provisionals espouse traditional republican principles, are now by far the larger and more important group, and are responsible for most Irish terrorist activity.

Whereas the official IRA with its Marxist creed has a built-in appeal to intellectuals, the provisionals are essentially a nonideological, populist, heavily working-class and sectarian movement. The Provisional IRA, to be sure, adheres to the ideals of old-time republicanism, giving it the appearance of an ideologically motivated group, but this is rather misleading. It has been attractive to Catholics in Ulster less because of its goals, which are unlikely to be realized, than because it is in fact the only effective organ of protest available to the Catholic minority with its deep-seated Catholic grievances. Though it is impossible at this stage to be precise about the composition of the provisionals, certain trends are apparent. Those involved are normally young men of modest educational achievements who are or were in comparatively low status, unskilled jobs. In short, they are much the same sort of men as those recruited into the British Army ranks. The terrorism of the Provisional IRA consists of an explosive mixture: half-baked history and ideology, genuine economic and social grievances, and the physical needs of young men to be involved in exciting action. In Ulster, this need among the male youth is exacerbated by the restrictive mores of the community and by the absence of competing entertainments to absorb the energies of its youth. A reasonable proportion of republican terrorism bears a great affinity to crowd hooliganism at football matches or the disorderly behavior and drunkenness of soldiers on British Rail trains. Some of the clashes between the provisionals and the British Army in particular are a lethal form of the gang warfare common to the poorer sections of Glasgow, New York, and Chicago. What distinguishes the provisionals is access to sophisticated military technology and sustained encouragement to use these weapons of destruction. No doubt, the longer the terrorist movement exists the more self-sustaining it becomes; many participants will be unwilling to part from the comradeship and sense of exhilaration provided. Furthermore, world economic troubles, particularly in Great Britain, and restrictive immigration laws in most English-speaking countries, have prevented the emigration of Irish youth, which previously served as an important safety valve. It would be a mistake to be misled by the veneer of sophistication and organization into seeing the provisionals as a united, ideological movement when in fact so much of its terrorism can more properly be viewed as a disastrous and deadly version of youthful high jinx. The equation of the provisionals with nationalists contains some but not all of the truth.

To argue that a great proportion of terrorism is gratuitous violence is not to ignore that the hard core element in republicanism is sincerely motivated. The motivated minority's power to wreak havoc, though considerable, is in the long term less dangerous than the purposeless populist terrorism that characterizes much of the provisional activity. Terrorist actions have taken on numerous forms, some being especially important. Populist terrorism is mainly confined to Ulster and is to be seen in the planting of bombs and in attacks on public houses, shops, and public buildings. In terms of injury and death, this populist activity takes the heaviest toll and is the most unpleasant face of the provisionals. Numerically then, the most staggering consequences are being suffered within the civilian community as a result of the actions of the least ideologically influenced and the most unstable portion of the movement.

A second but probably more important part of terrorist activity is directed against the old targets of the republicans—police, informers, the army, and the intelligence sections. This activity is a continuation of Collins's policy of selective assassination. No doubt concentration on these traditional targets has had some impact and is carried out mainly by hard-core republicans and certainly under their direction. Part-time reserve personnel living in remote or comparatively defenseless areas have been unusually vulnerable to attack. There is little evidence to suggest that morale amongst the police or the troops has deteriorated as a result of being in the front line against the terrorists, as was the case in 1919-1921, though the total impact of violence may have had some effect upon opinion in Britain as a whole.[17] But so long as the majority community is committed to remaining part of the United Kingdom, it is improbable that selective assassination can be more than a serious and unpleasant threat to stability.

Only a very tiny proportion of terrorist activity takes place outside Ulster and most of this has been in the form of bombing campaigns in mainland Great Britain. Such attacks have never been a major element in the terrorist strategy and are almost exclusively intended to maximize the propaganda effort of republicanism. Even republicans are divided amongst themselves as to the wisdom of broadening the front to include mainland Great Britain, although it must be admitted that such an extension has been extremely effective within its terms of reference. The public has been substantially inconvenienced on a long-term basis to the extent that packages and cases can no longer be deposited in public places and that the same are rigorously searched on entry to public buildings. At certain times, visiting particular places involves risk. The restrictions imposed have been applied almost universally even in places where there is no Irish population and which are improbable targets even in the event of an intense terrorist campaign. Thus, a small dose of terrorism has had a surprisingly widespread effect, at least for the time being, on the mainland. Nevertheless, attacks on the mainland, while a traditional element in IRA campaigns of the past, are unlikely to become a significant part of the present republican terrorist activity.

In theory, if terrorism is to have its maximum impact it must be unpredictable. As we have seen, Irish terrorism since the late 1960s has been highly predictable. The terrorists have been able to strike almost anywhere at any time, but in practice there have been periods of intensity and periods of quiet. The brunt of the campaign has been directed against traditional targets, which can be anticipated and guarded. Even the more dangerous populist terrorism has developed certain characteristics that make some targets particularly probable; city center shops in Belfast and public houses and other places of entertainment are particularly favored. Although the destruction caused has been truly horrific, there is little evidence that the community has been intimidated by these threats. On the contrary, favored targets remain very much in the front line simply because they continue to be frequented and are, therefore, vulnerable. In a sense this bespeaks republican failure although it also helps to maintain the high level of violence in the province. Terrorism in this context is essentially sectarian and ritualistic and helps to maintain Provisional IRA and Catholic morale. The actual success of such outrages is an almost incidental byproduct because the acts themselves have a participatory and emotional importance that far outweighs actual or expected results. Should terrorism of this kind disappear, unquestionably some acceptable substitute would soon be found.[18]

When we see populist terrorism in this light and realize its historical origins, populist activity in Northern Ireland seems a long way removed from that of movements elsewhere. But perhaps this is an illusion. Although there are some real distinctions, at least some of the Irish terrorism resembles that associated with the Baader-Meinhof gang in West Germany or with the Symbionese

Liberation Army in the United States. Perhaps it has most in common, however, with the occasional eruptions of violence in the black areas of American cities. Much of the Irish activity is less properly described as terrorism than as a particularly unpleasant form of violence springing directly from the grievances of an oppressed minority or the frustrations of the young and unemployed.

Is terrorism in Ireland a distinguishable phenomenon? Certainly Walter Laqueur's attempt to argue a distinction between terrorism and guerrilla action does not hold water when applied to Ireland. The terrain does not make sustained guerrilla warfare feasible in Ulster, but attacks on army installations and police headquarters has more in common with this form of action than with the new style, popular terrorism. Terrorism in Northern Ireland is practiced by people who would elsewhere be engaged in guerrilla warfare. The same group is pragmatic in its choice of activity, however, and is not influenced by the arguments of intellectuals as to what is acceptable terrorist behavior. We are not arguing that in this respect the Irish are any different necessarily from members of other terrorist movements: Laqueur's definition may fit no actual instance very well.

That the Provisional IRA has been able to maintain itself for so long at such an intense level of activity can be attributed to several factors. Chief among these must be the failure of the Northern Ireland and British governments to identify and assuage the grievances of the Catholic community and thereby remove the stuff upon which the IRA feeds. In the first instance, the IRA Provisionals were able to establish themselves as the defenders of their community's interests and they now hold that section of the population to ransom as much as they do the whole province. They have demonstrated their power, and ordinary people are now unlikely to place their trust in an official government that has proved patently unable in the past to fulfil its role as defender of life and property.[19] Then, too, both Catholic politicians and the Catholic Church in Ulster must bear some of the responsibility for the growth of republican terrorism. Both have appeared to believe that a small dose of terror in Ulster would increase their own respective bargaining positions within the state and that they would be able to control that violence. Politicians were as familiar with the legends of Parnell and Collins as any and, although they did not begin the shooting, they believed that they, like earlier Irish leaders, might use the violence to personal advantage. Their early ambiguity of attitude may have enabled politicians to remain in touch with popular opinion and have been essential to the credibility of individual leaders, but it also conferred a degree of legitimacy upon the Provisional IRA. The Church hierarchy and lower clergy for long have had an ambiguous relationship with movements of violence in Ireland.[20] Churchmen, too, must bend with the wind to retain the confidence of their flock, but they can also provide leadership. Clerical leadership has been notably deficient in the present crisis and many pronouncements from both higher and lower clergy may be construed in a light that is favorable to the aims if not the means of the republicans. In a sense, then, for much of the last decade, the Provisional IRA has presented the only viable leadership and policy to the Catholic community. With this effective monopoly, it is hardly surprising that terrorists have often had a sympathetic community behind them.

Successive British cabinets have been undecided as to the best approach to the crisis. British weakness here, however, seems to be merely a reflection of other and greater psychological disturbances in society as a whole. In the face of economic difficulties and internal friction, governments have been consistently taken by surprise by Irish developments and unable or unwilling to provide appropriate personnel and leadership for the province. Some politicians sent to administer Northern Ireland have received extravagant public praise on the mainland for reasons that totally escape the outsider. This perhaps reflects the meager pool of talent available.

The future of terrorism in Northern Ireland remains uncertain. Terrorist activity has perhaps weakened the resolve of the British to remain in Ireland, but, given the anticipated continued resistance of the majority in Ulster to a United Ireland, the republicans are unlikely to achieve their cherished objective. Terrorism has had a quite profound impact upon the governmental arrangements for Northern Ireland and the old regime cannot be restored in toto. Alternatives put forward to date, normally based on power sharing, have no special appeal for the Catholic minority, and it is possible that direct rule from Westminster would provide the most satisfactory solution.[21] The ideals of the IRA are likely to remain steadfast, but there are signs that war-weariness is sapping the strength of populist terrorism; its detachment and pacification would be a crucial step in the struggle against violence. All, however, depends on British policy and its implementation and there is as yet little evidence of sustained or constructive thinking in that quarter. Alternatively, Irish terrorism might itself be transformed into an international movement that attracted wider interest and support. In this latter (unlikely) event, the history of the province might develop unexpected twists and dramatic turns, and British cabinets would be compelled to take up a creative stance in order to avert larger problems both at home and abroad.

Notes

1. See Paul Wilkinson, *Terrorism and the Liberal State* (London 1977).

2. Walter Laqueur, *Terrorism* (London 1977).

3. Wilkinson, op. cit., p. 87.

4. Ibid.

5. The most extensive recent account of Parnell's life is F.S.L. Lyons, *Charles Stewart Parnell* (London, 1977).

6. A recent useful book is Leon Ó Broin, *Revolutionary Underground* (Dublin, 1976).

7. It is possible, however, that this aspect of the Parnellite movement has been overstressed. See Alan O'Day, *The English Face of Irish Nationalism* (Dublin, 1977).

8. A facet of Protestant life in the republic is attractively treated in R. B. McDowell, *The Church of Ireland, 1869-1969* (London, 1975).

9. Recent public statements by Conor Cruise O'Brien lend authority to this view. Also, see his *States of Ireland* (London, 1972) for a statement of the view that Ireland as an island contains two distinct peoples.

10. Conor Cruise O'Brien has recently given eloquent voice to this line and perhaps as a consequence been widely heralded by the British establishment and press. There is nothing quite so sure to end one's effective influence in Ireland as the good words of the British establishment!

11. See Tom Bowden, *The Breakdown of Public Security: The Case of Ireland 1916-1921 and Palestine 1936-1939* (London, 1977), which offers a convincing analysis of Collins's policy and successfully revises some of the views to be found in Charles Townshend, *The British Campaign in Ireland 1919-1921* (London, 1975).

12. Townshend, op cit., is valuable on British military direction and policy but must be read alongside Bowden, op. cit.

13. See J. Bowyer Bell, *The Secret Army* (London, 1970), and his essay "Revolutionary Organizations: Special Cases and Imperfect Models," in David Carlton and Carlo Schaerf, eds., *International Terrorism and World Security* (London, 1975).

14. An interesting recent account of 1916 is Ruth Dudley Edwards, *Patrick Pearse* (London, 1977).

15. From a different perspective, Conor Cruise O'Brien lends substantial authority to this view. *The Times* (London), 18 January 1978.

16. For some alternatives, see Richard Rose, *Northern Ireland: A Time of Choice* (London, 1976). Another useful book is I. Budge and C. O'Leary, *Belfast: Approach to Crisis* (London, 1973).

17. Curiously, those pillars of the respectable right and left, Lord Blake and A.J.P. Taylor, have both shown signs of this in their newspaper writings. Both Blake and Taylor remain important beacons of establishment opinion.

18. David Carlton (see Ch. 9) offers the convincing thought that the likely result is the tacit acceptance of an "acceptable" level of violence in order to avoid the need to find a substitute.

19. Wilkinson, op. cit.

20. See David Miller, *Church, State and Nation in Ireland 1898-1921* (Dublin, 1973).

21. So-called "power sharing," where both communities would have a defined place in the government and administration (presumably based on relative population), would not by itself improve the position of the minority or make it feel directly involved and responsible for the regime. The principle seems to resemble a permanent coalition government—something that most British politicians reject in other circumstances. Moreover, the prime notion in British representative democracy is that majorities rule alone and are thereby responsible. Either power sharing is something of a fraud, unlikely to lull Irish Catholics to sleep, or it is such a good idea that it ought to be applied to all of the United Kingdom and benefit the many minorities there. On the whole, power sharing is the example par excellence of the muddled thinking of British leaders about Northern Ireland.

6
Hostage Negotiations and the Concept of Transference

Abraham H. Miller

Frank Bolz is a garrulous jokester who embraces life with warmth, zest, and passion. He is, in his own inimitable way, a raconteur par excellence. He is a social being who thrives on the ambience of human interaction. Frank, a detective captain with the New York City Police Department, is its chief hostage negotiator. To date he has successfully negotiated, without loss of life, over several hundred hostage situations.

Many good experienced police in other cities will tell you in all candor and sincerity that the NYPD has gained a lot of mileage out of an especially talented individual. Frank, even with some discount for his tendency for modesty, will sincerely say otherwise. Talent is an undeniable and necessary ingredient in the repertoire of hostage negotiation resources. But beyond talent is a need for good procedures, training, and the ability to work in an environment where the political structure is supportive of the basic quest—success comes when everyone walks alive.

Frank Bolz's role as comic and raconteur ends when he talks about hostage negotiation techniques. Frank is not simply a believer in hostage negotiation as policy; he is an active proselytizer. The record underscores his conviction. Wherever hostage negotiation techniques

This research was supported by grant number 76-NI-99-0108 awarded by the Law Enforcement Assistance Administration, U.S. Department of Justice, under the Omnibus Crime Control and Safe Streets Act of 1968, as amended. Points of view or opinions stated in this document are those of the author and do not necessarily represent the official position or policies of the U.S. Department of Justice.

The author wishes to acknowledge the support of Dr. Alfred Tuchfarber, director of the Behavioral Sciences Laboratory, University of Cincinnati, and his staff.

have replaced assault, the result is almost invariably the same—more people come out alive.

Before the initiation of hostage negotiation techniques, police relied on raw courage, stealth, and the assault. Many people died in those assaults. They still do. Recent figures released by the RAND Corporation[1] indicate that more hostages die as a result of assaults than from direct killing by terrorists. The assault does not appear to be a deterrent, despite its heavy cost in life and limb. Countries in which the government has refused to negotiate—Argentina, Colombia, Israel, Jordan, Turkey, and Uruguay—were nevertheless targets of more hostage episodes.

Statistical evidence aside, the primary feeling on the part of police negotiators is that assaults are an absolute last resort. Assaults as a *primary* strategy do not work; negotiations do.

As Lieutenant Richard Klapp, head hostage negotiation training officer for the San Francisco Police Department noted, "Negotiation is the most compassionate, most humane and most professional way to handle these things. We know that we have saved lives and that is the way we know we have to go."[2]

Men like Frank Bolz and Richard Klapp have set a new image for the conduct of police work. Indeed, one of the most intriguing aspects of the emphasis on negotiation is that it has redefined the role and image within police departments of good police work. This has meant a change in emphasis from physical tactics to psychological tactics. It has meant a redefinition, at least in some quarters, of a good police officer. Negotiators emphasize such attributes as empathy, compassion, sensitivity, intelligence, and psychological insight as the skills of a good policeman. They generally play down anything remotely indicative of the use of force. Negotiation replaces physical prowess with intellectual skill and represents a set of values that—while not at variance with all perceptions police maintain of their work—is not universally adhered to in police circles.

The change in emphasis has also meant a greater recognition of the reality of police work, emphasizing the kinds of skills police actually use rather than some romantic image of the police. A significant portion of day-to-day police work requires crisis intervention— breaking up a family quarrel, keeping neighbors from fighting with each other, or, as one Scotland Yard officer put it, "Convincing people to do what is in their own best interest" (said with a strong emphasis on *convincing*). Crisis intervention requires crisis negotiation, the skilled dialogue that substitutes intellect and sensitivity for bravado. And just as men reasoned logically long before Aristotle, police were engaged in crisis intervention and crisis negotiation long

before it was defined in such terms.

Despite the almost unparalleled success of hostage negotiation techniques, there is emerging in some public and even police headquarters a reaction against the policy of negotiation. Some of this grows out of a concern for the potential undermining of the strong, action-oriented image of police work. There is also concern that the rise in the number of hostage situations and the often spectacular drama in which they are enveloped is attributable to the contagion effect wrought by publicity and the reliance on negotiation instead of force.

In otherwise informed and sophisticated police and military circles, one hears bandied about, with hackneyed frequency, "If the Israelis can do it, why can't we?" This sentiment has taken on such proportions that I was recently asked by one metropolitan police department to assist them in informing the public as to the value and utility of negotiation. The sentiment for a policy based on containment and assault has recently found substantial support not only within the mass public that shares the perception that publicity and softness create hostage situations, but among rank and file police officers who perceive the assault is a deterrent and believe that current practices based on negotiation only play into the hands of terrorists and invite future episodes.

Such sentiments have no confirmation in fact. The impact of the press is debatable and is a subject that goes beyond the scope of this chapter. However, it might be worth noting that from 1973 to 1977, in virtually any week in any month, someplace in the world, someone was being taken hostage and it was being reported.[3] The so-called contagion effect is perhaps only a result of our sensitivity to the number of hostage situations given prominent play once a major episode makes the news. The argument that hostage episodes have increased over the past several years both in number and severity because of negotiations places the cart before the horse. It should be recalled that the tactic of negotiation came about after the rise in the number of hostage situations and the increase in their seriousness. The tactic of negotiation was developed in response to crisis and because the traditional mode of dealing with barricade and hostage situations resulted in casualties. Negotiations came about because police believed there had to be a better way.

How It Came About

On January 19, 1973, four formidably armed men entered John and Al's Sporting Goods Store in Brooklyn, New York. One man carried a sawed-off shotgun, the others handguns.

At 5:25 P.M., the police radio broadcasted a code 10-30 (robbery in progress) and thus began the chronicle of events that became known as the Williamsburg incident. It would last forty-seven hours and result in the death of one officer and injury to two others. Despite these unfortunate casualties, the Williamsburg incident began and ended as a model tactical operation that has been studied as an example worthy of emulation. It was meticulously planned, well executed, and illustrated the effectiveness of controlled fire power in the hands of a well-trained and disciplined tactical force.[4]

The quality of the operation was no accident. To a large extent, it was the result of work previously undertaken by a man whose role in the tactical scenario of hostage negotiations is little known, even in police circles. It was New York Police Department Chief Inspector Simon Eisdorfer who began promoting within the department the idea of an efficient tactical response to hostage situations. Eisdorfer's concern emanated from the tragic events of the 1972 Munich Olympiad, where an episode involving Palestinian terrorists who had seized Israeli athletes as hostages ended in the shocking death of all the athletes and several of the terrorists. Rightly or wrongly, it was the impression of many that the Munich police's tactical response was sorely inept and that better training and contingency planning for such situations might have minimized the loss of life, if not prevented the tragedy entirely. As headquarters for the United Nations and as the seat of several consulates, New York appeared likely to be the scene of a terrorist incident.

Under Eisdorfer's stimulus, basic tactics were developed for using specially trained personnel to contain the scene and provide disciplined fire power. These tactics were later applied to the Williamsburg siege.

The Williamsburg incident, however, came on the heels of another dramatic hostage situation played out in a Brooklyn bank and later captured for the screen as *Dog Day Afternoon*. In response to the succession of incidents, Police Commissioner Patrick Murphy requested that a detailed policy and methodology for dealing with hostage situations be developed.

When the Williamsburg episode unfolded, Harvey Schlossberg was a uniformed patrolman assigned to a squad car. Patrolman Schlossberg, however, was not a typical uniformed police officer. He held a Ph.D. in clinical psychology, and when Commissioner Murphy decided to develop a strategy for hostage negotiations, Schlossberg's talents were recruited to assist the process.

What Eisdorfer, in his role of commanding officer of the Special Operations Division, did for the tactical procedures, Schlossberg would do for the process of negotiation. By the time Schlossberg finished developing, executing, and preaching his plans for negotiation, officers in four hundred American and Canadian police departments would go about the procedures of hostage negotiation differently. The full impact of Schlossberg's work was only beginning. Supported by grants from the Law Enforcement Assistance Administration, law enforcement and military personnel from all over the free world passed through the classrooms in the Emergency Services Unit Building in Brooklyn. Some of Schlossberg's techniques found their way into the policies and procedures of police in Great Britain, the Netherlands, and West Germany. Even members of the Israeli police passed through the school and pondered whether the Israeli policy of nonnegotiation was indeed the only way to proceed.

The essence of Schlossberg's technique is to establish communications and to keep communications going for as long as it takes to get the subject to surrender. In one incident in New York, it took eleven days. Time is an expendable commodity—life is not. There is much talk about throwing away the clock, letting the dialogue progress, and directing the captors into realizing that capitulation is better than death. The underlying implication of Schlossberg's technique is that time is generally on the side of the authorities. (There has been, recently, as a result of the experience of European police and studies by psychologists of individuals exposed to prolonged stress, some rethinking about the impact of imminent confrontation with uncertainty and death on the mental health of hostages. For this reason, among others, the Dutch government decided to have its troops storm a train and school where South Moluccans had held hostages for almost three weeks in late May and early June of 1977. This reassessment will be discussed below.)

The Process of Transference

The perception that time is on the side of the authorities is based on the psychological concept of transference, a mental process through which a sense of closeness and attachment develops between the hostage and his captor. As time wears on, both captive and captor find themselves locked in a mutual fate. The captive feels powerless before the captor, begins to identify with him, and perceives that his hopes for survival reside with the captor. The captor is seen as having the opportunity to offer life to the captive—if only the authorities will accede to the captor's demands. The fact that the captive has been put by the captor in a situation where the captive's life has become a commodity of exchange is ignored. It is no longer the captor, but the authorities who are perceived to be at fault. The authorities are perceived to be standing in the way of survival and holding out the prospect of death.

The transference process is not necessarily asymmetrical. A similar bond can be created between the hostage taker and the hostage. The impact of sharing physical space under conditions of mutual crisis and stress builds intimacy and an emotional bond that generally serves as a prophylaxis against the hostage being killed. The strength of this bond is said to increase with time. In fact, it is commonly said among those experienced with hostage negotiations that if a hostage is not killed during the first fifteen minutes of an episode, the odds are that he will not be killed.

There is yet another reason why time is perceived to be on the side of the authorities. As the situation progresses and the prospect of imminent death continues, all but suicidally inclined captors desire some way out of the situation. Also, as time wears on, the police can rotate personnel. The hostage takers, unless well equipped, trained, and in significant numbers, will find that their capacity to act decisively and think clearly will erode with time.

Transference as a Function of Other Variables

The process of transference is not simply a function of time. It is also dependent on the nature of the interaction between hostage taker and hostage. All things being equal, the longer the period of time in which the interaction between hostage and captor take place, the greater the degree of transference. Time, however, is linked to the process of transference by the quality of the interaction. If the interaction is hostile, transference will generally not take place.

Interviews conducted by the Federal Bureau of Investigation with passengers on a Trans World Airlines flight skyjacked to Paris by Croatian separatists on September 10, 1976, illustrate the relationship between transference and the quality of interaction.[5]

One of the skyjackers, Marc Vlasic, was described as abusive, arrogant, and threatening. He had a penchant for fingering the phony dynamite brought on board in such a fashion as to add to the passengers' anxieties. Individuals who had substantial contact with Vlasic did not experience transference.

In direct contrast, the feelings of the passengers toward skyjacker Julie Busic, who was warm and outgoing while she played hostess to the passengers, were very positive. She was referred to by some of the passengers as "the perfect hostess."

Another one of the skyjackers, Petar Matvic, was also warm and positive in his reactions to the passengers and was in turn viewed very positively by those passengers who had contact with him.

Similar examples can be culled by contrasting the reaction of hostages in the first South Moluccan episode (December 2, 1975) in the Netherlands with the second (May/June 1977). In the first situation, there were several killings by the terrorists and at least one of the hostages was conspicuously abused. In the second episode, the hostages were relatively well treated until the assault by the troops when a terrorist deliberately killed one of the hostages. In the first South Moluccan episode, there were no reported incidents of transference. However, there were several in the second incident—a function of the difference in the quality of the interaction between captive and captor. Transference on the part of the hostages appears to be a selective process, contingent not simply on the amount of time or the nature and degree of the crisis, but also (among other things) on the quality of the interaction between captive and captor. When the interaction is hostile and negative, transference will probably not take place. Moreover, when the interaction is not simply positive, but the captive actively seeks it out, it appears that transference will be strongest.

Transference will generally not take place when there are predetermined racial or ethnic hostilities between captive and captor. Israeli officials inform me that there has not been one instance of transference by an Israeli hostage toward an Arab captor. Transference will also be precluded when the hostage is capable of maintaining some intellectual distance, which enables the objective assessment of one's plight as having been wrought by one's captors.

Richard Brockman, a twenty-nine-year-old psychiatric resident at New York's Columbia Presbyterian Hospital was aboard the ill-fated Trans World Airlines Flight 355 when the Croation terrorists seized it. In an article titled, "Notes While Being Hijacked,"[6] he detailed his response to thirty terrifying hours on board the flight. At the conclusion of the episode, the intercom blared and Brockman recalled:

"This is the captain speaking." His voice is clean, no cracks. "We have all been through an incredible experience. But it is over for us.

No one is hurt. However, it is not over for our hijackers. Their ordeal
is just beginning. They have a cause. They are brave committed people.
Idealistic dedicated people. Like the people who helped to shape our
country. They are trying to do the same for theirs. I think we should all
give them a hand."

    I look around me. The hijackers are smiling. The audience is
applauding. It has come full turn. We arrive at the theater. Stop
clapping, you fools. The cadence continues. The cadence continues.
Tinker. Tailor. Actor. Fool. Let me out of here. Open the gate. Please
let me out of here. No, the last curtain call.[7]

So, for Dr. Brockman, the episode came to an end. And even in the
surge of relief, he could not develop the emotional affinity for his
tormentors that many of the other passengers did. To the end, he was
distant and objective, aware that his life had been negotiated for some
higher objective in which he was only a participant as an accident
of circumstance.

    Some additional items about transference also emerged from the
Croatian episode. In debriefing passengers and crew, agents of the
Federal Bureau of Investigation noted that individuals who actively
and consciously went out of their way to interact with the terrorists
were most likely to experience transference. This is not to say that
transference was absent among other individuals, but rather that it
was most likely to take place among those who sought it.

    It appears from case by case observations that a number of variables
enter into determining whether transference will take place: (1) the
length of time the hostage and captors are confined; (2) the quality of
the interaction—Were the hostages well treated?; (3) the existence of
predetermined racial or ethnic hostilities between hostage and captor;
(4) the predisposition on the part of some hostages to seek out and
relate to their captors.

    The mechanism of transference that hostage negotiators like Frank
Bolz and Richard Klapp rely upon when the clock is thrown away is
not always a reciprocated relationship. Transference can and often
does take place on the part of the hostage toward the captor without
the sentiment being returned by the captor toward the hostage. In
fact, clever hostage takers have not been reluctant to let the process of
transference work to their own advantage, nurturing transference
among their captives while maintaining, behind outward signs of
friendship, a sense of deceitful manipulation of the hostages. In the
case of the first South Moluccan seizure of a Dutch train, one of the
terrorists pointedly told the captives that he could not kill any Dutch
people because he was married to a Dutch woman. This was not true.

    One of the results of transference is that negotiators learn that they must be leery of trusting hostages. Hostages can easily become unwitting accomplices of their captors, especially when transference takes place to the extent that the hostages perceive the police and not their captors as being the primary obstacle to freedom.

Transference becomes an effective vehicle in the process of negotiation when it is shared by both hostage and captor. It is in those situations that throwing away the clock is effective.

The Stockholm Syndrome

The process of transference was first noticed as a result of a bank robbery in Stockholm. The attempted robbery developed into a barricade and hostage situation. During the course of the episode, a young woman hostage allegedly initiated sexual relations with her captor. The motivation was not response to fear or coercion, but an intimacy that developed as a result of sharing a common fate in a situation of mutual crisis and the projected dependence of the woman captive on her captor. The relationship persisted after the bank robber's incarceration.

FBI agents note that had observers been attuned to the problem of transference earlier, the syndrome would have been called Shade Gap syndrome rather than Stockholm syndrome. Their reference is to a kidnapping that took place in Shade Gap, Pennsylvania, in 1967. When law enforcement officials came upon the kidnapper in a wooded area, he was hurriedly walking to escape pursuit and encirclement. A considerable distance behind him was the kidnap victim, straining to keep up. The victim had only to turn 180 degrees and walk off to freedom.

The most publicized episode of transference by a hostage to her captors is that demonstrated by newspaper heiress Patricia Hearst, who not only took a lover from among her captors but also provided them with covering gunfire when they were about to be seized for shoplifting. Patricia Hearst's behavior was different only in degree from what is commonly observed in hostages under long-term stress. And if Patricia Hearst's responses were more extreme, it is also true that the conditions of her captivity, both in terms of the severity of deprivation and duration, were also extreme. These factors were probably exacerbated by her age and lack of experience.

Transference and Hostage Negotiation Perspectives

Time and the intensity of the crisis can also function to promote transference between the hostage negotiator and the hostage taker, which builds the trust that eventually results in the hostage taker's surrender. But even experienced negotiators succumb to the experience. One seasoned negotiator told me that in one situation he had developed such a close emotional relationship to the captor that he found it difficult to testify against him. The officer knew he had to do it and he knew he would do it. However, before going into court he went to the subject and said, "_____, you know I have to testify against you. I'm sorry but it's my job." The subject responded by saying, "Yes, I know. It's okay." The factors that enter into the transference syndrome are also illustrative of the dimensions that affect the likely outcome of hostage situations. These dimensions are: (1) Who are the hostage takers and what are their motives? (2) Who are the hostages? (3) What demands are being made on whom?

Who Are the Hostage Takers?

Although experienced police negotiators continually point out that each hostage episode is idiosyncratic, they are also quick to note that there is a typology of hostage takers. Knowledge of the type of hostage taker is important in determining how the situation is to be handled. The most common type of hostage taker that the police encounter is the professional felon.

The felon is basically uninterested in seizing hostages. He usually takes hostages because his escape route while committing a crime has been blocked. The hostages appear initially to provide an alternate means of escape. As time wears on, they become a liability—the felon eventually comes to grips with the reality of his situation. What started out as armed robbery now has the potential to become murder. Armed robbery is easier to face. The felon only wants to be reassured that the massive phalanx of police that surrounds him will let him capitulate without killing him. It is the task of the negotiator to build the felon's trust to where he will accept that reality. Felons are generally the easiest individuals to bring to capitulation. They are rational, did not initially seek to take hostages, and want to spare themselves the grief of a longer prison term for a more serious offense.

A more serious hostage taker is the psychopathic individual who seeks to commit suicide but is afraid. He embarks on a course of action that he hopes will bring the police to the point of doing it for him. He is irrational and generally a threat to the hostage and to himself. Often, in this type of situation, negotiation may have to yield to assault.

The political terrorist is generally viewed by the police as the most threatening and dangerous hostage taker. Police unfortunately assume that political terrorists only embark on suicide missions. There is strong evidence to suggest that this is not the case. Few terrorist missions are suicidal. Most terrorist missions are against so-called soft targets and embody fairly elaborate escape plans. The threat of the political terrorist generally emanates less from his desire for suicide than from his preparation, both mental and physical, to take hostages and wait out the dialogue of negotiation. And, perhaps, the characteristic that most distinguishes them from other hostage takers is the ability (somewhat reduced recently) of political terrorists to find some country willing to grant them sanctuary. This has been a formidable weapon in the political terrorists' arsenal.

In some intelligence circles, it is argued that in part the more serious threat of the political terrorist comes from the pressure of his colleagues who, in his eyes, will not accept capitulation. This conclusion must be approached with caution as there have been sufficient instances of terrorist capitulation to cast doubt upon this observation. What is, however, more likely to happen is that as the siege continues, dissension and conflict will break out among the captors. Some members will wish to continue the siege or even escalate the violence, while others will seek a way out. Such was the case in the Netherlands in late May of 1977 when a band of South Moluccan terrorists seized 170 hostages, including 105 children, in a train and school.

The episode pitted noted Dutch psychiatrist and negotiator Dirk Mulder against twenty-four-year-old Max Papilaya, the terrorist leader. After twenty days, the Dutch government no longer found it could go along with the policy of throwing away the clock and resorted to an armed assault by specially trained marines. The assault came about when, during the final forty-eight hours, the situation inside the train seemed to be falling apart. Papilaya's fellow terrorists were beginning to question his authority. Papilaya showed signs of being willing to release the hostages while his comrades were not. In the end, Mulder felt this internal conflict would eventually obviate any chance for successful negotiations.[8]

The possibility of internal dissension among the terrorists cuts two ways. In the second Moluccan situation, the conflict led to the Dutch government's use of force. In other situations, the conflict has been adroitly exploited to lead to capitulation. The fact that similar circumstances can lead to diametrically opposite results illustrates how tenuous, fragile, and idiosyncratic the process of negotiation can be.

One fundamental factor that is an important determinant of the

behavior of political hostage takers is that they have set out to pur-
posely take hostages, which indicates mental and physical preparation; in addition, there was evidence in the course of the second South
Moluccan episode that the terrorists now are assiduously studying
the psychological procedures used by the police to negotiate for the
release of hostages. This is another important factor that makes the
terrorist hostage situation difficult.

Who Are the Hostages?

Who the hostages are influences the terrorists' actions against
them. The Hanafi Muslim (March 10, 1977; Washington, D.C.)
episode illustrates this. The Hanafis seized hostages at three locations: the B'nai Brith Building, the District of Columbia Building,
and the Islamic Center. At the B'nai Brith Building, some of the
hostages were beaten and tortured. At the district building, there was
similar physical abuse meted out and, there, in addition, one man
was killed and another was wounded. However, at the Islamic Center,
where the hostages and hostage takers shared a religious bond, the
interaction bordered on being so cordial that there was some initial
concern as to whether any useful court testimony would be obtained
from these hostages.[9] As is generally seen in the process of transference, the quality of interaction between hostage and hostage taker
is the dominant factor in building positive attachments. The nature
of interaction is determined by who the hostages are. Thus, Israeli
officials appear to be on rather firm ground in their assertions that
Israeli hostages of Arab terrorists do not manifest signs of transference.

There is yet another aspect of the identity of the hostages that will
influence the final outcome. It is widely believed that the more vulnerable or the more prominent the hostage, the more likely a
government's response will be in favor of negotiation. Thus, even the
Israelis are reported to have negotiated in earnest for the children at
Maalot (May 15, 1974). The Israelis said they could not conduct war
over the heads of their children. Whatever a government does will
largely be influenced by what its populace will tolerate. A nation is
far and away more likely to tolerate nonnegotiation as policy when
the lives being negotiated for are those of government officials than
when it is the lives of its children.

Beyond that, the taking of certain officials who possess stature,
visibility, and access to secret information will undoubtedly incur a
response from most governments indicating a willingness to nego-

tiate. Although former Secretary of State Henry Kissinger (undoubtedly with great sincerity) espoused a policy of nonnegotiation, few believe that if he were taken hostage, the policy would be adhered to.[10] Such factors, of course, mean that the policy of nonnegotiation may ultimately be little more than a stimulus for terrorists to seize hostages for whom the government would be more likely to negotiate—irrespective of espoused policy. The seizure of such hostages, however, is not a guarantee that negotiations will take place. There is the temptation on the part of any government, which can convince its citizenry of the wisdom of nonnegotiation, to avoid negotiation even in highly visible instances where the character of the hostages imposes an impetus for negotiation. For in such circumstances, the inviolability of the policy of nonnegotiation can be decisively demonstrated. Whether a government will, of course, exercise or even confront such an option is another matter entirely. There was strong opposition, in some quarters of the populace, to Israel's stand of nonnegotiation for the captives at Entebbe (July 1976) when that appeared to be the case.

What Are the Demands and On Whom Are They Being Made?

It is my position that in those cases where the primary demands can be deflected to the acceptance of symbolic demands, as occurred in the Hanafi Muslim episode, acquiescence of the terrorists to symbolic victory is a possible way of achieving denouement of the confrontation. There are, of course, situations (the Baader-Meinhof operation against the West German embassy in Stockholm in April 1975 and the events at Maalot and Entebbe) where it was extraordinarily difficult, if not impossible, to establish meaningful negotiations. In Stockholm, the terrorists were unwilling to yield; and at both Maalot and Entebbe, the terrorists demonstrated bad faith by increasing their demands once it was apparent that the Israelis were actually interested in negotiating. Between the extremes of total capitulation, as the Black September Organization (BSO) demonstrated at Bangkok (December 1972) and the seemingly suicidal undertaking at the West German embassy in Stockholm by Baader-Meinhof, there may well be means for achieving accommodation, without a government totally compromising itself and appearing politically vulnerable and without the terrorists completely losing face. The exposure of a government's vulnerability or the terrorists' loss of credibility can only lead to a hardening of positions in the next encounter. The West German government adopted a hard line in Stockholm because of a previous total capitulation to Baader-Meinhof when they kidnapped mayoral candidate Peter Lorenz (February 1975), and the BSO adopted a hard line at Khartoum after its prior capitulation in Bangkok.[11]

In situations where the interaction between terrorists and government is largely a means of the terrorists' enactment of a ritual to gain access to the public agenda, it is possible to obtain the surrender of the terrorists without resorting to force. The crucial factor is, perhaps, for such rituals to become more institutionalized. Ritualistic violence, as practiced for many years by Zengakuren (the Japanese leftist student group) and the Japanese police, can sometimes take place within a strictly defined set of parameters. Zengakuren knew that they could not defeat the better trained, disciplined, and equipped police.[12] The police also knew that the task of subduing the students and engaging in combat, fought by both sides with sticks and rocks, would be more or less formidable but would ultimately end in victory for the police. The encounter was largely a ritual by which the students made their demands known. The police learned that the students could be beaten but should not be beaten so badly as to lose face and consequently be forced to return once again to the street in order to regain it.

Consequently, the type of demand made and the context in which it occurs (that is, ritualistic or nonritualistic) will provide or terminate opportunities for negotiation with the terrorists.

That, of course, is one perspective on the subject. Israeli officials will strongly argue that it is the wrong one. The political terrorists they encounter appear to them to have little latitude to negotiate or compromise. Moreover, capitulation has consequences for them that are quite different from those encountered by other types of hostage takers. A political terrorist in Israel, and in many other countries as well, will end up in a prison with other terrorists. If he is not put into prison and is sent home, he will invariably face a court martial. As a result, there is a psychological frame of reference established that imposes strong negative motivations to surrender. For these reasons, the Israelis are adamant about their general refusal to negotiate—a refusal that is largely, although not wholly, immutable to considerations of who the terrorists and the hostages are or what the demands are.

Hostage Coping

The experience of being a hostage does not end with the resolution

of the situation. Many hostages relive the experience through daily psychological anxiety and sleepless nights. Studies are currently underway both here and abroad to ascertain how potential hostages might better cope with the experience of being in captivity. Throwing away the clock in negotiations may ultimately save the most lives; but what will be the quality of the life that is left? The longer the exposure to stress, the greater the prospect of long-term psychological damage to the victims. It was, in part, for this reason that after some twenty days the Dutch government resorted to force to free fifty-five hostages held by South Moluccan terrorists on a train in northern Holland. As Dr. Dirk Mulder, the government psychiatrist who negotiated with the terrorists was later to note, "How long could they [the hostages] stand it without longlasting physical and psychic problems?"[13] He felt that after twenty days the situation had to be resolved within the next week, in part, because the stress was becoming unbearable for some of the hostages.

Generally, the reaction of hostages to their plight appears to be as varied as the personalities. Some hostages have long bouts of psychological stress afterward. If taken captive at work, the work environment becomes so evocative for some that they refuse to return to it. In one case in New York, a woman even refused to pick up her pay because it meant returning to where she worked and had been taken hostage. One trained law enforcement officer who had been taken hostage in a cell block described getting dressed in the morning to go to work and being unable to go. Another officer who had undergone the same experience in the cell block claimed that after a full day's rest he went back to work and suffered no adverse effects then and has suffered none since. He further says that he is slightly more cautious around the prisoners, but fundamentally his behavior is the same. A woman who had been a hostage at Entebbe told me that after seven months she still awakens in the middle of the night to the sound of the voice of the German woman who had uniformly abused the hostages. Yet her husband, who underwent the same experience of captivity, claimed to have suffered no aftereffects. In Atlanta, Georgia, a bank holdup developed into a hostage situation and ended with the robber being shot in the presence of the hostages. Yet all the hostages returned to work.

The divergencies in response to the experience of being a hostage appear to be indistinguishable from the differences in responses to any form of severe stress. It would appear that any study of the responses of hostages to captivity would most accurately be accomplished from the vantage point of some baseline data. This would enable researchers to assess the stress in the individual's life prior to captivity.

Obtaining a suitable baseline may perhaps not be as difficult as it appears. The number of hostage victims would appear to be extensive enough so that a certain percentage would probably have at some time prior to captivity undergone psychiatric examination. From the psychological records, baseline data would be established and responses to stress would then be assessed against such data. It would be very important to continue the observation of the hostage for several years to fully determine the impact of the experience and its lingering effects. It is conceivable, if the psychiatric experiences of concentration camp survivors is at all relevant, that the impact of captivity might not manifest itself for years. Etinger's[14] work on concentration camp survivors shows that some victims did not manifest responses associated with the experience until twenty years later.

There is some question as to whether it is useful to prepare hostages for captivity. Certainly, such a program would be of highly limited utility for the larger population, but could be of value to specific target populations such as high-ranking business executives, diplomatic personnel, and military officers stationed abroad.

If an individual is a potential hostage, there will generally be some indication of the increasing probability of the threat. Terrorists undertake detailed and extensive preparations prior to kidnapping prominent individuals. Such preparations provide signs of the terrorists' intentions (for example, surveillance or new and strange people suddenly showing up at or near the victim's home). From the vantage point of hindsight, many prominent hostages recalled incidents that upon reflection would have signaled them that they were being stalked as victims.

Prevention also requires changing routes to and from work and establishing patterns that make one a more difficult target. But even when that is all said and done, there is the likelihood that barring what some see as a suicidal "fire fight" with the terrorists, if one is willing to take the risks and invest the resources, virtually every potential victim can be confronted with the alternatives of acquiescing to captivity or choosing to be killed in an attempt at resistance. To some degree, then, captivity is virtually inescapable.

If this is a fair assumption, then for some people, preparing for captivity is as important as preparing to avoid being captured. This means that captives should realize what their own instinctive and natural reactions will be during captivity, what their captor will probably do to them, the reactions their captors expect, and what hostages can do to counteract the psychological and physical pressure brought by their captors.

Terrorists use varying mechanisms to disorient their captives. Generally, the captive will be placed in an environment that precludes any sense of time and space. This means that the individual is not only cut off from contact with his loved ones and the supportive elements of a familiar external world, but is also disoriented as to the psychologically vital parameters of time and space. This disorientation is aggravated by guards, who may even torture the captive, and by isolation from other prisoners.

If subjected to interrogation, the hostage is also at a disadvantage. he will generally face a skilled and experienced interrogator. Here the process of transference can work decisively against the hostage. Feeling totally dependent on the captor, the hostage's will might bend and yield completely. Again, we are reminded of the Patricia Hearst episode. Her initial days of captivity exposed her to extreme sensory deprivation. She was completely disoriented to the passage of time. Her age and the ethically ambiguous circumstance of her life in Berkeley's Telegraph district did not provide the strong set of ethics that makes one resistant to manipulation by psychological transference.

As was observed in the case of American soldiers in the Korean war who were subjected to psychological manipulation by the Chinese communists, individuals with strong belief systems were highly resilient to brainwashing techniques. In contrast, those whose beliefs were open and flexible were far and away more likely to submit to indoctrination.[15] In two well-known hostage incidents, involving the capture, by Uruguayan Tupamaros, of Dr. Claude Fly, an American agronomist, and British Ambassador Geoffrey Jackson, the individuals not only resisted psychological manipulation but were of such firm character that they began exercising a strong influence over their guards. The terrorists found it necessary to remove some of the guards who had fallen under the prisoners' influence. For, as Dutch psychiatrist Dirk Mulder has noted, some of the toughness and anger of terrorists in the initial moments of a takeover are an attempt to deal not only with their fear, but also with their guilt at having seized innocents.[16] Both Fly and Jackson worked at breaking down the hostility that their guards held towards them.[17]

Both Fly and Jackson were men of strong religious conviction (Fly even wrote a book on Christian ethics during his captivity). Both men had strong family ties, had achieved a degree of personal success in their professional lives, and understood how their captors were attempting to manipulate them.

One of the greatest difficulties in dealing with any alien situation is the inability to find the psychological anchors that we all require in order to deal with life. Uncertainty, as a number of students of man and his interaction with his environment have observed, is a most difficult and anxiety ridden circumstance. The degree of anxiety produced in such situations is said to be so great that even situations that produce clearcut negative expectations are perceived as being easier to manage.[18] The benefit derived from preparing for captivity is to no small degree found in the reduction of uncertainty. The captive can anticipate and understand what his captors are doing and what is likely to follow. To the extent that this is possible and that the process is reinforced by the hostage having made accurate predictions, the level of uncertainty, disorientation, and anxiety is sharply reduced.

It is also important for the individual to make some mental link to the outside world. Sir Geoffrey instructed his wife to return to England in the event of his captivity and to paint the interior of the house. She was further instructed as to the sequence in which the rooms were to be painted. This provided him with a picture of what she was doing on each day of his captivity, and it provided him with a link to her. It is also important that a captive engage in physical and mental exercises. This contributes to maintenance of mental and physical health during confinement. Sir Geoffrey wrote children's stories and followed the Canadian Air Force Exercise Program. Although his captors took his writing materials away, Sir Geoffrey persisted by writing in his head and published his work shortly after his release. Dr. Fly wrote a book on Christian ethics while in captivity. His own conduct during his ordeal was so in accord with the principles he espoused that even the terrorists referred to him as a saint.

The Tupamaros released both men, Fly because of his ill health and Jackson following a triumphal jail break by 106 political prisoners. The latter episode served as a major propaganda victory for the Tupamaros.

As in most such cases, the captives were pawns, used for propaganda and to wrest concessions from the government. Most terrorists do not desire to kill preselected prominent hostages, unless the hostages were specifically seized as targets for assassination. (The seizure and subsequent assassination of the American policeman Dan Mitrione who was assigned as a consultant to the Uruguayan police is a case in point.) It appears that there is a reasonably good chance that a hostage will be released even if the demands are not acceded to;

however, there is some controversy over this point. The Tupamaros claim that the Uruguayan government had, in fact, entered into negotiations for the release of Fly. Whether anything came of these alleged negotiations was not revealed. Observers generally argue that it is reasonable to assume that if a specifically selected individual is seized as a political hostage and not executed shortly thereafter, then he most likely will not be executed. When execution is decidedly going to be carried out, it is usually done swiftly and publicly without negotiation being entertained. After all, the execution of a publicly visible individual renders a different type of political statement than the seizing of a hostage for the purpose of gaining concessions from a government.

Hostage Coping: The Mass Public

It may be useful for individuals who are especially vulnerable to becoming hostages to prepare themselves for being taken captive and for facing treatment by captors. Such preparations, as procedural mechanisms, are peripheral to the interests of the mass public. But the public is involved in any politically salient hostage situation. Targets are selected because they can be used to threaten public authority and public safety. Terrorism by definition is an act that seeks to influence a population significantly larger than the immediate target. Thus, the quality of the public's understanding and its response to terrorism of all varieties is highly significant. Ultimately, it is public opinion in a democracy that will help shape the political environment within which government officials must act. As Dr. Frank Ochberg has noted,

> A public which overreacts in outrage against the victim's helplessness may precipitate harsh, simplistic counter terrorist measures. A public which joins the victim in identifying with the terrorist-aggressor may undermine the morale and confidence of the police. A public perplexed and alienated by the entire process may interfere with the bond of trust between government and governed which is necessary for the survival of democratic institutions. But, on the other hand, a public that is reasonably well aware of the repertoire of human responses which are effectively used by men and women under stress— even under the stress of terrorist threat and captivity—such a public will be able to participate in rational decision making about national policy on terrorism.[19]

Dr. Ochberg's point is well taken. Too often the public implications of the terrorist act are ignored. Worse, yet, the terrorist's victim is generally a substitute for the state, but few nations assume any responsibility for their citizens who become the unwitting victims of terrorism. The effects of the experience of being victimized by terrorists extend beyond the mere time in captivity. Psychological problems tend to persist, but our society generally does not wish to assume responsibility for them. In addition, it is alleged that there is a lack of concern by some governments for employees who have been taken hostage because of their role as representatives of government. U.S. Department of State employees who have been taken hostage allege that there is a bureaucratic insensitivity to their plight. They have become pariahs because their very presence is a reminder to others of everyone's vulnerability to terrorism. These same individuals further add that their careers have, as a result of their ill fate, reached a trajectory, and there is no promise of advancement. These allegations, if true, coupled with the formal policy of nonnegotiation, are said to have an adverse influence on morale in the U.S. Department of State.

The fact, however, that such issues have come to the public's attention indicates at least a concern about the policy and an initiative toward change. Certainly, developing tolerance in the mass public for the plight of victims is not likely when a governmental agency whose employees are the target of terrorist activities is not responsive to the ensuing difficulties of its own employees.

The government may not have much control over the image of terrorism conveyed by the popular media. After all, terrorism is news and the media is there to convey the news generally in a form that sells copy. However, the government can make the public aware of the difficulties and problems faced in hostage situations. In this way, the public, while not exposed to the same information with which potential targets are provided, will have access to sufficiently high quality information that discussion can take place in an informed manner, leading to the type of environment that assists in maintaining intelligent and objective responses to a problem too easily caught up with emotional fervor. Such discussion, hopefully, will lead to a less vindictive response toward hostages who are compromised by the process of transference and to the establishment of public attitudes that will recognize that extinguishing liberty in the rush to combat terrorism only accomplishes for the terrorists what they are unable to accomplish for themselves.

Notes

1. Brian Jenkins, Janera Johnson, and David Ronfeldt, "Num-

bered Lives: Some Statistical Observations from Seventy-seven International Hostage Episodes" (Santa Monica: The RAND Corporation, July 1977).

2. From a personal interview with Lieutenant Richard Klapp, January 28, 1977. See also Ralph Craib, "Crisis Negotiators in Hostage Cases," *The San Francisco Chronicle*, January 29, 1977, p. 2.

3. M. Jane Stewart, "Hostage Episodes: 1973-1977: A Chronology" (unpublished).

4. The depiction of the Williamsburg incident is from personal interviews. See also John A. Culley, "Defusing Human Bombs—Hostage Negotiations," *FBI Law Enforcement Bulletin*, December 1974; and Donald F. Cawley, "Anatomy of a Siege," *The Police Chief*, January 1974.

5. I am indebted to Special Agents Conrad Hassel and Thomas Strentz of the FBI Academy for their insights on the process of transference.

6. Richard Brockman, "Notes While Being Hijacked," *The Atlantic*, December 1976, pp. 68-75.

7. Ibid., p. 75.

8. "Psyching Out Terrorists," *Medical World News*, June 27, 1977.

9. The Hanafi episode is described in Abraham H. Miller, "Negotiating for Hostages: Implications from the Police Experience" (paper presented to the International Studies Association, March 1977).

10. Kissinger's position as cited in Robert A. Fearey "International Terrorism," *Department of State Bulletin*, March 29, 1976, p. 397.

11. On March 2, 1973, three diplomats—two Americans and one Belgian—were murdered in the Saudi embassy in Khartoum by agents of Black September after an official announcement by President Richard Nixon of the U.S. government's refusal to negotiate. The announcement came while a U.S. Department of State negotiator was en route. Many observers have concluded that the action taken by Black September was to demonstrate that their capitulation in Bangkok was not typical of their pattern of operations.

12. Michiya Shimbori, "The Sociology of a Student Movement—A Japanese Case Study," *Daedalus*, Winter 1968.

13. "Psyching Out Terrorists," p. 17.

14. Leo Etinger remarks to the Fourth International Seminar on Terrorism, sponsored by the Centre International de Criminologie Comparée, Evian, France, June 1977).

15. E. H. Schein, Winifred F. Hill, H. L. Williams, and A. Lubin, "Distinguishing Characteristics of Collaborators and Resisters among American Prisoners of War," *The Journal of Abnormal*

Social Psychology, 1957, vol. 55, pp. 197-201.

16. "Psyching Out Terrorists."

17. U.S., Congress, Senate, Committee on the Judiciary, *Hearings on Terrorist Activity, Hostage Defense Measures*, 94th Cong., 1st sess., July 25, 1975.

18. In this regard, see Ivo K. Feierabend, et al., "Social Change and Political Violence: Cross-National Patterns," in *The History of Violence in America*, Hugh Davis Graham and Ted Robert Gurr, eds. (New York: Bantam Books, 1970); and Abraham H. Miller et al., "The J-Curve Theory and the Black Urban Riots," *The American Political Science Review*, vol. 71, no. 3 (September 1977), pp. 964-982.

19. Frank Ochberg (remarks to the Fourth International Seminar on Terrorism, sponsored by the Centre International de Criminologie Comparée, Evian, France, June 1977).

7
Terrorism and the Media: Some Considerations

Yonah Alexander

Terrorism, as an expedient tactical and strategic tool of politics in the struggle for power within and among nations, is not new in the history of man's inhumanity to man. From time immemorial, opposition groups, functioning under varying degrees of stress, have intentionally utilized instruments of psychological and physical force—including intimidation, coercion, repression, and, ultimately, destruction of lives and property—for the purpose of attaining real or imaginary ideological and political goals. That is, as agitational and disruptive civil violence, terrorism has been employed by subnational groups either seeking to effect limited changes within the existing political structure or desiring to abolish completely the established system, principally, but not exclusively, as part of a national or transnational revolutionary strategy.

Unlike older historical precedents, nonstate terrorists, who sanctified their actions in the name of higher principles, have introduced into contemporary life a new breed of violence in terms of technology, victimization, threat, and response. The brutalization and globalization of modern violence makes it amply clear that we have entered a unique Age of Terrorism with all its formidable problems and frightening ramifications. To be sure, it is generally recognized that terrorism poses many threats to contemporary society and is likely to have a serious impact on the quality of life and on orderly civilized existence. Perhaps the most significant dangers are those relating to the safety, welfare, and rights of ordinary people, the stability of the state system, the health and pace of economic development, and the expansion, or even the survival of democracy.[1]

An earlier version of this chapter entitled "Terrorism, the Media and the Police" was presented at the nineteenth Annual Meeting of the International Studies Association, Washington, D.C., February 29, 1978.

But, in spite of various national and international efforts to deal with the dangers of terrorism, the level of nonstate violence remains high. The reasons for these conditions are diverse but include at least ten factors: disagreement about who is a terrorist, lack of understanding of the causes of terrorism, the support of terrorism by some states, the existence of an international network of terrorism, the politicization of religion, double standards of morality, loss of resolve by governments, weak punishment of terrorists, flouting of world law, and the roles of the mass media.[2] While all these factors deserve serious and thorough study, this chapter will focus on the interaction of terrorism and the media, specifically as related to the police handling of incidents.

Clearly, modern technology has provided terror groups with a critical communications instrument—the media—which willingly or unwillingly serves their specific or general propaganda and psychological warfare needs.[3] More specifically, the strategy of terrorism followed by subnational groups does not prescribe instant victories over established regimes or states. On the contrary, the struggle for intended ends is seen as complicated and protracted. Terrorist groups, by their very nature, are too small and too weak to achieve an upper hand in an eyeball-to-eyeball confrontation on the battlefield. Since sheer violence can accomplish little or nothing in terms of ultimate goals, an extension of the duration and impact of the violent deed is therefore mandatory in the terrorist strategy. As Walter Laqueur stated, "The media are the terrorist's best friend. The terrorist's act by itself is nothing; publicity is all."[4]

It is because of this realization that terrorist operations have been broadly symbolic rather than physically oriented. In relying on immediate and extensive coverage of television, radio, and the press for the maximum amount of propagandizing and publicizing, terrorists can rapidly and effectively reach watching, listening, and reading audiences at home and abroad and thereby hope to attain essentially one or two of the following communications purposes: First, to enhance the effectiveness of their violence by creating an emotional state of extreme fear in target groups, and thereby ultimately alter their behavior and dispositions, or bring about a general or particular change in the structure of government or society; and, second, to draw forcibly and instantaneously the attention of the "whole world" to themselves in the expectation that these audiences will be prepared to act or, in some cases, to refrain from acting in a manner that will promote the cause they presumably represent.

Terrorism, then, like advertising, increases the effectiveness of its messages by focusing on spectacular incidents and by keeping particular issues alive through repetition. Carlos Marighella, in his much publicized *Minimanual of the Urban Guerrilla*, expressed this strategy:

> The coordination of urban guerrilla action, including each armed action, is the principle way of making armed propaganda.
>
> These actions, carried out with specific and determined objectives, inevitably become propaganda material for the mass communication system.
>
> Bank assaults, ambushes, desertions and diverting of arms, the rescue of prisoners, executions, kidnappings, sabotage, terrorism, and the war of nerves, are all cases in point.
>
> Airplanes diverted in flight by revolutionary action, moving ships and trains assaulted and seized by guerrillas, can also be solely for propaganda effects. . . .
>
> The war of nerves or psychological war is an aggressive technique, based on the direct or indirect use of mass means of communication and news transmitted orally in order to demoralize the government.
>
> In psychological warfare, the government is always at a disadvantage since it imposes censorship on the mass media and winds up in a defensive position by not allowing anything against it to filter through.
>
> At this point it becomes desperate, is involved in greater contradictions and loss of prestige, and loses time and energy in an exhausting effort at control which is subject to being broken at any moment.[5]

The utilization and manipulation of the media, as directed by Marighella and other proponents of political and ideological violence, have been practiced by practically all terrorist movements. They have sought not only to spread fear among the primary target, but also to publicize their discontent as well as their ideologies with a view to making their violent deeds appear heroic.

One dramatic instance of media manipulation is the Patricia Hearst–SLA episode. Her kidnapping in February 1974 was used as a form of propaganda for the revolution of the SLA. The terrorists insisted that the media carry in full their messages—both tapes and printed material—lest the safety of the prisoner be jeopardized. For several years, the media have continued to magnify the case out of proportion to its real significance, thus providing sensational mass entertainment and serving the publicity needs of the SLA and its successors as well. What is most disturbing about this case is the fact that the media have given a small group of criminal misfits a Robin Hood image and transformed it into an internationally known movement possessing power and posing an insurmountable problem to the authorities.

Overseas terrorist operations also have not been perpetrated for the sake of immediate results or for the purpose of violence itself. Thus, in November 1975, the Montoneros in Buenos Aires kidnapped the industrial director of Germany's Mercedes-Benz and released him after the company (among other things) published advertisements in newspapers in Europe, Washington, D.C., and Mexico denouncing the "economic imperialism" of multinational corporations in developing countries.

In another episode, which occurred in February 1975, the Baader-Meinhof terrorists kidnapped a West Berlin politician in order to secure the release of their imprisoned comrades and also "hijacked" a local television network. Describing this incident, one West German editor related, "for 72 hours, we lost control of the medium. We shifted shows to meet their timetable. [They demanded that] our cameras be in position to record each of the prisoners as they boarded a plane, and our news coverage had to include prepared statements of their direction."[6]

It can be concluded that the communications purposes that revolutionary terror groups seek through the media are attention, recognition, and legitimacy. As Weisband and Roguly succinctly observed,

> For the terrorist, the path to legitimacy is through one's reputation for resilience, for self-sacrifice and daring, for brutality, and, above all, for effective discipline over words and actions. The terrorist is his own torch and bomb; he ignites the flames of national passion and, if possible, of political sympathy, and he does it by violating universal human sensibilities. It is the credibility that violence produces whenever it appalls that renders terrorism horrifying yet powerful and, if successful, self-legitimating.[7]

To what extent does the media's extensive coverage of terrorism influence public attitudes? Although there is no definite answer to this question, according to nationwide public opinion polls conducted by Yankelovich, Shelly & White, Inc., with regard to American public attitudes towards the Palestine Liberation Organization (PLO),[8] there seems to be a close relationship, at least in terms of a greater awareness.[9]

The first poll in January 1975 was taken shortly after widespread media coverage of Yasir Arafat's triumphal appearance before the UN General Assembly in November 1974. The second poll was conducted a year later, toward the end of January 1976, after the UN Security

Council had invited the PLO to participate in its debate on the Middle East. In the intervening period, the PLO had succeeded in gaining admission to other UN-sponsored conferences and had opened offices in many countries in Europe and the Third World. But the PLO was also becoming more and more embroiled in the Lebanese civil war, which was increasingly in the news at the time.

As one might expect, the continuing attention given to the PLO by the mass media over the year was reflected in increased public awareness of the group's existence. In January 1975, only about one-half of the American public (52 percent) said that it had heard of the PLO. By January 1976, the figure had gone up to 63 percent. Again, as might be expected, the higher the educational level of the respondents, the greater the likelihood that they were aware of the PLO, with 88 percent of college graduates answering in the affirmative.

Another major consequence of extensive media coverage of terrorism is the exportation of violent techniques which, in turn, often triggers similar extreme actions by other individuals and groups. As Richard Clutterbuck asserted, "ideas travel . . . through the normal news media . . . people watching and listening to the reports get ideas about doing the same things themselves."[10] That is, the more publicity given to bomb scares, the more bomb scares there are likely to be, and reports about plane hijackings lead to more plane hijackings.

The excessive media coverage of the two attempts on President Ford's life in 1975 caused deep concern that the publicity might set off similar actions by other would-be assassins. As Vice President Rockefeller stated, "Let's stop talking about it. Let's stop putting it on the front pages and on television. Psychiatrists say every time there is any publicity, it is stimulating to the unstable." A similar view was expressed by Secretary of the Treasury William E. Simon: "It's the responsibility of the press, certainly, to tell the American people indeed what is happening. . . . But when these people are glamorized on the front pages of our national magazines, I think that this has to be thought of as doing great harm."[11]

The Hanafi Muslim takeover of three buildings in Washington, D.C., in March 1977 also became a major media event with similar implications. "The media," Charles Seib of the *Washington Post* wrote, "were as much a part of it as the terrorists, the victims and the authorities. The news business did what it always does when it deals with violence, bloodshed and suspense: It covered it excessively."[12] Ambassador Andrew Young, expressing concern about the contagious effect of such coverage, stated that it is tantamount to "advertising to neurotic people" who are inspired to attempt "suicidal and ridiculous" acts.[13]

An estimate of the impact on the mass audience was made recently.

> Typical reporting of a terrorist event here in the United States might reach an audience of, say, conservatively, forty million people. What's the chance that it may come to the attention of some borderline psychopath who may be stimulated to take part in some future episode? If we were to consider that just one-tenth of one percent of the audience were borderline psychopaths, that would be forty thousand potential maniacs. If we took one one-thousandth of one percent we've still got four hundred. If we took one one-hundred-thousandth of one percent, we would still have the four that are necessary to carry out a typical terrorist episode.[14]

To be sure, because terrorism, however local, is by its very nature a worldwide theatrical attraction, it tends to encourage angry and frustrated groups in other countries to undertake similar acts as a way out of their helplessness and alienation. For example, several weeks after Argentina's Montoneros removed the body of ex-President Pedro Aramburu to secure the return of Eva Peron's body from Spain, Burmese terrorists stole the body of U Thant for the purpose of using it in negotiations with the Burmese government.

Another major issue related to the problem of terrorism and the media is the particular interaction of both with police agencies. In every terrorist incident, an inevitable critical relationship develops between the media responsible for reporting the episode and the law enforcement personnel handling the incident. Not infrequently, the media, especially the broadcasters, hinder effective police responses to terrorist activities. The media can, for instance, detrimentally affect siege-management situations by: (1) interfering with on-going operations; (2) exacerbating the pressure on the responsible authorities and contributing to impaired decision making; and (3) harassing relatives of victims by pressing for interviews.

During the Hanafi episode, the media unknowingly worked at cross purposes to officials. They furnished the terrorists with direct intelligence information by continuing on-site television coverage, thus adding to the terrorists' feeling of power. Some members of the media also made direct telephone calls to interview the terrorists and thereby tied up communication between the police negotiators and the criminals.

Some details concerning this case were provided by Charles Fenyvesi, a reporter who had been a hostage at the B'nai Brith building during the siege.

The most damaging case concerned the TV reporter who caught sight of a basket lifted up by rope to the fifth floor, where, the world later learned, some people evaded the round-up and barricaded themselves in a room. Their presence apparently was not known to the gunmen, who held their prisoners on the eighth floor but patrolled the lower floors until late Wednesday afternoon. The gunmen were probably informed of the TV reporter's scoop by their fellow Hanafis who monitored the new media outside the captured buildings. Fortunately the gunmen did not break through the door.

Another case of a reporter endangering lives occurred when Khaalis was asked, during a live telephone interview with a leading local radio station, "Have you set a deadline?" The police and all the other experts had thought that the absence of a deadline was one encouraging sign. Fortunately, Khaalis was too engrossed in his rhetoric to pay any attention to the question.

A third example: One prominent Washington newscaster called Khaalis a Black Muslim. Khaalis, whose family was murdered by Black Muslims, flew into a rage and stormed into the room where we hostages were held. He declared that he would kill one of us in retaliation for the newsman's words. The police, meanwhile, advised the newscaster to promptly issue an apology, and Khaalis was eventually mollified.[15]

Robert L. Rabe, assistant chief of police, Metropolitan Police Department, who was personally involved in handling the incident, complained about another instance of media irresponsibility during the Hanafi siege: ". . . a local reporter took it upon himself to report live over the radio and television what appeared to him to be boxes of ammunition being taken into the B'nai Brith building in preparation for an all-out police assault, when, in fact, what was being taken were boxes of food for the hostages. Just imagine what the repercussions could have been if the terrorists had been monitoring their radios and televisions at that precise moment."[16]

It is noteworthy that, after the Hanafi hostages were freed, they were warned by the police not to give interviews to the media lest the prosecutor's task in dealing with the case become more difficult and complicated. According to complaints by the hostages, some members of the media were insistent on obtaining interviews. In one particular case, a network representative justified his request for an interview by asserting, "the public has the right to know." The harassed hostage declined to grant the interview, replying, "Is it in the Constitution that the public has the right to invade my privacy, to insist on exposing people already humiliated, to wallow in their pain and misery?"[17]

Finally, it is also evident that the media have jeopardized the authorities' management of terrorist incidents abroad. In the October 1977 hijacking of the Lufthansa jet, for instance, the media directly contributed to the death of a hostage because they did not realize that certain information, especially in regard to tactical operations, had to remain outside public knowledge. In this case, the terrorists on board the jet heard over the public radio broadcasts to which they had access that the German captain was passing valuable intelligence information to the authorities on the ground through his normal radio transmissions. Subsequently, the terrorists executed the captain.

To be sure, the media are not always detrimental. There are situations where the media, by publicizing an incident, have, in the words of Special Agent of the FBI, Conrad Hassel, "relaxed the pressure of the terrorist finger."[18] Harold Coffman, professor of law and psychiatry at Georgetown University, stated "coverage of such events is helpful. It allows these people to have some method of ventilating their anger and frustration, in making known their grievances. The more coverage given, the more they are likely to see themselves part of, rather than outside, the system."[19]

One such example is the Croatian TWA case of September 1976. The hijackers insisted that specific demands be met as the price for terminating the hijacking, including, among other things, that two propaganda tracts be published on the front page of a number of newspapers. The *New York Times*, the *Washington Post*, and the *Chicago Tribune*, to mention a few, complied and thereby contributed to a satisfactory management of the incident.

The media also played a helpful role in establishing a vital link between authorities and the public-at-large in connection with the May-June 1977 South Moluccan incident in Holland. During that episode, daily news releases containing bits of information on details not crucial to developing strategy and tactics satisfied the public appetite for information, as well as conveyed an image of official responsibility and effective crisis management.

In light of these ramifications, what role should the media in democratic systems have in combating terrorism? Two major factors must be considered in this connection. First are the facts that, to terrorists, an extensive coverage by the media is the major reward and that "establishment" communications channels willingly or unwillingly become tools in the terrorist strategy, and that advertising terrorism increases the effectiveness of its message through repetition and imitation. The second concerns the vital importance of protecting the people's right to know and a free press in open societies. A closely critical issue is the relationship between the media and law enforcement agencies. Although each has a duty to perform and a right to perform that duty, the legitimate roles of both entities are seemingly diametrically opposed.

In sum, how can the media in a democratic society devise new methods of fair and credible reporting of terrorist activities without jeopardizing their responsibilities to the public and without adversely affecting the current criminal justice processes.

It is obvious that there are no easy answers to these vital concerns, only very difficult choices. Indeed, the various issues have been highly controversial. For example, in April 1977, a Gallup poll found that Americans were divided about whether the media should give complete, detailed coverage of terrorism.[20] More definitive in their responses are the administrators of justice, as seen in the results of a survey of police chiefs in thirty American cities.

1. Ninety-three percent of the police chiefs believed live TV coverage of terrorist acts encourages terrorism.

2. None of the police chiefs of large cities surveyed believed that coverage of terrorist acts should be televised live. Sixty percent thought such TV coverage should be delayed or videotaped, and 27 percent believed terrorist acts should not be covered by television.

3. Forty-six percent of police chiefs considered live television coverage of terrorist acts "a great threat" to hostage safety and 33 percent considered it "a moderate threat." Only 7 percent considered it a minimal threat.

4. More than half of the police chiefs had generally unfavorable judgments of on-the-scene television reporters covering terrorists. Twenty percent of the police chiefs believed television reporters covering terrorist acts were "poor" and 33 percent believed they were "average." Only 20 percent believed that TV journalists covering terrorists were good.

5. Sixty-seven percent of the police chiefs said TV journalists should only communicate with terrorists with official consent. Another 33 percent believed that under no circumstances should TV journalists communicate with terrorists while they are engaged in criminal activity.[21]

Although this survey is limited in scope, it is reasonable to assume that, in general, law enforcement officers, who now lack both the legal authority and the practical ability to control coverage of terrorist activities, look upon the media "as a powerful force, sometimes more influential than government itself,"[22] which should somehow be restrained. This attitude was verbalized by Ambassador Andrew Young, who asserted that "the First Amendment has got to be clarified by the Supreme Court in light of the power of the mass media"; he stated that media personnel should censor themselves.[23]

To be sure, some newsmen seem to realize that the media have much too much influence in domestic and international affairs.[24] A few are even prepared not to cover terrorism at all. One television news director in Cleveland explained, "We feel that the coverage we give such incidents is partly to blame, for we are glorifying lawbreakers, we are making heroes out of nonheroes. In effect we are losing control over our news departments. We are being used."[25]

While most journalists recognize the perils involved in covering terrorist incidents, the media in general reject as unthinkable any curtailment of their reporting. The National News Council, for example, warned "the dangers of suppression should be self-evident: doubts over what the media have withheld and the motives for such a blackout; questions about other types of news which might also have been withheld ostensibly in the public interest; and the greater possible risks involved in wild and reckless rumors and exaggerated, provocative word-of-mouth reports."[26]

To some journalists, even the suggestion that guidelines be adopted to prevent excesses in terrorist incident coverage implies censorship and, ultimately, suppression. This sentiment was expressed by A. M. Rosenthal, executive editor of the *New York Times*: "The last thing in the world I want is guidelines. I don't want guidelines from the government and I don't want any from professional organizations or anyone else. The strength of the press is its diversity. As soon as you start imposing guidelines, they become peer-group pressures and then quasi-legal restrictions."[27]

In light of these and similar concerns, it is highly unlikely that governments in Western democracies, believing that free and dynamic media are vital to the success of their systems, will institute any form of official management of news. It has been reported, for instance, that President Carter "has no desire to seek legislation or to otherwise impose a solution and hopes those who make news decisions will themselves determine definable boundaries of legitimate coverage."[28]

A rare example of a democratic government's request of a news ban occurred in connection with the Schleyer kidnapping and the Lufthansa hijacking in October 1977. In this case, the threat of terrorism was so grave that the West German government, for the first time, appealed to the media to impose a strict silence on themselves. This request was almost universally accepted. Subsequently, the government published, as originally promised, a detailed account of the events and decisions related to these specific terrorist incidents.[29]

In spite of this unique experience, the complex question of the role of the media in influencing terrorist results and societal intiative behavior remains largely unresolved, although the interaction between the media and domestic violence has been the subject of serious discussion and substantial research since 1968.[30] However, the role of the media during terrorist crisis conditions, particularly as it affects incident-management situations, has not, thus far, at least, been suitably explored and systematically studied. Only isolated initiatives have been undertaken in this area. Several conferences and limited research activities dealing with some aspects of the problem[31] have generated useful suggestions for responsible reporting of terrorist incidents. Moreover, some news organizations have adopted specific policies with a view toward better management of such situations. The *Chicago Sun-Times, Chicago Daily News,* the *Courier-Journal,* the *Louisville Times,* United Press International, and CBS News have unilaterally determined internal guidelines for coverage.[32] Other media entities such as the *Washington Post* and WMAL-TV of Washington, D.C., have established temporary rules to handle specific incidents as, for instance, the Hanafi episode.[33]

The research conducted by scholars on this subject is rather fragmentary, consisting of portions of reports,[34] occasional articles,[35] and several chapters in books.[36] Perhaps the most comprehensive study is *Disorders and Terrorism,* published by the National Advisory Committee on Criminal Justice Standards and Goals.[37] While the task force examines some aspects of news coverage during commission of acts of terrorism, contemporaneous coverage, and follow-up reporting,[38] it fails to assess fully the role of the media as it affects the management of terrorist activities by the authorities.

While the foregoing activities are, indeed, commendable for contributing preliminary relevant material, there exists no multidisciplinary data base of past efforts, no serious analysis of success and failure of handling specific terrorist incidents from the perspectives of the media and law enforcement officials themselves, and no acceptable and tested models of media and policy management of terrorist situations. In view of this condition, there is an immediate need to undertake a rigorous study on the interaction of terrorism, the media, and police, and thereby fill the gap in scholarship perti-

nent to current criminal justice processes. A new urgency is given
to this need by the warning of Walter Scheel, president of West
Germany: "unless this flame [of terrorism] is stamped out in time,
it will spread like a brush fire all over the world."[39] Indeed, this
message forces us to ponder the future with grave concern and to
determine appropriate courses of action.

Research on terrorism and the media should take into account the
following observations and considerations: First, terrorism is essentially violence for effect and is directed not only at the instant victims
of it and their family members, but, by extension, also at a wider
audience. Second, terrorism is a theater, at least in its embryonic
stages, and, consequently, terrorists are making a conscious and deliberate effort to manipulate the media for their intended ends. Third,
since the media are based on competition and profit, it is inevitable
that they become an integral part of any terrorist act, providing star
actors, script writers, and directors. Fourth, by providing extensive
coverage of incidents the media give the impression that they sympathize with the terrorist cause, thereby creating a climate congenial
to further violence. Fifth, the media often hinder the work of law
enforcement agencies, thus jeopardizing successful outcomes of incidents. Sixth, the media have occasionally been helpful to the
authorities in managing incidents without abandoning their responsibilities to the public's right to know. Seventh, the media should
objectively, accurately, and credibly report about terrorist acts lest
the public panic and lose trust and confidence in both the press and
government. Eighth, any attempts to impose media blackouts are
likely to force terrorists to escalate the levels of violence in order
to attract more attention. Ninth, since a major goal of terrorism is
to undermine authority and cause anarchy, an unjustifiable limitation or even destruction of free media will ultimately result in the
victory of terrorism. Tenth, the media, without surrendering their
prerogatives, should help criminal justice processes in dealing with
terrorism, and, conversely, the administration of justice officials
should turn to the media for professional assistance in handling the
incidents and in limiting their derivative societal repercussions.
Eleventh, given the nature and complexity of modern terrorism, the
determination of a proper role for the media should not be left to
their judgment alone, nor is it desirable that law enforcement
agencies should unilaterally develop policies on this matter. And,
twelfth, the threat of contemporary terrorism requires the openness,

understanding, and cooperation of society, so that we can deal with this important area of public concern more hopefully and realistically.

Notes

1. For details, see Yonah Alexander, ed., *International Terrorism* (New York: Praeger Publishers, 1976); Yonah Alexander and Seymour M. Finger, *Terrorism: Interdisciplinary Perspectives* (New York and London: John Jay Press and McGraw Hill, 1977); and Yonah Alexander and Herbert M. Levine, "Prepare for the Next Entebbe," *Chitty's Law Journal*, vol. 25, no. 7 (September 1977); and *Terrorism: International Journal*, vol. 1, nos. 1 (November 1977) and 2 (February 1978).

2. The mass media in a broad context includes newspapers, magazines, books, radio, television, and films. Our discussion concerns the news media, for which hereafter we shall use the term media.

3. For a case study of the interaction between communications instruments and politics, see, for example, Yonah Alexander, *The Role of Communications in the Middle East Conflict: Ideological and Religious Perspectives* (New York: Praeger Publishers, 1973).

4. "The Futility of Terrorism," *Harper's*, vol. 252, no. 1510 (March 1976), p. 104.

5. Carlos Marighella, *Minimanual of the Urban Guerrilla* (Havana Tricontinental, n.d.), p. 103. For a similar discussion, see Jerry Rubin, *Do It!* (New York: Simon and Schuster, 1970).

6. Quoted in Neil Hickey, "Terrorism and Television," *TV Guide*, July 31, 1976, p. 4.

7. Edward Weisband and Damir Roguly, "Palestinian Terrorism: Violence, Verbal Strategy, and Legitimacy," in Alexander, *International Terrorism*, pp. 278-279.

8. One may regard the PLO as a terrorist organization or as a guerrilla group according to the measure of one's identification with the cause. The U.S. government, thus far at least, considers the PLO a terrorist movement.

9. Remarks by George E. Gruen delivered at the conference on International Terrorism organized by the City University of New York and the State University of New York, June 10, 1976.

10. "Terrorism Is Likely to Increase," *London Times*, April 10, 1975.

11. Quoted in the *New York Times*, October 8, 1975.

12. Charles B. Seib, "The Hanafi Episode: A Media Event," *Washington Post*, March 18, 1977, p. A27.

13. *New York Times*, March 15, 1977.

14. Statement by Michael T. McEwen at a seminar on Terrorism: Police and Press Problems sponsored by the Oklahoma Publishing Company and the University of Oklahoma, April 14, 1977. Unpublished proceedings, p. 32.

15. Quoted in "The Media and Terrorism," proceedings of a seminar sponsored by the *Chicago Sun-Times* and the *Chicago Daily News* (Spring 1977), pp. 28-29.

16. Remarks by Robert L. Rabe at the conference on Terrorism and the Media sponsored by the Ralph Bunche Institute on the UN (The City University of New York) and the Institute for Studies in International Terrorism (State University of New York) and held at the Graduate Center of The City University, November 17, 1977.

17. Quoted by Charles Fenyvesi in remarks presented at the conference on Terrorism and the Media.

18. Stated at a seminar on Terrorism and Business sponsored by the Center for Strategic and International Studies (Georgetown University) and the Institute for Studies in International Terrorism (State University of New York), held in Washington, D.C., December 14, 1977.

19. Quoted at a seminar on Terrorism: Police and Press Problems, p. 65, note 14.

20. *Editor and Publisher*, August 27, 1977, p. 12.

21. Ibid.

22. Remarks by Robert L. Rabe at the Conference on Terrorism and the Media.

23. *New York Times*, March 15, 1977.

24. See, for example, Barry Sussman, "Media Leaders Want Less Influence," *Washington Post*, September 29, 1976, p. A1.

25. Philip Revzin, "A Reporter Looks at Media Role in Terror Threats," *The Wall Street Journal*, March 14, 1977, p. 16.

26. The National News Council, "Paper on Terrorism," March 22, 1977, unpublished.

27. David Shaw, "Editors Face Terrorist Demand Dilemma," *Los Angeles Times*, September 15, 1976, p. 14.

28. *New York Times*, March 15, 1977.

29. *German Tribune*, November 13, 1977.

30. The list of research in this area includes, for instance, U.S. National Advisory Commission on Civil Disorders, *Report* (Wash-

ington, D.C.: U.S. Government Printing Office, 1968); thirteen volumes of reports from the U.S. National Commission on the Causes and Prevention of Violence, especially D. L. Lange, R. K. Baker, and S. J. Ball, *Mass Media and Violence*, vol. 9 (Washington, D.C.: U.S. Government Printing Office, 1969); U.S. Surgeon General's Scientific Advisory Committee on Television and Social Behavior, *Television and Social Behavior: Technical Reports to the Committee*, 5 vols. (Washington, D.C.: U.S. Government Printing Office, 1972); Otto Larsen, ed., *Violence and the Mass Media* (New York: Harper & Row, 1968); and Charles U. Daley, ed., *The Media and the Cities* (Chicago: University of Chicago Press, 1968).

31. For example, the Ralph Bunche Institute on the United Nations (City University of New York) and the Institute for Studies in International Terrorism (State University of New York), in cooperation with the *Courier-Journal*, the *Louisville Times*, and the Institute on Human Relations organized a Conference on Terrorism and the Media in November 1977 in New York City. Another meeting on The Media and Terrorism was organized in Spring 1977 by the *Chicago Sun-Times* and *Chicago Daily News*, and Field Enterprises, Inc. Similarly, The Oklahoma Publishing Company (*Daily Oklahoman–Oklahoma City Times*) and the University of Oklahoma co-sponsored a seminar on Terrorism: Police and Press Problems in April 1977. The Maryland Chapter Society of Professional Journalists sponsored a panel session on Police Relations with Press at the May 1977 meeting of the Maryland-Delaware-D.C. Press Association, held in Ocean City, Md. A meeting on Terrorists and Hostage Coverage, held in Washington, D.C., in Fall 1977 was organized by the Radio-Television News Directors' Association (RTNDA). Among the non-American conferences, mention should be made of the 1978 meeting of the International Press Institute on terrorism and the media held in London.

32. For a text of these guidelines, see the National News Council, "Paper on Terrorism."

33. For other policy positions of news organizations, see, for example, Ina Meyers, "Terrorism in the News," *Daily Times* (Mamaroneck, N.Y.), April 2, 1977.

34. See, for example, Robert J. Jackson et al., *Collective Conflict, Violence, and the Media in Canada* (Ottawa, Ont.: Carleton University, n.d.).

35. See, for instance, Yonah Alexander, "Communications Aspects of International Terrorism," *International Problems*, vol. 16, nos. 1-2 (Spring 1977), pp. 55-60; and H.H.A. Cooper, "Terrorism

and the Media," *Chitty's Law Journal*, vol. 24, no. 7 (1976), pp. 226-232.

36. See, for example, Alexander and Finger, *Terrorism*; and Cherif Bassiouni, *Terrorism and Political Crimes* (Springfield, Ill.: Charles C. Thomas, 1975), pp. 43-46.

37. *Disorders and Terrorism*, Report of the Task Force on Disorders and Terrorism (Washington, D.C.: National Advisory Committee on Criminal Justice Standards and Goals, 1976).

38. Ibid., pp. 366, 387-388, 401-402.

39. Quoted in the *New York Times*, October 25, 1977.

8
The Legalization of Terrorism

L. C. Green

Murray's Oxford English Dictionary defines terrorism as "Government by intimidation as directed and carried out by the party in power in France during the Revolution of 1789-1794; the system of the 'Terror.' A policy intended to strike with terror those against whom it is adopted; the employment of methods of intimidation. . . ." This definition is not very helpful and is perhaps somewhat circuitous, although it gives those with a knowledge of history a picture of unrestricted violence and horror, involving arbitrary executions on a large scale. More practically motivated is the Terrorists Order propounded by the British authorities to deal with the situation in Northern Ireland. This document defines terrorism as "the use of violence for political ends [including] any use of violence for the purpose of putting the public or any section of the public in fear."[1] However, this definition, too, is open to criticism and is somewhat extensive. Moreover, it is wide enough not only to embrace the atrocities against which it is directed and the victims of which are alleged to be innocent bystanders, but also to include within its ambit almost every case of one-to-one criminal confrontation as well as governmental oppression directed against the national population.

It must not be overlooked that those organizations that are commonly regarded as terrorist, such as the Weathermen, the Baader-Meinhof group, the Japanese Red Guard, the Tupamaros, and urban and street guerrillas, as well as those radical and libertarian movements that tend to support them (often completely ignorant of their true purpose but devoted to liberalism *in abstracto*) frequently maintain that such governmental oppression is the only true terrorism, for what the majority of the "establishment" regards as terrorism is nothing but the reaction to such governmental abuse. For this reason, these movements sympathize with those who are not anxious to see international cooperative action directed at suppressing terrorism, for the end justifies the means and if the causes of terrorism were dealt with, the manifestations would disappear. The definition of governmental terrorism tends to be somewhat subjective as is evident from the decision of the European Court of Human Rights in the dispute between Ireland and the United Kingdom. While the European Commission of Human Rights found that certain practices indulged in by Britain amounted to "torture" and, to some extent at least, may be considered to have "terrorized" some portions of the public, the court itself, regardless of the British decision not to contest this finding, held that the practices in question did not amount to torture, but only to cruel and degrading punishment. From this, one may assume that what the recipient regards as terrorism may not be so considered by the administrator. In any case, to the extent that governmental authority permits such intimidatory activity, it may be presumed that it is legalized terrorism, and it matters little that the world community or individual states condemn it as outrageous conduct.[2]

However, the world, and especially the public at large, is not excessively interested in governmental terrorism, which tends to be accepted as unavoidable and is often viewed as inevitable if a government is to retain its authority against threats emanating from woolly-headed or vicious revolutionaries. For the public, such acts of terrorism, if such they be described, are only likely to be condemned by revolutionaries (potential or active), idealists, libertarians, starry-eyed academics, and similar radicals. What the man in the street has become concerned about are acts that are officially directed against a government or some political movement and that work themselves out against innocent bystanders or are executed in the territory of a third state that is in no way directly involved in the conflict between the actor and the alleged object of his action. It is this sort of activity that he expects his and other states to take action to control. He is not concerned with the legality of Israel's raid upon Entebbe airport[3] nor the Egyptian commando operation in Cyprus. In his eyes, such actions are morally correct activities directed towards the suppression or frustration of terrorist acts.

It would appear that states and their governments tend to take a somewhat similar hands-off approach towards terrorism alleged to have been committed by the authorities of a fellow member of the family of nations. International law has long since recognized the right of a state to do what it desires with its own nationals and the principle of nonintervention in domestic affairs is perhaps one of the oldest, even though incursions into its ambit may have taken place in the last twenty or thirty years. Perhaps the most notorious examples of state-directed terrorism are to be found in the practices of Stalin's Russia, Hitler's Germany, or the so-called psychiatric hospitals of Brezhnev's Soviet Union. Nevertheless, to a very great extent, the world adopts the view that was exemplified by Great Britain just prior to World War II. While H. A. Smith was denouncing Nazi Germany for activities that, in his view, placed that country outside the orbit of civilized society,

> In practice we no longer insist that States shall conform to any common standards of justice, religious toleration and internal government. Whatever atrocities may be committed in foreign countries, we now say that they are no concern of ours. Conduct which in the nineteenth century would have placed a government outside the pale of civilised society is now deemed to be no obstacle to diplomatic friendship. This means, in effect, that we have now abandoned the old distinction between civilised and uncivilised States.[4]

This statement is equally applicable to many of the activities of the United Nations, its Human Rights Commission, and many of the so-called human rights and civil liberties organizations that now exist and that are highly eclectic in their choice of countries and activities for condemnation. At the time Smith was writing, the governments of Europe were maintaining either that what was alleged to be occurring in Germany was not in fact taking place, or that if the allegations were true then the events in question were within the domestic jurisdiction of the German government and, by international law, therefore outside the scope of third party criticism. Of course, as today, when political convenience demanded, the attitude changed. Thus, immediately upon the outbreak of World War II, Britain's reservations disappeared and His Majesty's Stationery Office issued a White Paper entitled The Treatment of German Nationals in Germany.[5] This "new" approach to domestic activities is reflected in the words of Sir Hartley (now Lord) Shawcross at Nuremberg:

> the right of humanitarian intervention on behalf of the rights of man trampled upon by a state in a manner shocking the sense of mankind has long been considered to form part of the recognised law of nations.[6]

This is in line with the views of Grotius, who stated in his *De Jure Belli ac Pacis,*

> Kings and those who are invested with a Power equal to that of Kings, have a Right to exact Punishments, not only for Injuries committed against themselves, but likewise, for those which do not particularly concern them but which are, in any Persons whatsoever, grievous violations of the Law of Nature or Nations. For the Liberty of consulting the Benefit of Human Society, by Punishments, . . . means that War is lawful against those who offend against Nature.[7]

While, in the nineteenth century, there were many attempts by the more powerful states—who described themselves as the guardians of civilization—to assert their right to intervene in the name of humanity, it is now little doubted that these claims were nothing but ideological covers for predatory assertions.[8] It is difficult, therefore, to perceive on what legal authority Shawcross made his assertion.

Since 1948, when the Universal Declaration of Human Rights[9] was adopted, the potential has existed for protests, if not action, against state-directed terrorism; but as such incidents as the Russian Wives case[10] (the United States and Australia condemned Soviet refusal to allow Russian women to join their husbands, at a time when some states in the United States were still punishing miscegenation and Australia was refusing to allow the Japanese wives and children of Australian servicemen to join their husbands and fathers in Australia) indicates the basis of such criticism is frequently nothing but the gaining of advantage points in the political confrontation. At the same time, these developments with regard to the paper protection of human rights have encouraged various organizations like the International Commission of Jurists and Amnesty International to organize mass publicity and condemnation campaigns against states that pursue policies of political terror against their own nationals, although there is some evidence in the publications and operations of such organizations that their targets are often somewhat one-sidedly selected. Moreover, the Charter of the United Nations clearly precludes[11] "intervention" into matters that are essentially within domestic jurisdiction unless there is a threat to peace. In the first place, it would be difficult for a politician to persuade his people that "terror" directed by a state against its own nationals really constitutes a threat to peace and warrants the imposition of international sanctions (the situation in South Africa is a case apart and cannot be taken as a precedent). Second, it must never be forgotten that no state is an isolated island unto itself. Each has a protector among the great powers. If its smaller friends fail it, and criticism of its policies should figure on the agenda of the Security Council, a state may rest assured that it will ultimately be protected by the veto of a friend among the Big Five.

The type of issue that has aroused concern is, for example, the hijacking of aircraft and the holding of passengers and crew, the kidnapping of diplomats, the use of the international mails for the dispatch of explosive materials, and the activities of dissident movements involving extreme violence allegedly under the guise of a campaign for political independence or reform. In the past, movements opposed to a government have tended to restrict themselves to individual acts of political assassination, organized rebellion, or civil war. While the latter have frequently been accompanied by acts of terror, perhaps due to the paucity of effective media cover, the protesters have not found it essential to indulge in isolated acts of outrage directed against the population or private nongovernmental establishments, with the aim of securing publicity for their alleged cause. In fact, when acts of individual terror were perpetrated during the nineteenth century, governments tended to react by describing them as anarchist and denying them the political protection[12] that they were inclined to offer to those whose activities were directed at governmental takeover.[13] While it is true that some of these acts might well have incurred general opprobrium, there was a feeling that John Stuart Mill's view that a political offense was "any offence committed in the course or furthering of civil war, insurrection, or political commotion"[14] had much to commend it, this went too far for a nineteenth century establishment to adopt, although there was sufficient sympathy for those committing violent acts that were politically motivated for the view to develop that if the act was committed in the course of an organized attempt to overthrow and replace the government, then international customary law, while not necessarily legalizing such acts of terrorism, should afford the offender protection from extradition.[15] There was, however, no attempt to embody this as a principle confirmed by a general or universal treaty.

When this attitude was developing during the nineteenth century, acts of terrorism, whether committed by a government under the umbrella of legislation or by dissidents acting on their own or in unison, remained territorial. The place of the act, normally speaking, was within the territory of the government concerned, while the victims were within the national territory. Private acts of terrorism tended to be committed against government institutions or official personalities. The situation has now changed. The modern terrorist seems to be completely unconcerned with the geographic location of his act and equally reckless as to the nationality of his victim. In fact, it would appear at times as if, perhaps in the hope of securing publicity or pressure upon his government, the terrorist intends to internationalize his act. This has become particularly true since resolutions of the United Nations concerning the right of self-determination appear to have given this right a status in law and morality that is not accorded to any other right or principle. It is not difficult today, in view of this, to echo the words of Mme. Roland on passing the statue of Liberty on her way to the scaffold during the Reign of Terror in 1793: *Ô Liberté! Ô Liberté! que de crimes on commet en ton nom.*

The Charter of the United Nations talks rather nebulously of respect for the principle of equal rights and self-determination for peoples, without making any attempt to define what was meant by peoples or self-determination. However, responding to the upsurge of anticolonialism, the General Assembly in 1960 adopted a Declaration on the granting of Independence to Colonial Countries and Peoples,[16] declaring that "all peoples have the right to self-determination; by virtue of that right they freely determine their political status . . . ," but pointing out that "any attempt at the partial or total disruption of the national unity and the territorial integrity of a country is incompatible with the purposes and principles of the Charter of the United Nations." A committee was established to supervise the implementation of this right. It soon became clear that the concept of decolonization was amenable to differing interpretations, while the meaning of self-determination was political in the extreme, with some states conceiving it to be no more than the withdrawal of a former European colonial power[17] and others as an exhortation to independence and self-government, regardless of whether the entity in question would be viable or whether its inhabitants were in favor of this interpretation of their destiny.[18] It was not long, however, before it became clear that in the eyes of many members of the United Nations, this declaration had heralded in what many might consider as an inevitable slide towards legalization and respectability for any act of terror committed by any dissident, provided the right ideological jargon was employed.

To emphasize the importance of the idea of self-determination and to remind the world that it was more than a political concept, the United Nations embodied this principle into the Covenant on Economic, Social, and Cultural Rights and the Covenant on Civil and Political Rights.[19] Article 1 of each of these covenants proclaims, "all peoples have the right to self-determination." To highlight the importance of this principle, it is included as one of the seven principles appearing in the Declaration on Principles of International Law Concerning Friendly Relations and Cooperation Among States in accordance with the Charter of the United Nations.[20] The declaration places this "principle of equal rights and self-determination of peoples" on the same level as the principles

> that States shall refrain in their international relations from the threat or use of force against the territorial integrity or political independence of any State, or in any other manner inconsistent with the Purposes of the United Nations . . . of sovereign equality of States . . . [and] that States shall fulfil in good faith the obligations assumed by them in accordance with the charter.

The elevation of the principle esconces it as a basic principle of international law equal in importance to such traditionally recognized basic principles as sovereignty—a fact that is reiterated in the declaration when it states that all seven principles are interrelated and "constitute basic principles of international law," which should be strictly observed.

The declaration explains what it means by the principle of self-determination. It adds little when it states that by virtue of this principle "all people have the right freely to determine, without external interference, their political status," but it goes on to impose upon every State

> the duty to promote . . . realization of the principle . . . in order . . . to bring a speedy end to colonialism, having due regard to the freely expressed will of the peoples concerned, and bearing in mind that subjection of peoples to alien subjugation, domination, and exploitation constitutes a violation of the principle, as well as a denial of fundamental human rights, and is contrary to the Charter.

Stated baldly in this fashion, the declaration might be considered as nothing but a pious invocation. However, it goes on, to affirm

> every state has the duty to refrain from any forcible action which deprives peoples . . . of their right to self-determination and freedom and independence. In their actions against, and resistance to, such forcible action in pursuit of their right to self-determination, such

peoples are entitled to seek and to receive support in accordance with
the purposes and principles of the Charter.

Presumably, it is in acknowledgment of these purposes and principles that the declaration, having apparently sanctified the use of
force in the search for self-determination, proclaims that it is not to

> be construed as authorizing or encouraging any action which would
> dismember or impair, totally or in part, the territorial integrity or
> political unity of sovereign and independent States conducting them-
> selves in compliance with the principle of equal rights and self-
> determination of peoples . . . and thus possessed of a government
> representing the whole people belonging to the territory without dis-
> tinction as to race, creed or color.

Critics might be forgiven if they feel that this caveat tends to reduce
the meaning of the principle of self-determination or else has little
intrinsic meaning of its own. Further, as if to reduce the obligation
of support placed upon third states, the declaration affirmed "every
state shall refrain from any action aimed at the partial or total
disruption of the national unity and territorial integrity of any other
state or country"—a further caveat that would, if it meant anything,
reduce the value of the commitments in the declaration almost to
vanishing point. In fact, if one looks at the modern world to ascertain
where movements on behalf of self-determination appear legitimate,
it would seem that this is true only in regard to the Republic of South
Africa, regardless of the fact that it is a member of the United Nations;
or Zimbabwe where the local inhabitants have reached an agreement
for temporary sharing of power with their white rulers prior to
complete independence under a black majority; or Israel where a
number of fellow members of the United Nations are providing arms,
men, and other supports to the Palestine Liberation Organization,
which claims to be engaged in a struggle for self-determination
which, according to the movement's own charter, is aimed at the
liquidation of a member of the United Nations. On the other hand,
the Organization of African Unity has made it clear that, no matter
what the complaints of any ethnic or tribal community within an
African state may be, no support will be given to any movement for
self-determination directed against a member of that organization,
for Article 3 of the Addis Ababa Charter listed as one of the principles
of the organization "respect for the sovereignty and territorial integrity of each state and for its inalienable right to independent
existence."[21]

When condemning colonial regimes and approving struggles for self-determination, international organizations have tended to avoid any specific recommendation or expression of approval that might indicate support for terrorism or violence as such. On the other hand, the form of words used has been sufficiently wide to embrace such activities. Thus, in 1972, when the Security Council met in Addis Ababa to discuss African problems, its resolution condemning apartheid[22] recognized "the legitimacy of the struggle of the oppressed people of South Africa in pursuance of their human and political rights as set forth in the Charter of the United Nations and the Universal Declaration of Human Rights," without making any reference to the nature or modalities of that struggle. On the same day it adopted another resolution[23] condemning Portuguese attempts to suppress the rebellious independence movements in Portugal's African colonies, recognized the "legitimacy of the struggle of [those] liberation movements," but again made no reference to the manner in which those movements sought to achieve their ends.

While the United Nations was concerned with the right of non-self-governing peoples to achieve their independence by whatever means they considered suitable, acts of terrorism (the despatch of letter bombs, attacks on diplomats, deviation of aircraft on international flights, and violent attacks on civilians) were being committed and were frequently explained away on the basis of national self-determination and the logical conclusion to the denial by a political opponent of the rights claimed by those committing the acts. There was a growing tendency among those sympathetic to the actors to suggest that the end justifies means, or that there was no point in seeking to suppress terrorist activities until the causes of such activities had been eradicated. From a practical point of view, it would seem that political problems that had proved well nigh insoluble through the years, such as the achievement of majority rule in South Africa, solution to the Middle East problem, and the like, were of more immediate concern than the question of releasing civilian hostages, rescuing kidnapped diplomats, or suppressing interference with air transport. Presumably all such incidents could continue pending the solution of the insoluble. This attitude is well illustrated by the General Assembly Resolution on measures to prevent international terrorism.[24] True, the assembly expressed

> deep concern over increasing acts of violence which endanger or take innocent human lives or jeopardize fundamental freedoms [and urged] States to devote their immediate attention to finding just and peaceful

solutions to the underlying causes which give rise to such acts of violence.

The motivation of this wording perhaps becomes clear from other clauses of the resolution. Thus, the General Assembly found it necessary immediately to

> reaffirm the inalienable right to self-determination and independence of all peoples under colonial and racist regimes and other forms of alien domination and uphold the legitimacy of their struggle, in particular the struggle of national liberation movements, in accordance with the purposes and principles of the Charter and the relevant resolutions of the organs of the United Nations [and] condemn the continuation of repressive and terrorist acts by colonial, racist and alien regimes in denying peoples their legitimate right to self-determination and independence and other human rights and fundamental freedoms.

Reminding itself that the resolution opens by stating that the General Assembly is "deeply perturbed over acts of international terrorism which are occurring with increasing frequency and which take a toll of innocent human lives"—and perhaps recalling that only three months earlier the United States had submitted a draft convention[25] embodying

> measures to prevent international terrorism which endangers or takes innocent human lives or jeopardizes fundamental freedoms and study of the underlying causes of those forms of terrorism and acts of violence which lie in misery, frustration, grievance, and despair and which cause some people to sacrifice human lives, including their own, in an attempt to effect radical changes

—the assembly went on to "invite States to become parties to the existing international conventions which relate to various aspects of the problem of international terrorism . . . [and] to take all appropriate measures at the national level with a view to the speedy and final elimination of the problem." However, this imprecation to states had attached to it a proviso reminding them that they were to "bear in mind" the provisions relating to "the inalienable right to self-determination and independence . . . in particular the struggle of national liberation movements."

By wording its resolution in this fashion, the General Assembly has clearly elevated the right to self-determination above human life. Moreover, while apparently condemning acts of terrorism, it has bluntly asserted that if undesirable acts—which some might describe as terrorism—are undertaken in the name of self-determination or national liberation, then such acts are beyond the scope of condemnation and are legal.

The international conventions to which the General Assembly was referring are those of Tokyo, The Hague, and Montreal in regard to aerial hijacking. After the Tokyo Convention of 1969,[26] which condemned acts jeopardizing the safety of aircraft and which made no reference to self-determination, the General Assembly itself condemned acts of hijacking as well as those which might "endanger the life and health of passengers and crew in disregard of commonly accepted humanitarian considerations,"[27] and saw no need to add a caveat in respect of self-determination. Similarly, the Security Council expressed concern at international hijackings and called for the release of all passengers and crews "without exception"[28] (a provision that appears to have been forgotten when the Security Council failed to support a United Kingdom–United States proposal to condemn the hijacking that was terminated by the Israeli rescue at Entebbe with some members more concerned with condemning Israel's act of "aggression,"[29] while the General Assembly by a resolution adopted *nemine contradicente*[30] condemned *"without exception whatsoever*, all acts of aerial hijacking" and urged states to deter and punish all such acts. In neither case was it deemed necessary to introduce political exceptions based on ideological sympathy for self-determination or national liberation. It was only after the Hague and Montreal conventions of 1970 and 1971[31] had widened the scope of condemnation, extended the nature of criminal jurisdiction (apparently making aerial hijacking and the like subject to universal jurisdiction), introduced the concept *aut dedere aut punire* ("extradite or prosecute"), and seemed to call for local criminal prosecution even when extradition might not be possible because the local legislation recognized the exception based on the political character of the offense,[32] that the General Assembly found it necessary to introduce its "safeguards" with regard to self-determination and national liberation.

These conventions, aimed at the suppression and punishment of aerial hijacking, were drawn up under the auspices of the International Civil Aviation Organization. But there is one international convention dealing with terrorism which is a United Nations Convention. In the past few years, a number of attacks have been made against diplomats (usually those of third countries) by terrorist activists seeking to apply pressure against their own government, anticipating that the diplomat's home country will add to this pressure in an attempt to ensure the safety of the diplomat in question. In addition, embassies abroad have been attacked and diplomats murdered sometimes merely to ensure publicity for the terrorist group concerned. This appears to be the difference between the attack upon the Israeli embassy in Thailand in 1972 and that upon the Saudi Arabian embassy in the Sudan in 1974, both of which were committed by the Black September group of Palestine terrorists. Since all countries make use of diplomats, and since the kidnappings of such persons by, for example, urban guerrillas in South America indicates that all are equally at risk, it is perhaps not surprising that the General Assembly in 1974 adopted by consensus a Convention on the Prevention and Punishment of Crimes against Internationally Protected Persons, including Diplomatic Agents.[33] Taken by itself, this convention appears to provide for making such offenses as much crimes by international law as is piracy *jure gentium*. However, the resolution to which the convention is annexed expressly provides that its provisions are "related" to the convention and "shall always be published together with it." Paragraph 4 of the resolution makes crystal clear the reason for this proviso. While the purpose of the resolution and the convention annexed thereto is to prevent and punish such crimes "in view of the serious threat to the maintenance of friendly relations and cooperation among States created by the commission of such crimes," paragraph 4

> recognizes that the provisions of the annexed Convention could not in any way prejudice the exercise of the legitimate right to self-determination and independence, in accordance with the purposes and principles of the United Nations and the Declaration on Principles of International Law concerning Friendly Relations and Cooperation among States in accordance with the Charter of the United Nations, by peoples struggling against colonialism, alien domination, foreign occupation, racial discrimination and apartheid.

Thus, once again we find that an act of terrorism that is considered likely to affect international relations and friendly cooperation among states, and that therefore might be considered contrary to the purposes and principles of the United Nations and of any Declaration of Principles in such a field, is sanctified and no longer regarded as a crime if it is committed in the sacred name of twentieth century holy writ: self-determination.

This same concern for the new gospel is to be found in the General Assembly Resolution defining aggression.[34] Since the days of the League of Nations, attempts have been made to define aggression and the International Military Tribunal at Nuremberg held "to initiate a war of aggression . . . is the supreme international crime differing only from other war crimes in that it contains within itself the accumulated evil of the whole."[35] After much debate and study, the General Assembly eventually, in 1974, came upon a definition that was adopted without a vote, pointing out that *"no consideration of whatever nature, whether political,* economic, military, *or otherwise,* may serve as a justification for aggression. A war of aggression is a crime against international peace." Nevertheless,

> nothing in this definition . . . could in any way prejudice the right to self-determination, freedom and independence, as derived from the Charter, of peoples forcibly deprived of that right and referred to in the Declaration on Principles of International Law concerning Friendly Relations and Co-operation among States in accordance with the Charter of the United Nations, particularly peoples under colonial and racist regimes or other forms of alien domination; nor *the right* of these peoples *to struggle to that end and to seek and receive support,* in accordance with the principles of the Charter and in conformity with the above-mentioned Declaration.

It is clear, therefore, that not only does the General Assembly recognize the plea of self-determination as justification for an act of terrorism which thereby ceases to carry such an obloquious description, but it goes further and the General Assembly concedes that under the claim of seeking self-determination the "supreme international crime," condemned as such by the assembly itself in 1946,[36] is in fact lawful and should "receive support." Can anything be a better example of "diplomatic double talk"[37]?

One of the main problems that arises in connection with these various measures legalizing terrorism is the definition of self-determination and national liberation. As yet, there is no accepted definition of either of these terms, although a number of rebellious organizations have described themselves as national liberation movements. It is clear, however, that such autonomous assumptions of this title are not adequate. Thus, the Biafran movement in Nigeria, the Eritrean and Somali national liberation movements in Ethiopia, or the Front de Libération Québécois in Canada have not been accepted as such by anybody, so that the latter's kidnapping of a British diplomat in 1970 would fall within the ban of the convention. Current practice, as illustrated by events in Angola, South Africa, and the Middle East, suggests that the test of whether an organization is entitled to describe itself as a national liberation movement, and thus entitled to carry out acts that would otherwise be condemned as terrorism or international crimes, is recognition by the local regional organization—a test that would ensure that a movement on the North American continent or in Europe would almost certainly never qualify.

In the eyes of most states and perhaps of the majority of the people in the world, the organization that has been responsible for most acts of international terrorism, and that in fact has not hesitated to claim responsibility for such, has been the Palestine Liberation Organization (PLO) or one or other of its dependent groups. This is the organization, moreover, that has been granted respectability and legalization by the United Nations. Despite its commitment to the overthrow and destruction of Israel, and despite their undertakings with regard to that member of the United Nations by its fellow members, the PLO has been afforded, by the General Assembly, a status of acceptability as a national liberation movement that authorizes it to commit virtually any act of terror with impunity, since the General Assembly has opened the door of the organization to claim that all its activities are directed towards self-determination and as such legalized by the United Nations. The first indication that this might occur is to be found in the Resolution on Basic Principles of the Legal Status of the Combatants Struggling against Colonial and Alien Domination and Racist Regimes.[38] Ostensibly, this resolution was based on recognition of the need to apply the basic humanitarian principles to all armed conflicts, and it reaffirms

> that the continuation of colonialism in all its forms and manifestations . . . is a crime and that *colonial peoples have the inherent right to struggle by all necessary means at their disposal* against colonial Powers and alien domination in exercise of their right of self-determination.

It goes on to assert that such struggles are

> legitimate and in full accordance with the principles of international law [and that] *any attempt to suppress the struggle* against colonial and alien domination and racist régimes are [sic.] incompatible with the Charter of the United Nations, the Declaration on Principles of International Law concerning Friendly Relations and Co-operation among States in accordance with the Charter of the United Nations, the Universal Declaration of Human Rights, the Declaration on the

Granting of Independence to Colonial Countries and Peoples and *constitutes a threat to international peace and security.*

As such, therefore, the attempt is amenable to the application of enforcement measures by the Security Council. This has the effect of placing such activities whatever the means employed by the independence seekers under the protection of the United Nations and entitled to full support by all its members. Moreover, such a struggle is declared to be an "international armed conflict," so that those committing acts of terror in its name cannot be tried for such crimes, since they are entitled to treatment as prisoners of war and immune from criminal action unless their acts constitute war crimes.

All that now remained was for the United Nations to declare that the Palestine Liberation Organization was in fact a national liberation movement and that the State of Israel was a colonial, alien, or racist regime. It did not take long for the United Nations to adopt such measures. On November 22, 1974,[39] the General Assembly by majority vote, "taking into consideration the universality of the United Nations prescribed in the Charter," invited the Palestine Liberation Organization "to participate in the sessions and the work of the General Assembly in the capacity of observer," and, in a related resolution, recognized "that the Palestinian people is entitled to self-determination . . . [and appealed] to all States and international organizations to extend their support to the Palestinian people in its struggle to restore its rights."[40] It should be pointed out that the charter does not provide for any entity to enjoy observer status with the General Assembly. Moreover, insofar as the charter looks to the universality of the organization, it must be remembered that membership is restricted to states, and it is difficult to see how the participation as observer or otherwise of a nonstate organization committed to violence and the extinction of an existing member of the United Nations can in any way contribute to the universality of membership. The resolution went on to declare that the Palestine Liberation Organization "is entitled to participate as an observer in the sessions and the work of all international conferences convened under the auspices of the organs of the United Nations." This resolution on observer status for the Palestine Liberation Organization was only one of a number relating to the status of national liberation movements vis-à-vis the United Nations and must be read in conjunction with that on Participation in the United Nations Conference on the

Representation of States in Their Relations with International Organizations.[41] This resolution provided for invitations to "all states," and "the national liberation movements in their respective regions recognized by the Organization of African Unity and/or by the League of Arab States in their respective regions to participate as observers in the Conference, in accordance with the practice of the United Nations." This resolution indicates the highly selective approach of the General Assembly to bodies claiming to be national liberation movements and clearly reflects the present voting power in the assembly. Consequent upon this resolution, the Palestine Liberation Organization has been invited to conferences of the International Labor Organization, though it is difficult to see in what way, whether as observer or anything else, it can contribute to that organization's activities, and of the International Civil Aviation Organization, although it has no aircraft (its activities in this sphere having been directed against the interests of that organization as expressed in the antihijacking conventions).

The activities of the General Assembly in legalizing the operations of the Palestine Liberation Organization culminated in the adoption of a resolution allegedly concerned with the Elimination of All Forms of Racial Discrimination[42] in furtherance of the Declaration of 1963 on this subject.[43] Having already condemned zionism for its "unholy alliance" with South African racism,[44] which, as everyone knows, is "a crime against humanity . . . violating the principles of international law . . . and constituting a serious threat to international peace and security,"[45] the General Assembly now saw fit to "determine that zionism is a form of racism and racial discrimination." This resolution only just achieved the requisite two-thirds majority needed for adoption, receiving seventy-two votes in favor, thirty-five against, and thirty-two abstentions. It is interesting to note that a number of African, Latin American, and non-aligned states generally were among those opposing or abstaining, for the resolution in its preambular phrases notes that, in 1975, the Assembly of Heads of State and Government of the Organization of African Unity at their meeting in Uganda considered

> that the racist regime in occupied Palestine and the racist regimes in Zimbabwe and South Africa have a common imperialist origin, forming a whole and having the same racist structure and being organically linked in their policy aimed at repression of the dignity and integrity of the human being

and that in the same year, the Conference of Ministers for Foreign

Affairs of Non-Aligned Countries meeting in Peru "severely condemned zionism as a threat to world peace and security and called upon all countries to oppose this racist and imperialist ideology." Having come to this world-shattering conclusion, the General Assembly by its resolution has placed Israel, as a state based on zionist philosophy, in the same class as states committed to colonialism, racism, and alien domination. The Palestine Liberation Organization as a national liberation movement committed to its overthrow and the achievement of self-determination for the Palestinians is thus now fully authorized to indulge in whatsoever acts of violence it may please, without any fear of condemnation that the acts in question constitute terrorism or any offense against international law.

It should not be assumed that the Palestine Liberation Organization is the only one that has been accorded recognition by the League of Arab States or the Organization of African Unity. The same status has been accorded to the South West African People's Organization, the Pan-Africanist Congress, the African National Congress, the African National Congress of Zimbabwe, and the Patriotic Front of Zimbabwe. All of these, therefore, are authorized to commit terrorist acts against the Republic of South Africa and Rhodesia with equal impunity. In fact, we now find that even though the representative organizations within Namibia and Zimbabwe appear to be satisfied with arrangements for the achievement of self-determination through cooperation with the former white rulers, the Organization of African Unity, the United Nations, and the president of the United States are not prepared to accept this and apparently would prefer to see the continuance of terrorism, so that the particular organization that enjoys favorite son status in the eyes of the local regional organization may assume power, regardless of the attitude or wishes of the local population in whose name the movement in question purports to be seeking self-determination. Once again, could there be clearer evidence of the legislation of terrorism and the application of diplomatic double talk?

While one may deplore the methods employed by *soi-disant* or recognized national liberation movements, it has to be remembered that some of these are engaged in actual armed conflict and their views may therefore be of significance in conferences related thereto. Little criticism can be made of the United Nations for resolving that the Palestine Liberation Organization should be involved in talks concerning peace in and the future of the Middle East. Nor can criticism be leveled at those who call for the involvement of the South West Africa People's Organization or the Patriotic Front in discussions concerning the future of Namibia and Zimbabwe. Equally, one can appreciate why the Geneva Conference on Humanitarian Law in Armed Conflict agreed to the demand that certain national liberation movements should be invited to participate, and since they were actively engaged in hostilities, it is perhaps understandable that they received a status between that of observer and full participant. What is perhaps not quite so acceptable was the decision of the conference to be controlled by the views of regional organizations, for this meant that invitations, as in the case of the United Nations, were not based on any objective standards but on the political predilections of a numerical voting majority. The resolution of the conference as it appears in the Final Act bears reproduction:

> In view of the paramount importance of ensuring broad participation in the work of the Conference, which was of a fundamentally humanitarian nature, and because the progressive development and codification of international humanitarian law applicable in armed conflicts is a universal task in which the national liberation movements can contribute positively, the Conference . . . decided to invite also the national liberation movements recognized by the regional intergovernmental organizations concerned to participate fully in the deliberations of the Conference and its Main Committees, it being understood that only delegations representing States were entitled to vote

but their status was further enhanced by their being allowed to sign the Final Act of the conference. In addition to the organizations already mentioned, invitations were extended to the Mozambique Liberation Front (FRELIMO) and both the Angola National Liberation Front (FNLA) and the People's Movement for the Liberation of Angola (MPLA), although in view of the securing of independence by Mozambique and Angola, these organizations only attended the first and second sessions.

In accordance with the view already expressed by the General Assembly that struggles for national liberation amount to international conflicts, the conference agreed in Article 1 of Protocol I[46] that this concept includes "armed conflicts in which peoples are fighting against colonial domination and alien occupation and against racist regimes in the exercise of their right of self-determination." It went on in Article 44 to redefine the nature of combatants and prisoners of war. Having said

> all combatants are obliged to comply with the rules of international law applicable in armed conflict, [it states] violations of these rules shall not deprive a combatant of his right to be a combatant or, if he

falls into the hands of an adverse party, of his right to be a prisoner of war.

It requires combatants "to distinguish themselves from the civilian population while they are engaged in an attack or in a military operation preparatory to attack." To this, there can of course be no objection. But,

> recognizing, however that there are situations in armed conflicts where, owing to the nature of the hostilities, an armed combatant cannot so distinguish himself, he shall retain his status as a combatant, provided that, in such situations, he carries his arms openly: (a) during each engagement, and (b) during such time as he is visible to the adversary while he is engaged in a military deployment preceding the launching of an attack in which he is to participate.

There is no guide as to the meaning of this latter provision. Moreover,

> any combatant who falls into the power of an adverse party while not engaged in an attack or in a military operation preparatory to an attack shall not forfeit his rights to be a combatant and a prisoner of war by virtue of his prior activities.

This means that any person in civilian clothing captured and charged with responsibility for terrorist activities will be able to plead that he is a member of a national liberation movement engaged in a struggle for self-determination and that acts with which he is charged were actually committed during a military engagement when he was in fact carrying his arms openly. As such, he will be able to maintain that he was not a terrorist subject to criminal law, but a legitimate combatant entitled to be treated as a prisoner of war. Once again, we have the situation where international law has granted legal status to terrorists and legalized their terrorist activities.

The implications of this provision have already become apparent in Europe. During the Folkerts case[47] before the District Court of Utrecht in 1977, the accused, whose extradition was sought by the Federal German Republic as a member of the Baader-Meinhof group, officially known as the Rote Armee Fraktion (RAF), contested the jurisdiction of the court on the ground that the RAF was engaged in a class war not only with the Federal Republic but with every state in the world where such a class war exists. On this basis, he contended that the RAF was engaged in an international armed conflict and protected by the Geneva Conventions and Protocol I. The court rejected this, first, on the ground that the protocol has not yet come into force, but, more importantly, because the RAF is not a movement which, in the exercise of its right to self-determination, is fighting against colonial domination, alien occupation, or racist regimes, nor had Folkerts been able to prove that at the time of his arrest he was engaged in such a conflict. It is perhaps only a matter of time before a court in a country sympathetic to some terrorist organization decides to the contrary. It would only need a situation in which the accused happened to be a member of what that particular country regarded as a national liberation movement.

It is not the only nonaligned majority in the United Nations, the Organization of African Unity, and the League of Arab States that is prepared to legalize acts of terrorism. In 1977, the Council of Europe adopted the European Convention on the Suppression of Terrorism,[48] according to Article 1 of which a number of acts generally recognized as being terrorist in character are condemned and rendered extraditable without any possibility of the claim being frustrated by the political offense plea. These offenses are listed as being within the scope of the Hague and Montreal antihijacking conventions: those involving attacks against the life, physical integrity, or liberty of internationally protected persons, including diplomatic agents; those involving kidnapping, the taking of hostages, or serious unlawful detention; and those involving the use of bombs, grenades, rockets, automatic firearms, or letter or parcel bombs if their use endangered persons. This treaty was signed by all the members of the Council of Europe except Ireland and Malta. Insofar as the former is concerned, it has made it clear to the United Kingdom that it is not prepared to regard acts that are committed by members of the Irish Republican Army and that fall within the treaty definition of terrorism or the British Terrorists Order[49] respecting Northern Ireland as other than political offenses. Yet again, political and ideological sympathy is considered more important than the suppression and punishment of terrorism, although in this case it might be argued that the acts have not been made lawful, but merely excepted from extradition.

There seems little chance of terrorism being controlled on anything like a universal basis so long as international organizations or individual states are prepared to apply a double standard whereby they confer legality and respectability upon acts of violence that are committed by those with whom they sympathize, especially when they can be presented in the language of the new international order that places self-determination and independence above any other principle or obligation. Nor can one expect the public to condemn such acts, when the media describe them as heroic activities full of glamour, rendered yet more respectable by abandoning the term "murder" in favor of the legal term "execution." One is tempted to remind such partisans of the comments of Milton and of Lord Acton:

Licence they mean when they cry Liberty.

There is no error so monstrous that it fails to find defenders among the ablest men. Murder may be done by legal means, by plausible and profitable war, by calumny, as well as by dose or dagger.

Notes

1. See Ireland v. United Kingdom (1978, European Court of Human Rights, official text, para. 85).

2. See, e.g., 1978 report of United States State Department on governmental derogation of human rights, *The Times* (London), 10 February 1978.

3. See, e.g., Green, "Rescue at Entebbe—Legal Aspects," 6 *Israel Yearbook on Human Rights* (1976), 312; Strebel: Nochmals zur Geiselbefreiung in Entebbe, 37 Z.A.Ö.R.V.R. (1977), 691.

4. 19 *The Listener* (1938), 183.

5. Cmd. 6120 (1939).

6. Concluding Speeches by the Chief Prosecutors (H.M.S.O., 1964), 63-4.

7. (1625) Lib. II, cap. 20, ss. 40 (1,4), Eng. tr. 1730, 436-7, 438 (Carnegie tr. 504, 506).

8. See, e.g. (Sir Wm. Harcourt) *Historicus on International Law* (1863), 6, 14; Lauterpacht, "General Rules of the Law of Peace," 1 *Collected Papers* (1970), 3-4 (English trans. of "general course" delivered at the Hague Academy, 1937).

9. G.A. Res. 217A (III).

10. (1949) Res. 285 (III), see Green, "Human Rights and the Color Problem," 3 *Current Legal Problems* (1950), 236, 245 et seqq.

11. Art. 2(7).

12. See, e.g., *Re Meunier* [1894] 2 Q.B. 415.

13. See, e.g., *Re Castioni* [1891] 1 Q.B. 149.

14. House of Commons, 6 Aug. 1866, 184 Hansard (3rd Ser.), col. 2115.

15. See, e.g., U.S. practice in absence of a treaty reservation, 4

Moore, *Digest of Int'l Law* (1906), 332 et seqq.; see also, British Despatch re Kossuth, 1849, 6 *Br. Digest of Int'l Law* (1965), 44.

16. Res. 1514 (XV).

17. E.g., Indonesian and West Irian.

18. E.g., Spain and Gibraltar.

19. Res. 2200, Annex.

20. Res. 2625 (XXV).

21. 1963, 2 Int'l Legal Materials 766.

22. Res. 311 (1972).

23. Res. 312 (1972).

24. Res. 3034 (XXVII).

25. UN Doc. A/C/6/L.850 (11 Int'l Legal Materials 1382).

26. 2 Int'l Legal Materials 1042.

27. Res. 2551 (XXIV).

28. Res. 286 (1970).

29. For a summary of debate and texts of draft resolutions, see 15 Int'l Legal Materials 1224 et seqq.

30. Res 2645 (XXV) (italics added).

31. 10 Int'l Legal Materials 133, 1151, resp.

32. See, e.g., Green, "Hijacking and the Right of Asylum," in McWhinney, *Air Piracy and International Law*, 1971, 124 et seqq.; "Piracy of Aircraft and the Law," 10 *Alberta Law Rev.*, 1972, 72 et seqq.; Joyner, *Aerial Hijacking as an International Crime*, 1974, 201-16.

33. Res. 3166 (XXVIII), Annex.

34. Res. 3314 (XXIX) (italics added).

35. H.M.S.O., Cmd. 6964 (1946), 13; 40 *Am. J. Int'l Law* (1946), 186.

36. Res. 95 (I).

37. Schwarzenberger, *Power Politics*, 1951, 716-20.

38. Res. 3108 (XXVIII) (italics added).

39. Res. 3237 (XXIX).

40. Res. 3236 (XXIX).

41. Res. 3247 (XXIX).

42. Res. 3379 (XXX).

43. Res. 1904 (XVIII).

44. Res. 3151 G (XXVIII).

45. International Convention on the Suppression and Punishment of the Crime against *Apartheid*. Art. 1, Res. 3068 (XXVIII), Annex.

46. 16 Int'l Legal Materials 1391.

47. 20 Dec. 1977, Rolno. 3853/77. I am grateful to Mr. Sam Bloembergen, legal adviser, Netherlands Ministry of Foreign Affairs, for providing me with the text and a summarized translation of this judgment.

48. European Treaty Series, No. 90.

49. See Ireland v. United Kingdom (1978, European Court of Human Rights, official text).

Part 5

The Future

9
The Future of Political Substate Violence
David Carlton

The phenomenon of political substate violence is as old as the state itself. In various periods and in different regions it has naturally taken a variety of forms: predominantly urban or predominantly rural; broadly supported by the community or perpetrated by a handful of alienated malcontents; executed with intensity or sophistication or practiced unskillfully. These variations often serve to give both the perpetrators and the victims of substate violence the false impression that they are dealing with a novel phenomenon. Counsels are often confused by the inevitable loose use of terms (such as civil war, revolution, guerrilla war, terror, and terrorism) that create the mistaken view that these are completely distinct. The term *terrorism* is at present in vogue, but there is no consensus among statesmen, lawyers, or scholars about its precise meaning.[1] After all, in the well-worn cliché, one man's terrorist is another man's freedom fighter. Efforts to qualify the term *terrorism* with adjectives (such as state, national, international, or transnational) may, to some extent, be helpful. But there inevitably remain grey areas between these categories, and also between all of them and other forms of substate violence commonly described in other terms than terrorism. We shall avoid these difficulties by using the term *terrorist* to denote any perpetrator of substate violence whose motives are broadly of a political character, even if they are often in common parlance described in other terms, such as guerrilla. Under this definition, however, sovereign states cannot be perpetrators of "terror" within their own boundaries (though they may sponsor or arrange for terrorist acts to be committed in other states). This is not to argue that some leaders of states do not, in practice, create what would commonly be called terror for their own citizens within their own countries or that such terror is necessarily ethically less (or more) reprehensible than that caused by substate actors. Terror by governments against their own citizens is of course a subject of universal interest and can, from some ethical standpoints, legitimately be compared to or even be seen as a justification for substate terror. But there is a clear definitional distinction between the two. In this chapter, we shall concern ourselves with the substate perspective, and the terms *terrorism* and *terrorists* will be used only in this sense.

Predicting in the field of international politics is necessarily hazardous. And certainly no scholar should attempt such an exercise without engaging in some preliminary reflection on the lack of success of many of those who have made similar attempts in the past, whether in works of fiction or of political science. For example, I. F. Clarke's study, *Voices Prophesying War,*[2] makes salutory reading. First, it is clear that most *detailed* predictions are almost certain to be unsound. Secondly, those who examine subjects such as war and violence may be consciously or subconsciously fascinated by apocalyptic possibilities and hence may tend greatly to underrate the evidence or trends that could lend themselves to unexciting conclusions. For example, the least diverting prediction for the future of terrorism would be one that foresaw neither uncontrolled escalation nor deescalation after a dramatic reassertion of authority by sovereign states, but rather one that foresaw a continuing untidy pattern of incidents largely unrelated to one another and each of only transient significance to an increasingly unconcerned world. Another lesson to be gleaned from a study of past prophets in the area of politics and international relations is that even the most successful rarely allow for the influence of random accidents as the cause of great events. Thus, while many forecast something like World War I, none could foresee that it would be triggered by quarrels arising out of the near-bungled assassination of an Austrian archduke rather than out of some great clash over high principle or a longstanding territorial dispute between great powers. Again, many forecast that a second world war would leave every British city in total ruins, but none guessed that the fortuitous invention of radar would play a substantial role in falsifying these predictions. The lesson for those in "futurology" is clear: avoid detailed predictions and hint knowingly at undefined developments that will surely surprise us all!

These cautionary remarks do not imply that nothing of value can be said about the future of terrorism. For the very act of contemplating the possibilities, whether by writers or by decision makers or even by terrorists or potential terrorists, may, as in other fields, help to shape the developments themselves. Thus, it may be of interest to try to discern the principal determinants of the future character of terrorism. We shall here examine four such broad determinants in the belief that in combination they will hold the key to whether the problem of terrorism will come to threaten the stability of sovereign states on a scale hitherto unknown. The four are (1) the rate of technological innovation as it affects terrorism; (2) self-imposed restraints on the part of terrorists; (3) countermeasures open to individual sovereign states; and (4) the international dimension of the prevention and the promotion of terrorism.

Technological Innovation

It is well to begin with a reminder that terrorist groups of whatever kind have not hitherto sought to impose the maximum possible slaughter on mankind in general or even, usually, on their particular adversaries. The explanations for this relative restraint are no doubt complicated and it may be that in the future some groups will behave differently. But these are matters we shall consider in some detail in due course. In this section we are merely concerned with the capabilities that may, as a result of continuing technological innovation, conceivably come to be possessed by terrorists *if* uncharacteristically they should seek to maximize their capacity to kill.

First, we may note that newly formed small terrorist groups will, in general, find it easier with each passing year to obtain at least minimum means for taking life. Small urban groups, not significantly linked to sponsoring states or groups abroad, may expect to benefit from contact with conventional criminals who appear to be increasing in numbers in most advanced societies, who are more and more willing to carry firearms, and who appear to have little difficulty in obtaining such weapons. It is also becoming fashionable, most notably in Italy, for criminal groups to take hostages as a means of gaining money by extortion. They may increasingly seek cynical links with small, politically motivated terrorist groups. The former, by adding a political element to their ransom notes, may carry more conviction; the latter gain funds and weapons in return, say, for occasionally allowing mere criminals to use their code words in negotiations.

Well-established terrorist groups, even those not engaged in traditional rural guerrilla campaigns, are also likely to find conventional weaponry easier to obtain—and in their case, the weapons may be highly sophisticated. For arms races among the world's sovereign states have been increasing steadily for many decades. So, too, has the arms trade between sovereign states. The result is that much supposedly obsolescent weaponry is constantly changing hands and can even more easily be diverted into the hands of terrorists. In some cases, the suppliers have only a commercial motive. In other cases, some sovereign states deliberately sponsor the provision of arms to at least the more well-established substate groups. And this is likely to become all the more widespread in a world where many guerrilla groups have successfully thrown off colonial regimes and established themselves as rulers of fully fledged sovereign states and where a substate group—the Palestine Liberation Organization (PLO)—has succeeded in blurring the distinction between itself and sovereign states by being allowed to present itself at the United Nations and elsewhere as if it actually had become a sovereign state. Moreover, the more "responsible" subnational groups may, in turn, at least to some extent serve as suppliers to smaller terrorist factions without the knowledge or approval of the original sponsors. Thus, we may conclude that, if other conditions favor such a development, lack of access to arms will not prove to be any stumbling block to a vast proliferation of terrorist groups at least as well equipped as the relatively small number active in the 1970s.

Will present and future groups gradually be able to obtain ever more sophisticated and devastating conventional weapons? Again, the answer would appear to be in the affirmative. True, a gap may be expected to grow in this respect between the well-established, state-sponsored groups and the tiny groups of fanatics such as the Symbionese Liberation Army (United States) and the Angry Brigade (Great Britain). For example, the PLO and related groups would probably have little difficulty in obtaining, say, a modern precision-guided munition (PGM). And it could also easily find or train operators skilled in its use. With a PGM, one man can hit a target from a great range—perhaps a low-flying aircraft from a distance of a mile or more. But such a powerful and self-confident group is perhaps less likely to favor an escalation in the level of violence in modern terrorism than a small gang of frenzied fanatics who may come to favor the idea of a larger number of casualties for its own sake. Yet most of the tiny groups may have to wait some decades before they can hope to move beyond the level of the gun or the homemade bomb. But the pace of technological change plainly suggests that even for them, PGMs may, in the fullness of time, become almost as easy to obtain as guns are today.

Finally, we must ask whether even the most sophisticated groups can hope to obtain weapons of mass destruction in the foreseeable future. This is a matter of much complexity and has been the subject of some controversy.[3] In the popular imagination, the question turns of course on the risk of terrorists acquiring nuclear weapons. Certainly, if this should happen, it would constitute a quantum leap of a most sensational kind. Whether it would be of much practical value to any rational terrorist group is another question—to which we shall return. It is also doubtful whether many, if any, terrorist groups are at present actively thirsting to obtain such a capability. But here we must concentrate on whether it is technically feasible. Plainly, there must be a finite chance that a present or future nuclear weapon state would actually supply a nuclear weapon to such a group. Again, it must be a possibility that, despite all precautions, such a bomb could be stolen intact. But these are surely remote contingencies. Of more interest is whether any terrorist group could make a bomb by its own exertions. Experts are not in full agreement on this matter. True, the theoretical basis of making a nuclear weapon is understood by many postgraduate physicists of average competence. A student at Massachusetts Institute of Technology (MIT), set the task, was without much difficulty able, on the basis of printed material in the American public domain, to design a nuclear bomb that might well have worked. But design and manufacture are not the same. For the MIT student had neither plutonium nor U-235 and could not, in practice, have obtained any. It is unclear whether a determined group could do so other than with the aid of a sovereign state (which, in that case, might just as well hand over not merely plutonium or U-235, but a fully fabricated bomb). Plainly, the terrorists, if not helped in this way, would need to arrange to steal the necessary material. A dramatic hijacking is a theoretical possibility. But it is much more plausible that terrorists would arrange for an agent within one of the world's many governmental atomic plants to divert the material, perhaps in small amounts over a protracted period. There have indeed been rumors that attempts along these lines may conceivably already have been made in more than one Western country. However this may be, we may conclude that if large numbers of terrorist groups are absolutely and singlemindedly determined to "go nuclear," one or another will, in the end, succeed. But it is also true that most sovereign states are in no way inferior in technological potential to even the most sophisticated terrorists and hence may have at least as much rational motive to obtain nuclear weapons. The chances are, therefore, that there will be many more nuclear weapon states before a substate actor joins the club.

There is, however, the possibility that a terrorist group will decide that concentration on the ownership of a nuclear bomb is not the

most expeditious means of inflicting mass destruction. And in this
they would probably be correct. What other possibilities exist? One is
a variant on the nuclear theme, namely, that terrorists might seek to
blow up nuclear reactors in the hope that this would trigger a full-
scale nuclear explosion. Another possibility is to engage chemical
experts in an attempt to acquire the ability to poison the water
supply of one or more cities. A third option would be to concentrate
on developing a biological warfare capability, with a view to being
able to cause an epidemic of, say, anthrax or bubonic plague. All
would probably involve less difficulty than making a nuclear bomb.
On the other hand, terrorists would probably have the least
difficult—though still formidable—task in bargaining effectively if
they had a small stock of nuclear bombs. The other possibilities may
carry rather less credibility and certainly that is the logic that has
led sovereign states that have sought weapons of mass destruction to
concentrate their attention on nuclear weapons rather than on, say,
indiscriminate biological weapons. But it must be stressed that
terrorist groups are not sovereign states and they may themselves
realize that bargaining with any weapons of mass destruction
presents exceptional problems. Of course, some terrorists may not
have bargaining in mind but may simply aim at eliminating as many
human beings as possible. But such utterly nihilistic terrorists are
relatively rare and are precisely the ones least likely to have the
means to obtain weapons of mass destruction.

Another feature of technological advance that is of relevance for
the future of terrorism is the pace at which more and more countries
are becoming increasingly vulnerable to disruption by small numbers of dissidents. Terrorists are by no means the only people to
recognize this vulnerability. In many advanced Western democracies,
trade unionists have already surprised their governments and perhaps
also themselves by revealing that small numbers of workers in key
positions can paralyze national industrial production and can even
pose a threat to civilized life in general. In Great Britain, for example,
coal miners and electricity supply workers found that they were able
to cause as much chaos by industrial action as in an earlier era could
only have been achieved by an all-out general strike. This led Edward
Heath to call a general election in February 1974 when most industrial workers, already on a three-day week, were facing the possibility
of a complete shutdown as a result of a coal miners' strike for higher
pay. He asked the electorate: Who governs the country, the elected
representatives (a majority of whom favored pay restraint) or the
National Union of Mineworkers? He lost the election and the new

government of Harold Wilson promptly defused the crisis by giving in to the miners' demands. Shortly thereafter, the British inflation rate rose to more than 20 percent per annum. Another example of overwhelming power in a few hands occurred in Ulster when the power workers went on strike not for higher wages but in support of a hardline Protestant reaction to Prime Minister Brian Faulkner's move towards power-sharing with Roman Catholics. The armed forces evidently did not have the expertize to take over. The result was chaos and industrial paralysis. Faulkner accordingly resigned; power-sharing was abandoned, and the strikers triumphed. Other small groups of key workers who may, in the future, demonstrate their indispensability are those engaged in water supply and sewage disposal. Plainly, it would be feasible for sophisticated terrorists in some cases, say, with the aid of PGMs, to achieve almost as much disruption as strikers if they choose their targets with care.

The fact is that advanced democracies—and maybe advanced totalitarian states as well—are much more vulnerable than states of the nineteenth century or even half a century ago. Large-scale industrialization has steadily grown and sophisticated processes are now commonplace. Any breakdown in communications or in the flow of components or in the supply of electricity or in the working of computers can instantly render idle thousands of workers at a given plant. Today, in contrast to the fairly recent past, the scope for pragmatic adaptation in the face of such difficulties is negligible in many factories. Again, the increasing sophistication of operations in some key industries makes it impractical for the state to send in the armed forces in the event of a strike. True, few countries are at present as vulnerable as such advanced West European democracies as Italy, Great Britain, or France. But many developing or semi-developed countries are aiming to travel the same road. Hence, in due time, more and more states will become similarly vulnerable to disruption. This is an encouraging prospect for terrorists. But it is by no means clear that it will be terrorists who will, in practice, pose the greatest threat. With or without terrorists, some communities may simply become ungovernable because of largely nonviolent conflicts of interests. Those states with democratic constitutional frameworks would seem to be much at risk both from terrorism and nonviolent conflict and some may be driven to seek authoritarian solutions. But advanced states without ballot-box democracy surely cannot count on total immunity from these various strains, given the extremely delicate balance that exists between parts of a modern advanced economy. Computers are a case in point.

As Bertil Häggman has written:

> The growing use of computers offers new and effective methods to small terrorist groups to create chaos and confusion in the industrialized world. When the main part of all economic transactions is dependent on the use of computers, confusion can easily be brought on through rather simple acts of sabotage. Production and distribution chains can be rendered useless. . . .[4]

For terrorists, technological advance has another important implication: some terrorists can already operate without much difficulty on a global scale, and present trends suggest that even the smallest groups will soon be able to internationalize their activities with ease. Travel time, by air, between regions is shrinking year by year. Means of communication are also constantly improving. This has two principal advantages for terrorists. First, they may find it increasingly easy to get in touch with controllers, sponsors, or potential havens at ever greater distances from the scene of a particular operation. Secondly, any outrage perpetrated in one country can now be immediately transmitted on television to millions of viewers on the other side of the planet. As more and more people in even the poorest countries will acquire television sets in the coming decades, terrorists can accordingly look forward to drawing attention to their causes with ever increasing facility. This may serve to make terrorism seem increasingly tempting to aggrieved groups of every variety.

On the other hand, technological advance is in one important respect unwelcome to terrorists. State authorities are now able to acquire, store, and retrieve information about larger numbers of politically motivated people. And the same improvements in international transportation and communication that in other respects are beneficial to terrorists serve to enable governments to communicate rapidly with one another and maybe concert their responses. The problem for the analyst of the future of terrorism is to assess whether these various advances are likely to be of net advantage to what we may term the offense (the terrorist) or the defense (the state). Experience of the last decade suggests that there is in fact a relationship between improvements in technology and the growth of transnational terrorism. And it is difficult to foresee any breakthrough that could enable the defense to reverse the trend and suddenly obtain a decisive advantage over the offense.

We may thus conclude that terrorism is bound to grow if the main determinant is seen as increasing ease of access to weaponry in general or, alternatively, to weapons of increasing sophistication. Indeed, it must be only a matter of time before a terrorist group obtains weapons of mass destruction, provided always that the desire to do so is sufficiently strongly felt. This clearly does represent a major change—at least at the conceptual level. For until recently, no terrorist group could even hope to obtain weaponry that would give it more destructive power than many sovereign states possess. Terrorism has traditionally been seen as the weapon of the weak. Now some of the weak are potentially extremely strong. But potential power is not always turned into reality. And it seems likely that other factors than what is in theory technologically possible will be more important in determining the future patterns of terrorist activity.

Self-imposed Restraints

Terrorists often give the appearance of being desperate, unscrupulous, and bound by no code of ethics. Hence some commentators are tempted to suppose that they would impose limitless suffering on all humanity if the means were available to them. But this is, in many cases, a superficial view. Certainly, the larger Palestinian groups or the Provisional Irish Republican Army (IRA) or the guerrilla movements in Africa are not mere nihilists. Their leaders have clear and maybe even attainable objectives which they pursue along lines that can be to a considerable degree rationally explained. The larger groups, moreover, are nearly all concerned with a limited "nationality" or "territorial" cause whatever other seemingly unlimited, ideological veneer accompanies it. No doubt they make errors of judgment from time to time both in strategic and tactical terms; and in some cases, their causes may seem to outsiders to be foredoomed to partial or total defeat. But the same is true of the behavior of the leaders of some sovereign states.

Some of the leaders of the larger terrorist organizations may indeed have personality disorders and some may be on the brink of insanity. But these descriptions also fit some leaders of sovereign states. The reality surely is that most of the well-known groups of substate actors are *not* run by madmen; rather they are run by people capable of engaging in rational calculation and debate. They are therefore much concerned with the relationship between ends and means. They may also paradoxically have an inclination towards conservatism in debates about techniques and methods. Hence the relative lack of variety in terroristic activity during the last ten years: bombing, airliner hijackings, and shooting often following an almost boringly repetitive pattern. And so far they have shown but little ingenuity or enterprise in trying wholly novel methods of terroristic bargaining. On the contrary, one group has tended to imitate another in its techniques even to the smallest detail. In short, they have tended to behave as terrorists or guerrillas are supposed to behave in an urban or rural context.

Trade unionists in Western democracies provide an interesting parallel. The use of withdrawal of labor, of picketing, and of the elaborate ritual of traditional bargaining techniques also seems to vary only marginally between countries and across the decades. Even militant minorities within trade unions seem to be infected with something of the same conservatism, not even contemplating, for example, the use of bombing to achieve higher wages. Superficially, this provides a contrast with discontented nationality groups who have long had a tendency to give rise to activists ready to perpetrate violent outrages rather than concentrate on more passive methods of persuasion. (Even Mahatma Gandhi's passive resistance to the British Raj was not universally supported: a militant faction favored more violent means.[5]) But this contrast between trade unionists and terrorist groups dedicated to "national liberation" serves only to highlight a similarity: both types of pressure group tend to be creatures of habit. It is this conservatism, more than ethical inhibitions, that makes it unlikely that, at any early date, we shall see from the larger terrorist groups a quantum leap in the use of mass violence or even the deliberate introduction of any significant innovations in bargaining techniques.

Smaller groups lacking any broad basis of support and thus probably obsessed with abstract ideology rather than aspirations of "national liberation" may be less conservative in principle, though in practice they may be unable to do little to make the distinction evident, particularly in respect to weaponry rather than bargaining techniques. Facing the despair of total defeat, which is a quite probable fate for such small groups, they may indeed develop thoughts along nihilistic lines. The Baader-Meinhof group provides an example of how increasing desperation can make a *Götterdämmerung* attractive. But in their case, the result was the suicide of the leaders rather than mass slaughter of the population in general— maybe because the latter was not a practical option.

Relative restraint among the larger terrorist groups may result from their essential conservatism. But this does not mean that rational justifications cannot be adduced to bolster this instinctive attitude. Above all, terrorists are often more interested in drawing attention to their cause than in the mass destruction of life for its own sake without reference to geography or nationality. For example, guerrillas fighting in South Africa may be tempted to engage in a spectacular hijacking or even a bombing in a distant continent. But a policy of killing as many people as possible in randomly selected cities, say, Paris, Moscow, and Calcutta would be absurd. We may consider the case of the Munich Olympics of 1972 when Palestinian terrorists killed eleven Israeli athletes and achieved massive world publicity. They would not have obtained more publicity if they had killed twice as many Israeli athletes nor if they had massacred hundreds of German spectators. For the publicity could scarcely have been greater than it was. It could, of course, be argued that killing on a much larger scale would have greatly increased the general fear of the Palestinian terrorists in West Germany and elsewhere. But it is not clear that maximizing fear to that extent would have served any particular purpose not achieved by the operation actually carried through. The resulting increase of hatred in West Germany might as easily have led to a stiffening of resistance to their aims as to a willingness to support them. In any case, it is doubtful whether West German policy towards the Palestinians, however it might have developed, would have made any decisive difference to the Middle East scene. It is therefore not surprising that most terrorist groups seem to regard the occasional killing of a few people—whether real adversaries or the totally uninvolved or those in an intermediate position—as not counterproductive to their aims but to draw the line at the policy of all-out maximization of slaughter of human beings in any and every country where the opportunity might exist. The number killed in an individual urban terrorist incident rarely reaches double figures. When it does, it may be an aberration caused perhaps by an overzealous subordinate or by an accidental failure to communicate a warning as was possibly the case in the Provisional IRA's massacre of twenty people in the Birmingham public house bombings of 1974. Hence, in almost every country, annual deaths from road accidents greatly exceed deaths from terrorism. This is not to argue that the death of two innocent people is ethically more acceptable than the death of twenty. It is simply to note that mainstream terrorists do not as yet seem to be obsessed by maximizing the numbers of victims. And this means that a spectacular quantum leap to mass destruction—which, as we have seen, may well soon be within the technological capability of terrorists—is not at present a likely prospect.

It may be argued, however, that terrorists will be driven to radical innovation by continuing failure to achieve success. Certainly, some terrorists are temperamentally impatient for rapid victory and too unstable to exercise patience over a period of years. But such terrorists are precisely those who are the least likely to be in top positions in groups that have a realistic capability for pursuing radically new strategies. The despairing apocalyptics are likely to be able to achieve little more in the foreseeable future than a once-for-all spectacular, which may indeed be sensational enough but which will be well short of a sustainable quantum leap. The larger groups, on the other hand, are not as lacking in patience as is often supposed. Some have been in existence for many years and have leaders who privately are quite reconciled to a long struggle or, alternatively, to a compromise settlement of their grievances. Some may even come to see their group as a permanent way of life with victory likely to be put off to the Greek kalends. For them the terroristic outrages may in time cease to be of central concern. For example, the IRA and its various associated organizations obviously have much general contact, established over many years, in Catholic/Republican enclaves in Ulster. There are no doubt many people who are sympathizers in varying degrees, but who are not practicing terrorists. It could even be that the "protection racket" aspect of their work will in practice grow in importance while the terrorist outrages meanwhile are likely neither to cease entirely nor greatly to increase in intensity. Paradoxical as it may appear, some of the larger terrorist groups may thus under certain scenarios be content, like many of their adversaries in governmental office, to float lazily downstream putting out the occasional boathook.

Does this mean that the terrorist scene will look much the same at, say, the turn of the century as it does now? No such conclusions can be safely drawn. For if there is now no important group visibly straining to find entirely new techniques or to achieve a breakthrough to mass destruction, there is likely nevertheless to be a gradual, largely unplanned evolution in a direction that will make terrorism a problem of increasing seriousness to governments. First, the rapid evolution of technology and the increasing availability of sophisticated weaponry may put temptation in the way of terrorist movements that might never have consciously gone out of their way to escalate their levels of violence. Secondly, once a particular inhibition has gone, it will not be easily restored. Thus, if one group should be presented with the chance to destroy a public procession of dignitaries by PGMs from a considerable distance, it may pragmatically decide to go ahead without fully realizing that this technique may then become fashionable with other groups. And, if at present the number of deaths in a terrorist outrage is rarely in double figures, we may slide step-by-step to a situation where we shall be able to state, probably in tones of some complacency, that the numbers rarely reach treble figures and that the overall total killed by terrorism is still less than that caused, if not by the motor car, then by a particular disease or by traditional wars. Bargaining techniques in hostage situations are also likely to alter, no doubt in fits and starts, in ways that will increase the sharpness of most incidents. Already we have seen this happening to some degree. Both terrorists and state authorities have learned some lessons and lost some inhibitions. Thus two encounters late in 1977, which saw a terrorist victory at Algiers and a terrorist defeat at Mogadishu, took a significantly different form from, say, the hijacking in 1970 that culminated at Dawson's Field. There was no single moment that signified the change—just an almost imperceptible evolution over seven years towards greater sophistication. The trend—which is unlikely to be reversed—is to greater and greater ruthlessness. In Mogadishu, for example—admittedly at a late stage in the operation—a corpse was pushed out of the airliner as a means of putting pressure on the West German government. Significantly, this was almost certainly not pre-planned. The corpse became available for use in bargaining as a result of a quarrel between the terrorist leader and the airline pilot, which culminated in the latter's death. On some future occasions, as a result of the piece of opportunism, the inhibition against the use of individual corpses in hijacking cases may no longer be thought to exist. If so, corpses may come to be used, deliberately rather than as an afterthought, on more occasions, early in the bargaining process and perhaps in ever increasing numbers. Thus at some future date, it may be commonplace for half a dozen bodies to be thrown out of a hijacked airliner or train in the first hours of an encounter—anything less may be then be thought to show that the terrorists are not in earnest! But if the past is any guide, we shall probably have come to such a point by gradual stages and not by a precalculated decision to take a spectacular leap up a ladder of ruthlessness.

We may thus conclude that most of the more important terrorist groups are at present relatively restrained in their use of violence. But inhibitions may gradually be broken down, probably more as a result of a cumulative series of random events rather than because of any deep yearning by most terrorist leaders to pursue uncontrolled escalation. There is here a parallel with the steady erosion of restraints exercised in wars between sovereign states during the twentieth century. Much less clear is whether a gradual escalation in ruthlessness will culminate in the true quantum leap to the use of weapons of mass destruction. Plainly, there is a distinct line between nuclear and nonnuclear weapons and hence this could not be crossed simply by incremental steps; and this may also apply, if a little less clearly, to the use of chemical or biological means of mass destruction. So we may hazard the guess that major terrorist groups will have to change greatly if such a quantum leap is to be attempted. But we cannot assume that they will not change. The appetite for slaughter may grow with the eating. Moreover, some mainstream terrorists may be driven to more desperate measures if sovereign states become more ruthless and more effective in their countermeasures, which may in turn result from the gradual growth of terrorist violence, even though short of mass destruction, that seems likely to occur with little or no conscious preplanning on the part of terrorists. It is to an examination of state countermeasures that we must now turn.

Countermeasures Open to Individual States

Some commentators argue that the future extent of terrorism will be decided by governments. The liberal-minded among them tend to plead for the creation of conditions in which there will fewer grievances likely to spawn terrorists, while the more conservative-minded argue that states need only exert themselves and behave with sufficient ruthlessness and resolve to contain the problem. Both groups may, however, be too sanguine about the power at the disposal of most states. For the probability is that neither reform nor repression could in practice be on the scale necessary to counter effectively other factors that favor the gradual growth of terrorism.

We may first consider the idea that it is practical to create conditions in which terrorism will not flourish. Plainly, some examples may be cited where this ought to be effective. For example, West Germany and even Italy ought to be able to improve conditions for full-time students in higher education and in the case of the former this has to some extent already occurred. This in turn will help to combat terrorism, for authorities on various extremist groups in those countries have noted that many individual terrorists set out on a radical road that eventually led them to violence as a result of extreme dissatisfaction at the widespread overcrowding and lack of opportunities in higher education.[6]

But many Third World countries could not afford to carry through educational reforms that are within the reach of Western European democracies. The West Germans may, by these means, be able to contain the flow of recruits into the Baader-Meinhof group, but this is not a remedy open to most states. And, of course, small groups of student extremists are only one part of the problem of terrorism. What, for example, could states do to create conditions in which the grievances of Irish or Palestinian terrorists would disappear? A superficial answer might be that the states concerned should seek acceptable settlements. But this will usually bring no guarantee of a decrease in terrorism. If, for example, a Middle East settlement should prove possible and a Palestinian state should be created, we might even see more not less terrorism. Some Israelis set on colonizing the West Bank might see their own leaders as traitors and initiate a terrorist campaign of their own. And even if Yasir Arafat expressed his satisfaction with the settlement and underwent the metamorphosis of becoming the respectable leader of a sovereign state, there would surely be other Palestinians who would accuse him of having betrayed the cause by settling for a Palestinian state within borders more limited than "justice" demands. Such Palestinian dissenters would presumably carry on with terrorist outrages—and the smaller in number and more desperate they were, the more extreme their tactics might become.

We may conclude, therefore, that it is impossible for states, particularly in the postcolonial era, to pursue policies that will, except in rare instances, remove many of the conditions and the grievances, real or imagined, that motivate terrorists. The question remains, however, whether such conditions in general, mostly beyond governmental powers to influence, are improving or worsening. The prognosis appears to be gloomy. For in much of the world, a population explosion is going hand in hand with increasing fears about whether food supplies and natural resources will be sufficient to sustain even present levels of subsistence. And even in the advanced countries, where no population explosion threatens, the energy crisis has caused economic stagnation and led to unemployment on a scale not known since World War II, raising doubts about the future stability of political systems. Moreover, in both advanced and developing countries, deference and passive acceptance of one's lot are becoming rare, and self-restraint imposed by religious beliefs is waning. Ever larger numbers of young people are achieving literacy and are acquiring at least a smattering of education that makes them uniquely envious of those who have greater opportunities or obtained jobs commensurate with their talents. In advanced as well as developing countries, there are vast numbers of people under thirty with high abilities and aspirations on a scale never previously known. Yet additional appropriate posts enabling them to make use of their talents have not been created, usually because governments could not afford to do so. Even West Germany, though it is able to afford to improve conditions in universities, cannot provide suitable employment for all the graduates. Again, university appointments in Western Europe or North America will now attract many more qualified candidates than a decade ago, and few experts believe that this is a temporary phenomenon. Much the same is true of posts in government, in the higher echelons of business, and in most prestigious professions. Here, then, are conditions in which discontents will flourish. No doubt many governments will face increasing difficulty in governing effectively with broad consent. That terrorism will grow in these conditions seems inevitable. But it must be stressed that it will be only one of many facets of increasing lawlessness and instability.

If governments cannot create idyllic conditions in which terrorism will lose its appeal, perhaps they will be able to halt its growth by repressive countermeasures. Here again the prognosis is not encouraging for governments. For in the conditions we are facing, terrorism could assume the character of a seven-headed hydra. Thus, though a state can, after considerable expenditure and deployment of personnel, greatly reduce the chances of aircraft skyjacking, it cannot successfully anticipate the direction in which terrorists will turn instead. The South Moluccans in the Netherlands, for example, did not hijack an airliner but chose trains and a school classroom. Such possibilities are clearly infinite, and only the imitative conservatism of terrorist groups has prevented this from being widely recognized. So government precautions can only have limited effect. This is not to say that states should make no effort to protect obvious targets. It is clearly necessary for the peace of mind of airline passengers to have quite strict security at airports. Likewise, it makes sense for all nuclear installations to have armed guards. But none of this will prevent determined terrorists from finding ways of making their presence felt. The state, then, should not become so obsessed by a particular threat as to lose sight of other objectives. For example, there has been a debate in Great Britain about the desirability of creating a so-called plutonium economy for supplying energy needs in the next century. This may or may not be a wise course because of the costs, the general safety risks, and possible alternative sources of energy. But what would be absurd would be to make such a momentous decision on the basis of whether it increased marginally the chances of terrorists seizing plutonium and thus being able to "go nuclear." For the fact is, as we have seen, the scope for well-organized terrorists obtaining weapons of mass destruction is already considerable—if they are of a mind to do it. And there are large numbers of countries, not only Great Britain, where they could seek their doomsday weaponry. So the substate genie is already potentially out of the bottle. Hence for one country drastically to impoverish itself in order to reduce terrorists' scope in one small part of a wide canvas would surely be unreasonable.

What of other possible countermeasures open to states acting on their own in the absence of international cooperation? Some authorities stress the importance of controlling the media, particularly in liberal democracies. There is a powerful case for seeking restraint on the part of the media revealing the detailed moves of government in a hijacking incident. Hence, only a few irresponsible sources broadcast the news that a rescue attempt was imminent at Mogadishu and, as it happened, this did not get through to the terrorists. But is there a case for trying to prevent news coverage of terrorists' actions altogether, given that publicity is often what they primarily seek? Liberal democracies will not of course wish to jeopardize the democratic value of a free press except in extreme circumstances and unless it is clear that the measure would be effective in reducing terrorism. Indeed, some will argue that freedom of the press is so sacrosanct that even limited curtailment would constitute a victory for terrorists who often hope to show that such states are in reality repressive and not democratic in character. Others, however, may adopt the neo-Kissingerian doctrine. According to Robert Skidelsky, the critical question is whether "citizens should acquiesce in unjust situations because the maintenance of security and general welfare takes priority over other claims."[7] But clearly liberal democrats who hold this opinion would need to be satisfied that selective authoritarian measures—for example, in the case of the press—would actually serve the purposes of greatly increasing the citizen's security against terrorism. And press control on its own probably would not make much difference. For it is difficult to imagine that any major terrorist outrage could remain secret for long. For example, the details of major guerrilla onslaughts in Rhodesia soon become known throughout the country and abroad despite censorship. Likewise, a large terrorist assault on, say, Moscow airport could not be kept from the Soviet people by silence on the part of the Soviet media: too many Soviet citizens would have firsthand knowledge and

too many listen to Western broadcasting stations. Rumors might even
serve to exaggerate perceptions of the extent of the damage done by
the terrorists. All that might be kept secret would be a relatively minor
terrorist incident in a remote place. This presumably does not constitute an effective deterrent to terrorism in the Soviet Union but
merely increases the chances that outrages will become more
spectacular. Some controls on the live televising of incidents may,
on the other hand, be justified.

Are there other actions that the state could take that would be effective? Certainly, life can be made more difficult for terrorists in a
number of ways. Some of the methods already tried include forcing
citizens to carry identity cards, holding baggage checks in public
places, and instituting bans on known extremists holding particular
jobs. But none of them is remotely capable of making terrorism
impossible. And it is at least open to doubt whether the complete
destruction of the liberal democratic state would even go very far
towards achieving that purpose. True, most of the urban terrorism in
the 1970s has been in so-called open societies. But the so-called
closed societies have not been immune. For example, the Soviet
Union suffered a bomb explosion in the Moscow subway in January
1977, and Yugoslavia has had much trouble with Croatian separatists. The present gaps in the incidence of terrorism in different
types of state could indeed lessen, particularly if there should be a
significant escalation in the state-sponsored form of terrorism. Again,
there is no guarantee that if, say, Great Britain adopted the Soviet
system, terrorism in Ulster would rapidly disappear. On the contrary,
increased surveillance and a more repressive atmosphere might even
serve only to make the hard-core IRA extremists more desperate and
hence more violent at least in the short run. Moreover, state-
sponsorship of transnational terrorism would certainly not disappear
with the end of liberal democracy, for not all of it is directed at states
having that system of government.

Similar arguments apply to the proposal to introduce capital
punishment for terrorism: martyrs would be created and the lust for
revenge might actually cause an escalation in the level of violence.
But there may be scope for experimentation by states in this area. One
might introduce suspended death sentences for captured terrorists,
which could be carried out by executive order in the event of a new
outrage from the same group or if a bid should be made to bargain
with hostages for the release of such convicted terrorists. Techniques
of this kind were of some value, for example, to the Irish Free State
in the period of conflict that followed partition in 1922. But no liberal

democracy, not even West Germany, seems at present to be in a sufficient state of despair to wish to act along these lines. And if matters did come to such a pass, it is far from clear that any means at all could easily guarantee success in restoring state authority.

We may finally consider whether states could achieve better results with radically new approaches to the problem of bargaining. Some commentators claim that great strides are already being made. When a major hijacking occurs, traveling circuses of experts, psychologists, and the like have tended recently to take charge and they have had a number of successes. Their aim appears to be "negotiate" with the hijackers but never actually to surrender to their main demands. Then, when the hijackers are exhausted, they are overpowered with a minimum loss of life. It is unlikely, however, that state authorities will continue to improve their performances at the expense of terrorists. For in most cases, terrorists have had good grounds for hoping, given the past record of government surrenders, that negotiations will end in success. If this expectation should change as a result of a series of terrorist defeats, we must expect that terrorists will refuse to play the game according to rules that suit the peripatetic psychiatrists. We must expect that, despite the admitted conservatism of their methods, terrorists will show fewer inhibitions and offer bloody tokens of their earnestness before they become exhausted. The Mogadishu affair might, for example, have had a different outcome if individual hostages had been regularly slaughtered from the first hours of the hijacking. Maybe Helmut Schmidt would still have refused to yield, but the pressure on him would have been enormous and certainly in the sophisticated process of bargaining the initiative would have lain with the terrorists rather than with the psychiatrists who would prefer a leisurely and ritualistic procedure.

We may indeed be driven to consider the view that in the long run the only effective technique for states is not to bargain or discuss at all with terrorists. This might at first be costly in innocent lives, but over time a government pursuing such a policy might expect to see a reduction at least in hostage-taking. The doctrine that no state should ever negotiate with a substate actor (save in the case of a colonial state deciding to grant independence and hence state sovereignty) has indeed a majestic simplicity and, if it had been consistently applied, might have prevented contemporary urban terrorism becoming such a vogue. But it is a counsel of perfection. For many states do not perceive that bargaining with and maybe surrendering to one group of terrorists will inevitably lead to even more frequent repeat performances. And in this they may be correct from their narrow national standpoint. For example, Greece and Austria have more than once seen fit to surrender to transnational terrorists whose main quarrels have not been with Athens or Vienna and hence these states have so far paid no heavy price for so doing. West Germany's experience has been different; but from the dovishness of their line in the aftermath of the Munich Olympics to the hawkishness of Mogadishu represented a long journey and not one that any government responsive to public opinion could easily have shortened—with the exception of Israel. The fact is that not all governments—not even the liberal democratic type—are certain to experience either sooner or even later the traumas suffered by West Germany. Every invertebrate surrender by, say, Greece or Austria will no doubt encourage terrorists in general; but the Greeks and Austrians may not themselves ever have to pay a high price. We may thus conclude that a hawkish policy of no bargaining has much to commend it, but it will be adopted by few liberal states unless they find themselves in extremis. Extremis may take two forms: relatively minor incidents (that is, limited demands set against the lives of at most a few hundred people) repeated with intolerable frequency, or a single major incident involving a weapon of mass destruction probably linked to a demand of comparable grandeur. West Germany constitutes an example of the first type and we have not yet seen an example of the second case. If the latter materializes, how should a government react? Bernard Feld of MIT has no doubts:

> What if the mayor of Boston received a note to the effect that a terrorist group had planted a nuclear bomb somewhere in central Boston—accompanied by a crude diagram which showed the bomb would work? . . . I would advise surrender to blackmail rather than the destruction of my hometown.[8]

But in practice much might turn on what was demanded. If the terrorist satisfied the authorities that they actually had a nuclear bomb that would work on a dramatic scale—and a diagram might not be sufficient to do this—and if they only wanted ransom money or even the release of a fellow terrorist, it might be thought prudent to comply (though there is a powerful case for refusing to bargain at all at the level of mass destruction threats because of the precedent that would be set). But what if the terrorists were Palestinians who, in a major Middle East crisis, required the American president to break off diplomatic relations with Israel and refuse her all future oil? If accepted, this would mean that a terrorist group had shaped American foreign policy in a major area. If successful, they or others would surely seek to repeat the operation with respect to some other aspect of high policy. And rival groups would soon appear. Presumably a Zionist group could soon find the means to present a convincing counterthreat: Boston would be no less certainly at risk if the president gave in to the Palestinian demand. From this scenario we may deduce that most states will continue to bargain empirically with terrorists over minor demands until it ceases to be a mere nuisance and become a real threat to the government's authority. When this happens sincere bargaining will probably have to cease. The United States government, in the example given, simply could not abdicate. But the fate of Boston, in such a scenario, is anyone's guess.

We may thus conclude that states have many options with which to combat terrorism, but that in practice these are likely to be only partially effective in dealing with relatively low-level incidents. It is, on the other hand, much more difficult to speculate about the result of a duel with substate actors involving weapons of mass destruction, for in this case we should be entering an entirely uncharted sea. But what seems overwhelmingly clear is that most individual sovereign states show no sign of being able to put an end to the growth of terrorism in its present form because, above all, they are fighting, in varying degrees, a losing battle against the disenchantment of their increasingly restless citizens; they simply cannot create conditions in which terrorism will cease to appeal to the more extreme dissenters. It is also because, to some extent, contrary to George Orwell's expectations, many states, even those of the advanced Marxist-Leninist variety, are simply not proving able to maintain the degree of physical control over potentially violent dissenters, let alone exercise total "thought control" on the scale necessary to guarantee that the threat of terrorism will fade away. No doubt, too, these weaknesses of sovereign states derive in part from the fact that many are at odds with one another about a variety of subjects and not merely with respect to ideology. Hence, they fail to offer each other full-scale cooperation against the substate menace. It is to this aspect that we must now turn.

The International Dimension

The future shape of terrorism probably depends crucially on the behavior of sovereign states in relation to terrorism occurring outside their own frontiers. There are obviously three broad possibilities: (1) matters will stay much as they are; (2) states will on balance increase their sponsorship of terrorism on the territory of adversaries;

or (3) states will on balance increasingly cooperate against the phenomenon. The present tendency is towards a steady increase in sponsorship and there is little evidence that such moves towards cooperation as there have been have so far had much effect in the opposite direction. Of course, sovereign states have always been willing to act as havens for groups of refugees out of favor with their state adversaries, and inevitably such groups have often plotted to bring revolution or terror to their native lands. Examples include Jacobites in the seventeenth and eighteenth centuries in Paris or Rome; emigres from czarist Russia in the nineteenth and early twentieth centuries in France or Switzerland; opponents of both Napoleon I and his nephew, Napoleon III, in nineteenth-century England; Bosnians in pre-1914 Serbia; and Croatian separatists in Budapest or Rome in the era of Horthy and Mussolini. The list could of course be greatly extended. But usually though not invariably the host government was, until recently, careful to insist on restraint and to avoid close sponsorship of such groups except in a situation where a formal state of war existed between it and the group's own state. Recently, such inhibitions have greatly decreased as formal declarations of war have gone out of fashion. Hence, some terrorist groups are now clearly linked to host governments and must be presumed to have relatively little independence. Examples are the Polisario Front based in Algeria and the Popular Front for the Liberation of Palestine and Black June based in Iraq and South Yemen. In addition, there are the more traditional guerrilla groups based, for example, in Mozambique and Zambia. We have seen, too, the growth of great power proxy conflicts. The West on the one hand and the Soviets and the Cubans on the other sponsored competing groups in, for example, Angola; in Indochina, the Soviets and the Chinese are supporting the Vietnamese and the Cambodians respectively in what is near to an undeclared war.

The fact is that the line separating wars between states and conflicts between subnational actors is in these cases becoming increasingly blurred. But it would be a mistake to suppose that sovereign states are powerless to halt this particular trend, especially if the main theater of action should cease to be the Third World. It seems unlikely that the advanced liberal democracies will simply stand idly by as transnational terrorists, sponsored by rival states, make civilized life increasingly impossible in their urban heartlands. It may make sense for the West from time to time to engage in a proxy conflict in Africa or to tolerate the occasional hijacking, assassination, or bombing at home. But it would be unwise for either the Soviet Union and her allies or for the so-called Third World "crazy states" to suppose that if they arranged for a massive escalation of terrorism in Western capitals, no effective response could be made. In the case of, say Libya, the West plainly has the means, if sufficiently provoked, to turn a covert war into an open one that could have only one result. Moscow is of course another matter. But the Soviet Union is unlikely to go very far down the road of sponsoring terrorism, particularly outside the Third World. True, their links with Cuba, Libya, or Algeria may mean that they could be indirectly associated with any escalation. But there are circumstances in which they could be expected to seek to restrain these states rather than encourage them to take steps that could drive the West to desperate responses. For the Soviet Union and other advanced Marxist-Leninist states could be as vulnerable to urban terror as the West. True, at the present nuisance level of activity, the West suffers more, though as we have seen Moscow has not been entirely immune. But in a situation of dramatic escalation in sponsored, transnational terrorism, the West would only have to conclude that the Soviets were primarily responsible, for an open or covert confrontation to become likely. The West would have the option of organizing terror squads of its own to operate, say, in Moscow and allied capitals—a more difficult exercise no doubt than for their opposite numbers but surely not impossible, especially now that groups campaigning for human rights are proliferating. Or the West might choose to take large-scale Soviet-sponsored terrorism as a provocation similar in character to the placing of missiles in Cuba in 1962 and respond with an open ultimatum. Perhaps the Soviets may one day be confident of the outcome of such a confrontation, but, if so, it is not clear why dramatically increased terrorism should be their chosen means of provoking a showdown rather than a move raising in acute form a traditional issue such as West Berlin.

The probability is, however, that the West could tolerate rather more transnational terrorism than it now faces. Hence, any early reaction or overreaction is unlikely. The fact of a degree of indirect Soviet linkage to terrorism will in practice be tolerated by the West in the future as in the past. But the aim of the West will be to ensure that the phenomenon does not get completely out of hand and to try to draw the Soviets into accepting formal or informal ground rules that are in the mutual interests, much as Moscow must have similar realistic aims for limiting rather than entirely halting Western encouragement of their own "human rights" dissidents. To this aspect of possible East-West understanding, we shall return. Meanwhile it must be emphasized that the West can afford to live with at least some degree of escalation in present levels of terrorism and that this is therefore likely to take place. But the state-sponsored aspect will probably not get out of hand. The interwar period provides a good precedent from this point of view. In 1934, King Alexander of Yugoslavia and Louis Barthou, foreign minister of France, were assassinated in Marseilles by the Croat separatist group, the Ustasha. The great powers all believed that Italy had played a major role in encouraging and training the Ustasha and it was suspected that Benito Mussolini may even have had advance knowledge of this particular outrage. But all concerned conspired for the sake of appearances to put the main blame on negligence by the Hungarian government, which was talked into publicly undertaking to mend its ways.[9] Thus it was found prudent not to put Mussolini in the dock in these circumstances, for to have done so would have been to place Italy, France, and Yugoslavia in a position where considerations of honor and inflamed public opinions would probably have required them to go to war. The game was not thought to be worth the candle by French and Yugoslav decision makers—not at least in a Europe where Adolf Hitler's Germany was growing in strength. But Mussolini, though he escaped retribution on this occasion, knew that he could not afford to be associated with further assassinations at this level and he accordingly recognized when to stop. There seems a good chance that modern governments, and especially the more powerful ones, will behave with similar maturity if ever an isolated major incident implicating one of their number occurs; and that the miscreant will not then push his luck too far by permitting a repeat performance.

Thus, while state-sponsored terrorism—probably the only potentially powerful kind at present—may increase, it is unlikely in the foreseeable future to become so widespread that advanced states will undergo a process of pastoralization because urban life will have become too dangerous to endure. Again, state-sponsored groups are unlikely to wish to threaten the use of weapons of mass destruction at any early date, and most nonsponsored groups would have the greatest practical difficulty in doing so.

What are the prospects for more positive cooperation between states as distinct from minimum mutual restraint based on a prudent recognition of the effective limits of sponsorship? Here the outlook is rather unpromising. First, as we have already seen, most sovereign states do not at present feel sufficiently threatened to sacrifice their narrow interests for the collective good. This need not surprise us.

For sovereign states have repeatedly demonstrated an unwillingness to give a high priority to the long-term interests of the global system as a whole, as the fate of collective security under the League of Nations, the search for arms control and disarmament throughout the twentieth century, and the result of age-old pleas for moves towards world government have all proved. States have not accepted the doctrine of Woodrow Wilson that peace is indivisible and will no more readily accept calls for equality of sacrifice in combatting terrorism that patently does not currently present a threat of equal magnitude to all states. Hence, the quest for the universal acceptance of an *effective* international instrument for the suppression of terrorism would be unlikely to succeed even if the problems of definition and of ideological divisions did not exist. Efforts to this end under both the League of Nations and the United Nations tend to confirm this judgment.[10] And even limited regional arrangements involving countries with similar views on ideology and the definitional aspect have not so far been particularly successful. For example, most West European countries have either signed or ratified the Council of Europe's Convention on the subject. But it may be doubted whether in practice states will adhere to it with any greater fidelity than was the case with, say, the league covenant. For example, France has already repeatedly fallen short of its obligations to try or permit the extradition of terrorists. This was most strikingly illustrated in 1977 when Abu Daoud, wanted by both West Germany and Israel for his alleged part in the Munich Olympics massacre, was permitted to leave France for Algiers.

A notable example in the other direction, however, was the decision (going beyond the letter of international obligations) by British Prime Minister James Callaghan to send qualified personnel to aid the West Germans in their assault on their hijacked airliner at Mogadishu. This was clearly not in the narrow British interest, for it could well have led to revenge strikes being made against a variety of British targets including Callaghan himself in circumstances where the British otherwise were not a prime concern of the Baader-Meinhof group. Helmut Schmidt was appropriately grateful, though it remains to be seen whether his country would show similar solidarity in a future crisis where roles were reversed. Noble though Callaghan's conduct was, it lies in the unique and probably declining Anglo-Saxon tradition of Wilsonian internationalism. Hence it seems unlikely that there will be many imitators of Callaghan except in the unlikely contingency that transnational terrorism becomes a menace to many sovereign states to a more or less even extent at much the same time.

There may be some chance, however, that the leading states of the West and the Soviets could reach some tacit or even formal bargains on the subject of terrorism that would not involve Wilsonian idealism but hard calculations concerning immediate mutual interests. One possibility, as already indicated, would be the establishment of ground rules for sponsorship of terrorist groups. It would be futile to expect the Soviets to renounce for all time and in all circumstances direct or indirect support of pro-Marxist guerrilla groups in Third World contexts. The West has of course the option to respond by giving varying degrees of support to their opponents. But it is probably in the interests of both Moscow and Washington to prevent these proxy conflicts spilling over in a major way into the advanced world. Cynical though it would be, the superpowers may delineate regions where proxy conflicts and sponsored terrorism should be virtually ruled out. For the Soviets have conservative as well as revolutionary interests. As Steven Rosen and Robert Frank have written:

> The Soviet Union, bound in Marxist-Leninist unity with all revolutionary movements against Western imperialism, still is constrained by other realitites. Could not the bombing of El Al offices and aircraft today be duplicated in Ukranian or Estonian or Jewish actions against Aeroflot tomorrow? What if Czech liberals or emigre Hungarian or East German nationalists in West Berlin discover that *their* target states also have sensitive economic and political processes that may be disrupted in one country or another? The Soviet Union, as the world's "other" great imperial power, cannot be unrestrained in its enthusiasm for the ability of small Davids to inconvenience big Goliaths.[11]

Another possibility for cooperation between the leading advanced states, irrespective of ideology, could lie in the protection of some of the privileges widely available to their own elites. Thus the safety of the world's airlines, international communication links, newspaper offices, publishing houses, universities, academic institutes, exclusive clubs, expensive shops, first-class hotels and restaurants, and the like are becoming as important to the small but growing Soviet elite as to their more numerous opposite numbers in the West. Thus we may see a tacit understanding not to sponsor terrorism against such targets. And over time we may even see the growth of all-out cooperation to suppress such outrages. Aircraft hijacking is a case in point. The Soviets have an agreement with Finland, which was invoked in 1977 when a would-be Soviet refugee who had hijacked a Soviet airliner to Helsinki was forcibly repatriated. And the Americans and the Cubans, though often actively on opposite sides in African and Latin American substate violence, have seen fit for a time to have a "civilized" agreement regarding air piracy in the Caribbean. More of this kind of limited collaboration seems likely. It may indeed be possible to stamp out air hijacking altogether. For a Warsaw Pact–NATO agreement to deny sanctuary to all hijackers and to suspend air links to those countries that did so would surely be sufficient to bring other states into line. Angry though they might be, Libya, South Yemen, Iraq, and Algeria could not for long afford to be isolated from communication with both parts of the world establishment. As Bismarck put it: "When the eagles agree, the sparrows must be silent." For the Soviets, there might of course be the difficulty that these Arab states might afterwards prove less friendly to Moscow with regard to other matters. And for the West, too, there would be a problem of convincing the public that traditional rights of asylum for refugees from Communism should be overridden. The West Germans, for example, at the very time of their trauma culminating at Mogadishu, granted sanctuary to a Czech hijacker—though he must expect to serve a prison sentence. Against the charge of hypocrisy, the West Germans can offer the defense that the Czech only sought his own freedom and made no demands on Prague. Nevertheless, he had brandished a weapon on board a civil airliner and must have carried conviction with the pilot that he might use it. To that extent, therefore, he was guilty of engaging in substate violence and in putting the lives of innocent passengers at some risk. On balance, therefore, liberal states could find an adequate ethical justification for agreeing to a comprehensive antihijacking pact. But a more important if probably less publicized justification would be that it would draw the Soviets along the path of helping to defend "civilization" at the expense of "revolutionary purity." In effect, this would help to confine most substate violence to the Third World. This would no doubt be hard on the Third World, but it would surely be both a Western and a Soviet interest in a divided world where the phenomenon cannot in practice be abolished. In the longer run it would also help to prepare the Soviets for the possible need for more far-reaching cooperation to deal with non-state-sponsored terrorist groups if these should, contrary to present indications, become so numerous and so well equipped that they would threaten the survival of normal urban life throughout the advanced world. For in those circumstances the Soviets and the West would have much in common. Vast as the ideological differences between Leninism and Western democracy are, they have been able to coexist uneasily for several decades, whereas it is doubtful whether either ideology could long coexist with vast numbers of half-crazed groups of wholly independent substate actors possessing means of mass destruction. Remote as such a world now seems, it is not demonstrably impossible. Thus Moscow and Washington may meanwhile find it prudent to take some preliminary steps to consider how to cooperate if it ever should arise.

Conclusion

We may tentatively advance these main propositions for the medium-term future.

1. Terrorism in general is likely to grow but in a somewhat uneven fashion.

2. Some countries will continue to be much less vulnerable than others even within ideological systems and the former are therefore less likely than the latter to respond to any incident with an eye to the long-term consequences.

3. Some sovereign states will continue to sponsor terrorist groups, but there are probably limits beyond which such states will find it prudent to not allow their friends to go. Hence, sponsorship may increasingly be seen in dramatic form only in the Third World arena.

4. State-sponsored terrorists are similarly likely to be discouraged from obtaining weapons of mass destruction and unsponsored groups may not be able to obtain them in the foreseeable future even if they should desire them.

5. The scope for universally accepted international agreements among governments is severely limited, but ad hoc deals to deal with particular aspects such as air hijacking may be attainable.

It is obviously more hazardous to make forecasts about the more distant future—say, beyond the turn of the century—when even small groups may have little difficulty in obtaining weapons of mass destruction. Brian Jenkins has asked:

> If governments cannot protect their citizens, as terrorists seem to be demonstrating, will governments as we know them become obsolete? The historical growth of national governments in the first place depended in part on national leadership, often a monarch, being able to monopolize the means of organized violence. If the military-power relationships are altered drastically in favor of small groups that obey no government, will we enter an era of international warlordism in which the people of the world and their governments are subjected to the extortion demands of many small groups?[12]

In short, are we at the beginning of the end of the sovereign national state, which until recently was thought to be threatened, if at all, not by substate warlords but by Hitler and/or Stalin seeking global hegemony or by the voluntary adoption of regional supranationalism perhaps leading eventually to world government? There is clearly a finite chance that Jenkins's vision will one day come about. We may indeed enter a new Dark Age. But so far this seems to be an extremely remote possibility. This is not to say that terrorism will fade away. On the contrary, we have adduced many factors that favor its gradual increase within certain limits. For our time, then, this phenomenon seems unlikely to bring about the end of civilized life as most of us living in urban centers know it, but to be set for a long run as international theater largely played out with ever greater ingenuity and sophistication on the television screens of a watching world.

Notes

1. See John Dugard, "International Terrorism: Problems of Definition," *International Affairs* 50 (1954):67-81.

2. I. F. Clarke, *Voices Prophesying War, 1963-1984* (London, 1966).

3. See, for example, Roberta Wohlstetter, "Terror on a Grand Scale," *Survival* 18 (1976):98-104; Paul Wilkinson, *Terrorism and the Liberal State* (London, 1977), p. 203; Mason Willrich and Theodore B. Taylor, *Nuclear Theft: Risks and Safeguards* (Cambridge, Mass., 1974); J. Bowyer Bell, "Proliferation: Sophisticated Weapons and Revolutionary Options—The Sub-State Perspective," in David Carlton and Carlo Schaerf (eds.), *Arms Control and Technological Innovation* (London and New York), pp. 157-58; M. C. Hutchinson, "Defining Future Threats: Terrorists and Nuclear Proliferation," in Yonah Alexander and Maxwell Finger (eds.), *Terrorism: Interdisciplinary Perspectives* (New York, 1977); and B. G. Blair and G. D. Brewer, "The Terrorist Threat to World Nuclear Programs," *Journal of Conflict Resolution* 21 (1977):379-403.

4. Bertil Häggman, "Slaves That Threaten the Masters?" *Security World,* May 1977.

5. Walter Laqueur, *Terrorism* (London, 1977), pp. 46-47.

6. See, for example, Jillian Becker, *Hitler's Children* (London, 1977).

7. *Spectator,* 7 January 1978.

8. Bernard Feld, quoted in Laqueur, op. cit., p. 227.

9. Bennet Kovrig, "Mediation by Obfuscation: The Resolution of

the Marseilles Crisis, October 1934 to May 1935," *Historical Journal* 19 (1976):191-221.

10. See Dugard, loc. cit.; and Fereydoun Hoveyda, "The Problem of International Terrorism at the United Nations," *Terrorism: An International Journal* 1 (1977-78):71-83.

11. Steven J. Rosen and Robert Frank, "Measures against International Terrorism," in David Carlton and Carlo Schaerf (eds.), *International Terrorism and World Security* (London and New York, 1975), p. 61.

12. Brian M. Jenkins, "International Terrorism: A New Mode of Conflict," in ibid; p. 34.

10
Coping with Terrorism: What Is To Be Done?

Robert A. Friedlander

> There was no pause, no pity, no interval of relenting rest. . . .
> In the universal fear and distrust that darkened the time,
> all the usual harmless ways of life were changed.
> —Charles Dickens, *A Tale of Two Cities*

"Terrorism is like the weather—everyone talks about it, but no one ever does anything to change it." This remark, made by a conference participant clearly illustrates the difficulties associated with the terrorist dilemma. According to almost every expert at the conference, and indeed elsewhere,[1] terrorist violence is rapidly escalating on a global scale. The warning of West German President Walter Scheel may well provide the epitaph of democratic pluralism: "Unless this [terrorist] flame is stamped out in time, it will spread like a brush fire all over the world."[2]

The tocsin has likewise been rung by UN Secretary General Kurt Waldheim:

> The world community is now required to deal with unprecedented problems arising from acts of international terrorism . . . which raise many issues of a humanitarian, moral, legal and political character for which, at the present time, no commonly agreed rules or solutions exist.[3]

Waldheim's dilemma stems directly from confusion over the nature

This article is adapted from a speech delivered at Michigan State University under the auspices of the Institute of Comparative and Area Studies and the Department of Criminal Justice of the School of Social Sciences, October 28, 1977. The author wishes to express his appreciation to Dr. Baljit Singh, assistant dean, College of Social Sciences, and to Dr. Iwao Ishino, director, Center for International Programs, Michigan State University.

of the terrorist challenge. To some it is a political issue; for others it is a moral question. A third view sees psychological disturbance as the root cause. But for lawyers, terrorist-violence must be deemed a violation of the rule of law. The issue then inevitably becomes: Whose rules and which laws?

Political and historical philosopher Hannah Arendt has written, "[w]here violence rules absolutely . . . everything and everybody must fall silent."[4] To my embarrassment and, I hope, that of my professional colleagues, the American Bar Association has been almost totally silent.[5] I personally subscribe to the philosophy that terrorist harm affects, in a real sense, all humankind.[6] Moreover, the Anglo-American common law tradition, which holds that under no circumstances can an innocent life be deliberately taken for any reason, conforms to the basic human rights concepts and principles that have become part of public international law since the end of World War II.[7]

What then, is to be done about the seemingly limitless acts of transnational mugging, as international terrorism can rightly be called? At what point will governments, national leaders, and societies subject to repeated political violence finally decide to take action and to develop protective measures? Is it impossible, within the context of the law, to deal with a fundamentally lawless situation? Is it true, as Roger Fisher maintains, that law—whether national or international—is an orderly way of dealing with disorder?[8]

Although applied more in the breach than in the practice, the traditional legal principle *aut dedere aut punire* ("extradite or prosecute") was originally meant to be applied to those offenders who, by the very nature of their offenses, are engaged in common crimes rather than in political protest.[9] My own feeling is there can be no difference between terrorism and common criminality, and that any exculpatory or conciliatory approach undermines the very existence of world public order.[10] When confronted with disrupters of the operative ruling system, Lewis Carroll's Queen of Hearts invariably cried, "Off with their heads!" Perhaps it is also time to terrorize the terrorizers. Action at Entebbe and Mogadishu, along with Syria's public hangings of terrorist guerrillas, was intended to achieve a similar purpose.[11]

At the very least, as with war criminals, terrorists should be declared outlaws before all the world and labeled *hostis generis humani* ("enemies of humanity"), analogous to pirates in public international law.[12] Why not figuratively brand them with the mark of Cain, so that none of humankind will want to share the earth with those who have perpetrated such monstrous acts?[13] As Alona Evans has pointedly observed, "[w]hen the price of crime becomes too high, the practitioners find something else to do."[14]

The proposal of an International Criminal Court, a favorite cause of many legal scholars and publicists, is at the present time a worthy ideal but a dubious prospect.[15] Why not provide an International Criminal Code to go along with an International Criminal Court?[16] Let the nations of the world promulgate precise, definite, binding statutes that would identify and penalize terrorist activities of all types and would make extradition compulsory if the host country refused to try the expatriate offender. As with war criminals of the past, alternative jurisdiction should be given to an International Criminal Court with jurists chosen not by their own governments, but by a nominating panel of international legal experts who would have a freedom of choice independent of their countries' national policies. A truly independent international court could serve as a global symbol for the rule of law.[17] Attorney Chester L. Smith's proposal for an international prison to confine convicted terrorists also merits thoughtful consideration.[18]

It is *not* enough to sign multilateral conventions if the signatory states are not willing to enforce their provisions (for example, Japan and Algeria in relation to the Japanese Red Army). It is *not* enough to proclaim that there can be no compromise with terrorist demands unless force is met with force (for example, Israel and West Germany at Entebbe and Mogadishu). What is needed is a combination of determined national policy, bold legislation (both foreign and domestic), and a *will* to enforce.

Suppose, for example, that an international convention incorporated Articles I and III of the Nuremberg Principles proposed by the International Law Commission in 1950.[19] Heads of state or government officials who perpetrate criminal acts would not escape international legal responsibility. Thus, if heads of state or government officials have committed an act that constitutes a crime under international law, they would be deemed criminally liable and therefore subject to punishment. Why not hold heads of state and all governmental officials to be accessories before and after the fact, if they help plan or assist in any terrorist act?[20] Jurisdiction over officials should be given to an international criminal court, or, alternatively, should be made universal, as it has been for pirates and war criminals.[21] Would such terrorist promoters as President Muammar el-Qaddafi of Libya and General Idi Amin Dada of Uganda then be willing to continue their reckless violations of international human rights?

Who would have thought a decade ago that all travelers on commercial airlines in the United States would be subjected to electronic or manual luggage inspection and to an electronic or physical body search? In some airports (such as Washington National and Miami International), individuals without purchased airline tickets can no longer greet incoming planes at arrival gates or escort companions to departure gates. Yet, only very few have raised any serious objections, and the courts have consistently upheld the right of airports and airlines to implement restrictive security measures against potential terrorist violence.[22]

The cost of countermeasures directed against terrorist activities is high, both materially and politically. It is far more expensive to defend against terrorist attack than it is to commit a terrorist act or support terrorist groups.[23] The hard fact and cold reality is that terrorism can never be eliminated, but it can be restrained and, perhaps, restrained effectively. Addressing the Palm Beach Roundtable in March 1976, FBI Director Clarence Kelley argued, "[i]f we are to have any degree of success in solving the cases now confronting us in terrorism . . . we must have all the tools available to us, including electronic surveillance."[24] Part of the cost of protecting the public against terrorist violence is the reduction of individual rights in a free society. The more effective the restraints, the greater the diminution of civil liberties.

At what point in a democratic society does the general welfare take precedence over citizens' rights? Arguing in favor of capital punishment, psychologist Ernest van den Haag asserts that more innocent lives are saved than lost when severe penalties are imposed for criminal acts, and thereby society gains, despite an occasional miscarriage of justice.[25] A. L. Goodhart similarly raises the specter of a greater social harm created by allowing ten guilty men to go free, rather than the lesser suffering of one innocent man wrongly convicted.[26] Supreme Court Justice Byron White warns, "[d]ue process does not require that every conceivable step be taken, at whatever cost, to eliminate the possibility of convicting an innocent person."[27] The analogy should be clear. If the state truly wishes to protect itself from the threat and destruction of terrorist violence, then social order must be strengthened at the expense of individual freedom. Philosopher Burton Leiser sees a strong justification in the death penalty, when applied to terrorists, for both its deterrent and its prophylactic community values.[28]

In a nondemocratic society, the temptation to meet violence with violence is often too great to resist. The Argentinian president, General Jorge Videla, distinguished himself by presiding over a short antiguerrilla military campaign in which no prisoners were taken. The Tucuman terrorist violence was effectively throttled by the Argentine army; in contrast, more than two thousand political murders were committed by the Montoneros and their opponents during the regime of Maria Estela Peron, and the police were almost totally helpless.[29] The Iranian army has summarily executed several hundred terrorist guerrillas.[30] After a decade of bloody and uncontrolled violence, the Uruguayan government crushed the Tupamaro rebellion. The price of success in restoring internal order has been the suspension of civil liberties and the end of Uruguayan democracy.[31]

According to the chief observer of the PLO at the United Nations, "[v]iolence is an essential part of a liberation movement."[32] The UN has steadfastly refused to condemn terrorism committed in the name of national liberation movements or even aggression directed against "colonial and racist regimes."[33] Such woolly-headed thinking has given rise to the oft-repeated cliche that one person's terrorist is another's national hero.[34] The implications for the international community are, I believe, severe. Political offense exceptions granted to the perpetrators of common criminality[35] may quite possibly result in dehumanizing the human rights guarantees established in international law since 1945 and recriminalizing the international state system despite the well-settled condemnation of crimes against humanity.

An exception to the political offense exception must be invoked to distinguish between revolutionary activity and common criminality. The test must also evaluate the harm inflicted upon innocent third parties and weigh the ideological motivation behind the act. On November 10, 1976, the nineteen-member Council of Europe unanimously adopted (subject to ratification) an antiterrorist convention. Its key provision essentially criminalizes politically motivated terrorism.[36] The ideological offender who slaughters ordinary citizens cannot be exculpated in any world societal structure, let alone sanctioned by an international organization that claims to be based upon the rule of law. Despite Third World pressures, self-determination must not be accepted as a license to kill.[37]

I personally favor the Single Convention proposed by Evans that would prohibit any acts of violence of an international character and would also contain specific punitive sanctions aimed at countries providing refuge for terrorist offenders.[38] (I likewise support a sanctions convention to deal exclusively with penalties for individual offenders and state parties.[39]) The proposal of the International Federation of Airline Pilots Association (IFALPA) to suspend all commercial air service to any state granting safe haven to skyjackers, disregarding any political motives, would be an effective deterrent at minimal cost with maximum effect.[40] It would serve notice on members of the world community that sheltering skyjackers is a tortious act, the remedy for which is a universally applied, collectively enforced economic sanction. Both the American and Canadian governments proposed a treaty to that effect in 1972.[41]

U.S. Senate Resolution 524, approved on September 17, 1976, urges the president and the secretary of transportation to apply such sanctions unilaterally to any future transgressors.[42] The Omnibus Anti-Terrorism Act, introduced by Senator Abraham A. Ribicoff and eight other senatorial cosponsors on October 25, 1977, calls for broad powers to be given both the president and the Congress for the purpose of restricting trade and travel with any country that has aided and abetted terrorist activity. (Parts of the bill relating to search and seizure of freight and mail from the offending country are at present of doubtful constitutionality.[43]) More effective and more realistic than an international criminal court would be a permanent international hijacking tribunal to try all illegal acts relating to interference with air transport.[44]

I strongly support the suggestion of Jordan Paust[45] to change the definition of "international protected persons" as specified in the Convention on the Prevention and Punishment of Crime Against Internationally Protected Persons, Including Diplomatic Agents[46] to include civilian populations rather than diplomats, heads of state, or other government personnel. An attack upon a public official can be dealt with under existing municipal enforcement procedures. International law should concentrate on protecting innocent parties rather than shielding public servants. There is no reason whatever not to designate children as an internationally protected class. If the world cannot protect its children, then the international legal system is a hollow vessel devoid of substance and of meaning.

Without publicity, terrorism becomes a weapon of the impotent. In a free society, the people's right to know and to be informed is essential to the survival of free institutions. In our contemporary world, however, democracy has come under siege, and terrorist violence is on the rise in democratic states.[47] Terrorism is quintessentially a *coup de théâtre*, which requires an impressionable audience for its dramatic impact. The communications media, whether consciously or otherwise, has well served the terrorist cause. Political terrorism is now viewed as an instant means of communication and is aided and abetted by contemporary technology, utilizing the dramatic force of the mass media.[48] Is self-restraint desirable or is strict government regulation inevitable? The basic issue, in the words of television critic Harry Waters, "is whether commercial television— after twenty-five years of scientific data linking video violence with anti-social behavior—will ever accept the fact that it can be a deadly potent carrier."[49]

Anglo-American law deals not with the possible but with the occurrence. In all rights-centered systems, as well as those affording minimal guarantees against the arbitrary exercise of governmental power, there are practical limits placed upon protective enforcement. A free society is always going to be at a disadvantage in combatting political violence. Unanimity in the world community is almost impossible to achieve.[50] Yet public opinion, whether national or international, can become an influential weapon in its own right. When the Japanese Red Army terrorists recently sought safe haven in their commandeered aircraft, out of several previously friendly regimes, only Algeria volunteered sanctuary.[51] Even Libya has temporarily withdrawn the skyjack welcome mat. And the UN debate on skyjacking, taken up by the General Assembly Political Committee, was a direct result of pressure in the form of a threatened global strike by the International Federation of Airline Pilots Association.[52]

Publicity can be turned against the terrorists instead of working for them. Alan Dershowitz has correctly stressed the need for moral outrage as an effective antidote to terrorism's psychological threat.[53] In the words of General Yehoshafat Harkabi, former chief of Israeli Military Intelligence, "[w]e need to downgrade terrorism on the intellectual level, on the popular level. . . . The first line of defense is in the minds of men."[54]

Given the tumultuous history of 1977, no one can deny that terrorist violence is on the increase throughout the globe. To say one thing and to do another, such as the narrow, exclusivist American approach to extradition,[55] merely increases the contempt for the rule of law that terrorism so dramatically demonstrates. The road to political violence and to international conflict has often been paved with good intentions. We must realize that terrorism is war and combatting terrorism is also war.[56] In the prophetic words of Nobel laureate Albert Camus, "on both sides, a reign of terror, as long as it lasts, changes the scale of values."[57] Hard choices have to be made, and none of us might again ever be the same. The still-unanswered question is, Are we willing to take that chance?

A special State Department Conference on International Terrorism was attended by two hundred government officials, lawyers, academics, businessmen, and security experts who could only agree to disagree. The participants were even uncertain about the nature of the threat, let alone its extent.[58] To establish any kind of priorities whatsoever, there first must be agreement on the matters for which the priorities are being established. As long as the world community continues to be divided over the issue of whether governmental or individual terrorism is the greater menace to the peace and security of humankind, there can be no meaningful international (as opposed to multinational) collaboration.[59]

The United States is correct to emphasize the individual threat.[60] National or state terror can be dealt with by invoking the doctrine of State Responsibility (being debated throughout this decade by the UN General Assembly's Sixth, or Legal, Committee), plus the principles and remedies set out in the Universal Declaration of Human Rights,[61] the Genocide Convention,[62] the International Covenant on Civil and Political Rights (which has just entered into force),[63] as well as the basic norms in the UN Charter itself. Time is of the essence. A bilateral approach is preferable to none at all; multilateral agreements can be built upon bilateral foundations; and regional enforcement may be more effective than universal declarations.

The manifold varieties of terrorism have created a plethora of scholarly classifications and analyses. Profiles have been developed, data banks have been created, and scenarios are repeatedly played out. There is more agreement on basics than is generally supposed, but, in the end, emphasis has been placed upon particular analytical theories rather than upon an evaluative consensus.[64] The problem of the typological approach to terrorism is, in the words of Chalmers Johnson, the problem of developing "a model of the social system that synthesizes the coercion theory and the value theory of social integration."[65] The time has come to go beyond the data bank approach and to put together a modality capable of monitoring, collating, and synthesizing the existing bodies of theories and analyses.

If the primary function of the law is to deal with problems in an orderly fashion, as Roger Fisher asserts,[66] then the international legal system is not yet doing its job. And several contemporary commentators have even inferred that international law is *unable* to deal with the nature of the problem.[67] Without the proper enforcement procedures, strongly worded statutes are not much help. The old common law adage that a law badly enforced is worse than no law at all still holds true.

The challenge of terrorism is fundamentally a challenge of the will.

If there is to be a test of strength between those who initiate terrorist violence and those who oppose it, then that challenge can only be met by the exercise of power which, in turn, is derived from a legal-political structure designed for regulation and not for reformation.

The debate over whether it is really possible to give a civilized response to an uncivilized act has yet to be resolved.[68] The issue is one of global survival, and its outcome affects us all.[69]

Notes

1. Cf. Johnson, "Perspectives on Terrorism," Summary Report of Conference on International Terrorism, Department of State, Washington, D.C., March 25-26, 1976; Central Intelligence Agency, *International Terrorism in 1976* (July 1977), herinafter cited as CIA Report, 1976; Mickolus, "Statistical Approaches to the Study of Terrorism," in *Terrorism: Interdisciplinary Perspectives* 212 (Y. Alexander and S. Finger, eds. 1977); Jenkins, "International Terrorism: A New Mode of Conflict," in *International Terrorism and World Security* 28-33 (D. Carlton and C. Schaerf eds. 1975).

2. *New York Times*, October 26, 1977, at 16A, col. 5.

3. Statement of July 9, 1976, made before the UN Security Council and reprinted in the *Wall Street Journal*, July 29, 1976, at 10, col. 4. See also Waldheim's strong remarks given at his press conference of October 19, 1977, wherein the secretary general reaffirmed his belief over "how right it was to draw the attention of the international community to this terrible phenomenon of our time." 14 UN *Chronicle* 13, 14 (November 1977).

4. H. Arendt, *On Revolution* 9 (1965).

5. See Friedlander, "Terrorism: What's Behind Our Passive Acceptance of Transnational Mugging?" 2 *Barrister* 11, 13 (Summer 1975). During the 1976 American Bar Association annual meeting in Atlanta, Georgia, the House of Delegates rejected a proposal by the section on international law to support a convention creating an international criminal court which would have jurisdiction over transnational terrorist crimes. Press Release, American Bar Association, n.d., at 5. The ABA recently reversed its position, with minimum publicity, and as of February 1978 favors a U.S. initiative to create an international criminal court for terrorists and hijackers when the number of victims exceeds five. 64 *A.B.A. J.* 323 (1978).

6. See the admonition of E. Cahn, *The Moral Decision* 71 (1955).

7. Paust, "A Survey of Possible Legal Responses to International Terrorism: Prevention, Punishment, and Cooperative Action," 5 *Ga.*

J. Int'l & Comp. L. 431, 462-469 (1975).

8. Fisher, comment, "Enhancing Order (and Law) in Future International Crises," 70 *Proc. Am. Soc. Int'l L.* 123, 135 (1976).

9. Schultz, "The General Framework of Extradition and Asylum," in 2 *A Treatise on International Criminal Law: Jurisdiction and Cooperation* 309-311 (M. C. Bassiouni and V. Nanda eds. 1973); M. C. Bassiouni, *International Extradition and World Public Order* 6-9 (1974); Costello, "International Terrorism and the Development of the Principle *Aut Dedere Aut Judicare*," 10 *J. Int'l L. & Econ.* 483 (1975); Schultz, "Les Problèmes actuels de l'extradition," 45 *Revue International de Droit Penal* 499, 501 (1974).

10. Cf. Friedlander, "Terrorism and Political Violence: Do the Ends Justify the Means?" 24 *Chitty's L. J.* 240 (1974); Friedlander, *supra* note 5.

11. For the Syrian hangings, see *New York Times,* September 28, 1976, at 1A, col. 4. Historian Walter Laqueur claims, "no West European, North American, Japanese or Middle Eastern terrorist of the 1960's or 1970's has been executed." W. Laqueur, *Terrorism* 131 (1977). His information is incorrect. Not only were Arab terrorists executed on two occasions in Syria, but five Basque terrorists were garroted in Spain in September 1975. See *New York Times,* September 27, 1975, at 1A, col. 6.

12. Cf. Leiser, "Terrorism, Guerrilla Warfare, and International Morality," 12 *Stan. J. Int'l Stud.* 39, 59-60 (1977); C. Emanuelli, *Les Moyens de Prévention et de Sanction en Cas D'Action Illicite Contre L'Aviation Civile Internationale* 76-83 (1974); Rubin, "International Terrorism and International Law," in Alexander and Finger, *supra* note 1, at 122-123. Former Secretary of State Henry Kissinger ultimately came to this conclusion before he left office. See his address before the American Bar Association annual meeting in Montreal, Canada, on August 11, 1975. H. Kissinger, *American Foreign Policy* 232 (3rd ed. 1977).

13. This suggestion was originally put forward by Hannah Arendt in a discussion of the fate of Adolf Eichmann. H. Arendt, *Eichmann in Jerusalem: A Report on the Banality of Evil* 278-279 (1965).

14. Evans, remarks at panel entitled "Approaches to the Problem of International Terrorism," Sixth Conference on the Law of the World, Washington, D.C., October 13, 1975.

15. Draft Statute for an International Criminal Court, 9 UN GAOR, Supp. No. 12, UN Doc. A/2645 (1973). See, particularly, the interesting exchange between Professors Gross, Murphy, Paust, Woetzel, Lador-Lederer, and Ciobanu, in 67 *Am. J. Int'l L.* at 508-511

(1973); 68, id. (1974), at 306-308, 502-503, 717-719; and 69 id. (1975) at 138-140.

16. Johnson, "Problems in the Enforcement of World Criminal Law," 8 *Aust. & N. Z. J. Crim.* 87, 96-98. Professor M. C. Bassiouni, secretary general of the International Association of Penal Law, has recently assembled a group of international legal scholars to draft a model international criminal code.

17. See the stimulating recommendations put forth by E. Deutsch, *An International Rule of Law* (1978).

18. Smith, "The Probable Necessity of an International Prison in Solving Aircraft Hijacking," 5 *Int'l Law* 269 (1971).

19. 5 UN GAOR, Supp. No. 12, UN Doc. A/1316 (1950).

20. Cf. Kutner, "Constructive Notice: A Proposal to End International Terrorism," 19 *N.Y. L. Forum* 325, 341-343 (1973); Lillich and Paxman, "State Responsibility for Injuries to Aliens Occasioned by Terrorist Activities," 26 *Am. U. L. Rev.* 217, 307n., 308-309 (1977).

21. Harvard Law School, *Research in International Law* 743-1013 (1932); 2 G. Schwarzenberger, *International Law as Applied by International Courts and Tribunals: The Law of Armed Conflict* 541-544 (1968).

22. See United States v. Lopez, 328 F. Supp. 1077 (1971); Brodsky, "Terry and the Pirates: Constitutionality of Airport Searches and Seizures," 62 *Ky. L. J.* 623 (1974); Gora, "The Fourth Amendment at the Airport: Arriving, Departing, or Cancelled," 18 *Vill. L. Rev.* 1036 (1973); Y. Kamisar, W. Lafave, and J. Israel, *Basic Criminal Procedure* 411-415 (4th ed. 1974).

23. R. Clutterbuck, *Protest and the Urban Guerrilla* (1974); A. Burton, *Urban Terrorism: Theory, Practice and Response* (1975) B. Crozier, *A Theory of Conflict* (1974); J. B. Bell, *Transnational Terror* (1975); and especially the studies in National Advisory Committee on Criminal Justice Standards and Goals, *Report of the Task Force on Disorders and Terrorism* (1976), hereinafter cited as Terrorism Report.

24. *Fort Lauderdale News*, March 22, 1976, at 3A, col. 2. See also *Electronic Surveillance Within the United States for Foreign Intelligence Purposes: Hearings on S. 3197* before the Subcommittee on Intelligence and the Rights of Americans of the Senate Committee on Intelligence, 94th Cong., 2d sess. (1976), hereinafter cited as Electronic Surveillance Hearings.

25. E. van den Haag, *Punishing Criminals* 39-41 (1975).

26. Goodhart, "Possession of Drugs and Absolute Liability," 84 *Law Q.* 382, 385-386 (1968).

27. Patterson v. New York, 45 *L. W.* 4708, 4711 (1977). Surprisingly, Mr. Justice Holmes expressed similar sentiments in 1904 when he made the observation "[a]t the present time in this country there is more danger that criminals will escape justice than that they will be subjected to tyranny." Kepner v. United States, 195 U.S. 100, 134 (1904) (Holmes, J., dissenting).

28. Leiser, "In Defense of Capital Punishment," 1 *Barrister* 10 (Fall 1974).

29. Amnesty International, *Report of an Amnesty International Mission to Argentina, 1-15 November 1976* (1977); *Washington Post*, March 25, 1976, at 21A, cols. 1-7; *New York Times*, November 14, 1976, at 4L, col. 1; Mort Rosenblum, "Terror in Argentina," *The New York Review of Books*, October 28, 1976, at 26-29.

30. Reza Baraheni, "Terror in Iran," id. at 21-25; Amnesty International, *Report on Torture* 227-229 (1975).

31. M. Weinstein, *Uruguay: The Politics of Failure* 120-139 (1975); E. Halperin, *Terrorism in Latin America* 37-46 (1976); F. Watson, *Political Terrorism: The Threat and the Response* 38-53 (1976); *Political Terrorism* 151-163 (L. Sobel ed. 1975).

32. Kirk, "PLO's Mild-Mannered Aggressor" (interview with Zehdi Labib Terzi), *Chicago Tribune*, April 4, 1976, Sec. 2, at 2, col. 4.

33. Cf. Measures to Prevent International Terrorism Which Endangers or Takes Innocent Human Lives or Jeopardizes Fundamental Freedoms, and Study of the Underlying Cause of Those Forms of Terrorism and Acts of Violence Which Lie in Misery, Frustration, Grievance and Despair, and Which Causes Some People to Sacrifice Human Lives, Including Their Own, in an Attempt to Effect Radical Changes, G.A. Res. 3034, 27 UN GAOR Supp. No. 30, UN Doc. A/8730 (1972); and resolution of the same title, G.A. Res. 31/102, 31 UN GAOR, UN Doc. A/31/429 (1976). The United States voted against both resolutions.

34. This phrase was repeatedly used by the participants at the conference entitled "Perspectives on Terrorism," held under the auspices of the International Institute of Higher Studies in Criminal Sciences, Syracuse, Italy, December 2-11, 1976. See *Fort Lauderdale News and Sun Sentinel*, December 18, 1977, at 1, col. 2. Cf. also Pierre, "The Politics of International Terrorism," 19 *ORBIS* 1251, 1254 (1976); Statement by John E. Karkashian, acting director, Office for Combatting Terrorism, made before the Subcommittee on Foreign Assistance, Senate Committee on Foreign Relations, Department of State, Bureau of Public Affairs, September 14, 1977, at 1. On the role of the revolutionary political criminal as hero, see E. Becker, *Escape from Evil* 146-168 (1975); S. Schafer, *The Political Criminal: The*

Problem of Morality and Crime 6-7 (1974); and E. Leach, *Custom Law and Terrorist Violence* (1977).

35. Deere, "Political Offenses in the Law and Practice of Extradition," 27 *Am. J. Int'l L.* 247, 250-251 (1933); Bassiouni, supra note 9, at 370-375.

36. European Convention on the Suppression of Terrorism, 15 *Int'l Legal Materials* 1272 (1976). Ireland and Malta later refused to sign.

37. Friedlander, "Self-Determination: A Legal-Political Inquiry," 1 *Det. Coll. L. Rev.* 71 (1975); G. Schwarzenberger, *International Law and Order* 219-234, 236 (1971).

38. Evans, supra note 14.

39. It must be recognized, of course, that the imposition of sanctions against an offending state party carries with it the possibility of a forceful countermeasure. In the words of Lord Lloyd of Hampstead, "the effect of applying sanctions, even on a limited scale . . . might in fact provoke the holocaust of war rather than preserving peace and order in the international community." Lloyd of Hampstead, *Introduction to Jurisprudence* 288 (3rd ed. 1972). But, see also, J. Starke, *Introduction to International Law* 32-34 (8th ed. 1977), for a contra view.

40. *New York Times*, November 2, 1977, at 8A, col. 2; id., November 4, 1977, at 3A, col. 1.

41. Their primary motivation came from a threatened global air strike by IFALPA in June 1972, and pilots of eighteen airlines (though not those of the United States, due to a court order) actually did participate in a work stoppage. This pressure, however, proved unavailing. See 68 *State Dep't Bull.* 1, 3 (January 1973); Bell, "The U.S. Response to Terrorism Against Civil Aviation," 19 *ORBIS* 1326, 1334-1335 (1976).

42. S. Res. 524, 94th Cong., 2d. sess., September 17, 1976.

43. S. Res. 2234, 94th Cong., 1st sess., October 25, 1977. I am indebted to Senator Ribicoff for providing me with a copy of the act.

44. The idea appears to have originated with UN Secretary General U Thant in a little-noticed passage of his speech commemorating the United Nations' twenty-fifth anniversary on September 14, 1970. See 8 *Public Papers of the Secretaries-General of the United Nations,* 1968-1971, at 472 (A. Cordier and M. Harrelson eds. 1977).

45. Paust, comment at Department of State Conference on International Terrorism, Washington, D.C., February 25, 1976.

46. Convention on the Prevention and Punishment of Crimes Against Internationally Protected Persons, Including Diplomatic

Agents, G.A. Res. 3166, 28 UN GAOR, Supp. No. 30, UN Doc. A/9030 (1973). The most extensive commentary on that convention is L. Bloomfield and G. Fitzgerald, *Crimes Against Internationally Protected Persons: Prevention and Punishment* (1975). As of this writing, the convention is two ratifications shy of entering into force.

47. CIA Report, supra note 1; Mickolus, supra note 1; Central Intelligence Agency Research Study, *International and Transnational Terrorism: Diagnosis and Prognosis* (April 1976). Between 1968 and 1975, American citizens and property had been the target in at least one-third of all transnational terrorist activities. Id. at 12. See also Cooper, "The International Experience with Terrorism: An Overview," Terrorism Report, supra note 23, at 419-442.

48. Cooper, "Terrorism and the Media," 24 *Chitty's L. J.* 226 (1976); Hickey, "Terrorism and Television," 24 *TV Guide* 2 (July 1976); F. Hacker, *Crusaders, Criminals, Crazies: Terror and Terrorism in our Time* xi, 161-162, 291-292, and 317 (1977).

49. Waters, "Gomorrah Revisited," *Newsweek*, April 5, 1976, at 61.

50. Cf. Kittrie, comment at panel entitled "Terrorism and Political Crimes in International Law," 67 *Proc. Am. Soc. Int'l L.* 87, 106 (1973); Murphy, "Professor Gross's Comments on International Terrorism and International Criminal Jurisdiction," 68 *Am. J. Int'l L.* 306, 308 (1974). However, for a contra position, see Whiteman, "*Jus Cogens* in International Law, with a Projected List," 7 *Ga. J. Int'l & Comp. L.* 609, 625 (1977), who considers piracy and political terrorism "to be outlawed by world consensus under international law (*jus cogens*)."

51. *Newsweek*, October 10, 1977, at 48; *Chicago Sun Times*, October 5, 1977, at 14, col. 1.

52. *New York Times*, November 2, 1977, at 8A, col. 2; id., November 4, 1977, at 3A, col. 1.

53. Dershowitz, "Legal and Jurisprudential Aspects of Terrorism," paper delivered at panel entitled "Terrorism: International and Comparative Perspectives," Association of American Law Schools, annual meeting, Washington, D.C., December 29, 1975.

54. Harkabi, comment at state department conference, supra note 45.

55. Bassiouni, supra note 9, at 25-45.

56. The eighteenth-century Scottish philosopher of rationalism, David Hume, foresaw the nature of the contemporary challenge: "were a civilized nation engaged with barbarians, who observed no rules even of war, the former must also suspend their observance of them . . ." *Hume Selections* 208 (C. Hendel, Jr. ed. 1955). The tough-minded (on crime and punishment) German *philosophe*, Immanuel

Kant, identified three models of world history, one of them being moral terrorism. F. Manuel, *Shapes of Philosophical History* 87 (1965). There is always a danger of overreacting to the terrorist menace, as demonstrated in the fatuous statement found in a best-selling historical study of terrorism: "By 1972 the reaction against terror and chaos manifested itself in the alarm of . . . the so-called silent majority, which then went to the polls to vote overwhelmingly for Nixon's second term in the White House [!]." A. Parry, *Terrorism: From Robespierre to Arafat* 341 (1977).

57. A. Camus, *Resistance, Rebellion, and Death* 113 (J. O'Brien trans. 1974).

58. Johnson, supra note 1.

59. Friedlander, "Terrorism and International Law: What Is Being Done?" 8 *Rut. Cam. L. J.* 383, 388-392 (1977).

60. UN Doc. A/C.6/L850 (1972). For an analysis of the American position, cf. Franck and Lockwood, "Preliminary Thoughts Towards an International Convention on Terrorism," 68 *Am. J. Int'l L.* 69, 76-87 (1974); Comment, "Terrorism: A Step Towards International Control," 14 *Harv. Int'l L. J.* 585 (1973).

61. G.A. Res. 217A, 3 UN GAOR, UN Doc. A/810 (1948).

62. G.A. Res. 260A, 3 UN GAOR, UN Doc. A/810 (1948).

63. G.A. Res. 2200, 21 UN GAOR Supp. No. 16, 49 UN Doc. A/6316 (1966).

64. Miller, "On Terrorism," *Pub. Admin. Rev.* 429, 432-433 (July/August 1977).

65. C. Johnson, *Revolutionary Change* 39 (1966).

66. Fisher, supra note 8, at 135.

67. Cf. Parry, supra note 56, at 548-552; Hacker, supra note 48, at 313-316, 340. Letter from David Martin, editor of *Student Lawyer*, to author, March 3, 1977, claims that international law "isn't set up to deal with terrorist activities."

68. See the remarks of former Senator Walter Mondale, Electronic Surveillance Hearings, supra note 24, at 63.

69. Perhaps the last word should be that of nineteenth-century liberal philosopher John Stuart Mill: "[a] civilization that can thus succumb . . . must first have become so degenerate that neither its appointed priests and teachers, nor anybody else, has the capacity, or will take the trouble, to stand up for it. If this be so, the sooner such a civilization receives notice to quit, the better." J. S. Mill, *On Liberty* 162-163 (G. Himmelfarb ed. 1974).

Selected Bibliography

Books

Adamic, Louis, *Dynamite: The Story of Class Violence in America.* New York: Viking Press, 1934.

Adelson, Alan, *S.D.S.: A Profile.* New York: Scribner's Sons, 1972.

Agirre, Julen, *Operation Agro: The Execution of Luis Carrero Blanco.* New York: Quadrangle, 1975.

Alexander, Robert J. *The Bolivian National Revolution.* New Brunswick, N.J.: Rutgers University Press, 1958.

Alexander, Yonah, *The Role of Communications in the Middle East Conflict: Ideological and Religious Aspects.* New York: Praeger Publishers, 1973.

————, ed., *Terrorism: National and Global Perspectives.* New York: Praeger Publishers, 1976.

Alexander, Yonah, and Nicholas N. Kittrie, *Crescent and Star: Arab-Israeli Perspectives on the Middle East Conflict.* New York: A.M.S. Press, 1972.

Alexander, Yonah, and Seymour M. Finger, eds., *Terrorism: Interdisciplinary Perspectives.* New York: John Jay Press, 1977.

Ali, Tariq, ed., *The New Revolutionaries: A Handbook of the International Radical Left.* New York: William Morrow & Co., 1969.

Allen, Rodney F., and Charles H. Adair, eds., *Violence and Riots in Urban America.* Worthington, Ohio: Jones Publishing, 1969.

Allon, Yigal, *Shield of David.* New York: Random House, 1970.

Alper, Benedict S., and Jerry F. Boren, *Crime: International Agenda.* Lexington, Mass.: Lexington Books; D. C. Heath, 1972.

Alves, Márcio Moreira, *A Grain of Mustard Seed.* Garden City, N.Y.: Doubleday Anchor, 1973.

Anderson, W., *Age of Protest.* Pacific Palisades, Calif.: Goodyear Publishing, 1969.

Andics, Hellmut, *Rule of Terror.* New York: Holt, Rinehart & Winston, 1969.

Andreski, Stanislav, *Parasitism and Subversion: The Case of Latin America.* New York: Pantheon, 1967.

Annual of Power and Conflict, 1974-75: A Survey of Political Violence and International Influence. London: Institute for Study of Conflicts, 1976.

Antonius, George, *The Arab Awakening.* Beirut: Khayat, 1955.

Arendt, Hannah, *On Revolution.* New York: Viking Press, 1963.

——, *On Violence.* New York: Harcourt Brace Jovanovich, 1969.

——, *The Origins of Totalitarianism.* New York: Harcourt Brace Jovanovich, 1966.

Arey, James A., *The Sky Pirates.* New York: Scribner's Sons, 1972.

Ariel, Dan, *Explosion!* Tel Aviv: Olive Books, 1972.

Aron, Raymond, *History and the Dialectic of Violence:* An Analysis of Sartre's "Critique de la Raison Dialectique." Translated by Garry Cooper. London: Blackwell, 1975.

Atala, Charles, *Terrorisme et Guerrilla: La Révolte Armée Devant les Nations.* Ottawa: Leméac, 1973.

Avineri, Shlomo, ed., *Israel and the Palestinians: Reflections on the Clash of Two National Movements.* New York: St. Martin's, 1971.

Avner [pseud.], *Memoirs of an Assassin.* New York: Yoseloff, 1959.

Avrich, Paul. *The Russian Anarchists.* Princeton, N.J.: Princeton University Press, 1967.

Avriel, Ehud, *Open the Gates! The Dramatic Personal Story of "Illegal" Immigration to Israel.* London: Weidenfeld & Nicholson, 1975.

Azad, Abul Kalam, *India Wins Freedom.* Calcutta: Orient Longmans, 1959.

Bagts, Alfred, *A History of Militarism, Civilian and Military.* London: Hollis and Carter, 1959.

Bain, Chester A., *Vietnam: The Roots of Conflict.* Englewood Cliffs, N.J.: Prentice-Hall, 1967.

Bander, Edward J., ed., *Turmoil on the Campus.* New York: H. W. Wilson, 1970.

Bandura, Albert, *Aggression: A Social Learning Analysis.* Englewood Cliffs, N.J.: Prentice-Hall, 1973.

Barnett, Correlli, *The Collapse of British Power.* New York: William Morrow & Co., 1972.

Barron, John, *K.G.B.: The Secret Work of Soviet Secret Agents.* New York: Reader's Digest Press, 1974.

Bassiouni, Cherif M., ed., *International Terrorism and Political Crimes* Third Conference on Terrorism and Political Crimes, held in Syracuse, Sicily. Springfield, Ill.: Charles C. Thomas, 1975.

——, *The Law of Dissent and Riots.* Springfield, Ill.: Charles C. Thomas, 1971.

Bassiouni, M. C., and V. P. Nanda, *A Treatise on International Criminal Law, Jurisdiction, and Cooperation.* Springfield, Ill.: Charles C. Thomas, 1973.

Bandovin, Jean, *Terrorisme et Justice.* Montreal: Editions du Jour, 1970.

Bauer, Yehuda, *From Diplomacy to Resistance: A History of Jewish Palestine, 1939-1945.* Philadelphia: Jewish Publication Society, 1970.

Baumann, Carol Edler, *The Diplomatic Kidnappings: A Revolutionary Tactic of Urban Terrorism.* The Hague: Martinius Nijhoff, 1973.

Bayo, Alberto, *150 Questions to a Guerrilla.* Translated by R. I. Madigan and Angel de Lumus Medina. Montgomery, Ala.: Air University, n.d.

Becker, Jillian, *Hitler's Children: The Story of the Baader-Meinhof Gang.* London: Granada Publishing, 1978.

Begin, Menachem, *The Revolt.* New York: Henry Schuman, 1951.

Bell, J. Bowyer, *On Revolt: Strategies of National Liberation.* Cambridge, Mass.: Harvard University Press, 1976.

———, *The Secret Army: A History of the IRA.* Cambridge, Mass.: M.I.T. Press, 1974.

———, *Terror Out of Zion: Irgun, Lehi, and the Palestine Underground, 1929-1949.* New York: St. Martin's, 1976.

———, *Transnational Terror.* Washington, D.C.: American Enterprise Institute for Public Policy Research, 1975.

Ben-Dak, Joseph D., ed., *The Future of Collective Violence: Societal and International Perspectives.* New York: Humanities, 1974.

Bennett, George, *The Concept of Empire: Burke to Atlee, 1774-1947.* New York: Barnes & Noble Books, 1962.

Bennett, Richard Lawrence, *The Black and Tans.* Boston: Houghton Mifflin Co., 1959.

Benson, Mary, *South Africa: The Struggle for a Birthright.* London: Penguin, 1966.

Beqiraj, Mehmet, *Peasantry in Revolution.* Ithaca: Center for International Studies, Cornell University, 1966.

Berger, Peter L., and Richard J. Heuhaus, *Movement and Revolution.* Garden City, N.Y.: Doubleday & Co., 1970.

Berkman, Alexander, *Now and After: The ABC of Communist Anarchism.* New York: Vanguard Press, 1929.

Berkowitz, B. J., et al., *Superviolence: The Civil Threat of Mass Destruction Weapons.* Santa Barbara, Calif.: A.S.C.O.N. Corporation, 1972.

Berkowitz, Leonard, *A Social Psychological Analysis.* New York: McGraw-Hill Book Co., 1962.

Bern, Major H. von Dach, *Total Resistance.* Boulder, Colo.: Panther, 1965.

Bettelheim, Bruno, *The Informed Heart.* New York: Free Press, 1960.

Bienen, Henry, *Violence and Social Change.* Chicago: University of Chicago Press, 1968.

Bingham, Jonathan B., and Alfred M. Bingham, *Violence and Democracy.* New York: World, 1971.

Black, Cyril E., and Thompson P. Thornton, *Communism and Revolution.* Princeton: Princeton University Press, 1964.

Blanchard, W. H., *Rousseau and the Spirit of Revolt.* Ann Arbor: University of Michigan Press, 1967.

Bloomfield, Louis M., and Gerald F. Fitzgerald, *Crimes Against Internationally Protected Persons: Prevention and Punishment.* New York: Praeger Publishers, 1975.

Bocca, Geoffrey, *The Secret Army.* Englewood Cliffs, N.J.: Prentice-Hall 1968.

Boesel, David, and Peter H. Rossi, eds., *Cities Under Siege: An Anatomy of the Ghetto Riots, 1964-1968*. New York: Basic Books, 1971.

Borisov, J., *Palestine Underground: The Story of Jewish Resistance*. New York: Judea Publishing, 1947.

Boston, Guy D., Marvin Marcus, and Robert J. Wheaton, *Terrorism: A Selected Bibliography*. Washington, D.C.: National Criminal Reference Service, March 1976.

Boulton, David, *The Ulster Volunteer Force, 1966-1973*. Dublin: Gill and McMillan, 1973.

Bowen, D., and L. H. Masotti, *Civil Violence: A Theoretical Overview*. Cleveland, Ohio: Case Western Reserve Civil Violence Research Center, 1968.

Brennan, Ray, *Castro, Cuba, and Justice*. Garden City, N.Y.: Doubleday & Co., 1959.

Brinton, Crane, *The Anatomy of a Revolution*. Englewood Cliffs, N.J.: Prentice-Hall, 1965.

Brodie, F. G., *Bombs and Bombings*. Springfield, Ill.: Charles C. Thomas, 1972.

Broehl, Wayne G., *The Molly Maguires*. Cambridge: Harvard University Press, 1964.

Brogan, Dennis W., *The Price of Revolution*. New York: Harper & Row, 1951.

Brown, Richard M., *Strain of Violence: Historical Studies of American Violence and Vigilantism*. London: Oxford University Press, 1975.

Browne, Jeffrey T., *International Terrorism: The American Response*. School of International Service, Washington, D.C.: The American University, December 1973.

Browne, Malcolm W., *The New Face of War*. Indianapolis: Bobbs-Merrill Co., 1965.

Bunting, Brian, *The Rise of the South African Reich*. London: Penguin, 1964.

Burckhardt, Jacob, *Force and Freedom*. New York: Random House, 1943.

Burns, Alan, *In Defense of Colonies*. London: Allen and Unwin, 1957.

Burton, Anthony M., *Urban Terrorism*. New York: Macmillan, 1975; Free Press, 1976.

Camus, Albert, *Neither Victims nor Executioners*. Chicago: World Without War, 1968.

Carlton, David, and Carlo Schaerf, eds., *International Terrorism and World Security*. New York: John Wiley & Sons, 1975.

Carr, E. H., *Studies in Revolution*. New York: Grosset & Dunlap, 1964.

Carr, Gordon, *The Angry Brigade: A History of Britain's First Urban Guerrilla Group*. London: Housmans, 1970.

Carter, April, David Haggett, and Adam Roberts, *Non-Violent Action: A Selected Bibliography*. London: Housmans, 1970.

Chailand, Gerard, *The Palestinian Resistance*. Baltimore, Md.: Penguin Books, 1972.

Chakhotin, S., *The Rape of the Masses.* New York: Haskell, 1971.

Chalmers, D. M., *Hooded Americanism.* New York: Quadrangle, 1968.

Chambard, Claude, *The Maquis: A History of the French Resistance Movement.* Indianapolis: Bobbs-Merrill Co., 1976.

Chorley, Katherine, *Armies and the Art of Revolution.* London: Faber & Faber, 1943.

Choucri, Nazli, and Robert C. North, *Nations in Conflict.* San Francisco: W. H. Freeman and Co., 1945.

Clark, Michael K., *Algeria in Turmoil.* New York: Praeger Publishers, 1959.

Clutterbuck, Richard, *Living With Terrorism.* London: Faber & Faber, 1975.

―――, *Protest and The Urban Guerrilla.* London: Cassell, 1973.

Clyne, Peter, *An Anatomy of Skyjacking.* London: Abelard-Schuman, 1973.

Coblentz, S. A., *The Militant Dissenters.* South Brunswick, N.J.: Barner, 1976.

Cohen, Geula, *Women of Violence: Memoirs of a Young Terrorist, 1943-1948.* London: Hart-Davis, 1966.

Collier, Richard, *The Great Indian Mutiny.* New York: E. P. Dutton & Co., 1964.

Conant, R., *The Prospects for Revolution: A Study of Riots, Civil Disobedience and Insurrection in Contemporary America.* New York: Harper's Magazine Press, 1971.

Connery, Robert H., ed., *Urban Riots: Violence and Social Change.* New York: Random House, 1969.

Conquest, Robert, *The Great Terror.* New York: Macmillan, 1968.

Coogan, Tim Patrick, *The I.R.A.* New York: Praeger Publishers, 1970.

Cooley, John K., *Green March, Black September: The Story of Palestinian Arabs.* London: Frank Cass, 1973.

Crelinsten, Ronald D., Danielle Laberge-Altmejd, and Denis Szabo, *Terrorism and Criminal Justice.* Lexington, Mass.: Lexington Books, 1978.

Critchley, T. A., *Conquest of Violence: Order and Liberty in Britain.* New York: Schocken Books, 1970.

Crosby, John, *An Affair of Strangers.* Briarcliff Manor, N.Y.: Stein & Day, 1975.

Cross, Colin, *The Fall of the Empire.* New York: Coward, McCann & Geoghenan, 1969.

Cross, James Eliot, *Conflict in the Shadows.* New York: Doubleday & Co., 1963.

Crotty, William J., ed., *Assassinations and the Political Order.* New York: Harper & Row, 1971.

Crozier, Brian, *The Rebels: A Study of Post-War Insurrections.* London: Chatto & Windus, 1960.

―――, *South-East Asia in Turmoil.* Baltimore, Md.: Penguin Books, 1965.

―――, *A Theory of Conflict.* London: Hamish Hamilton, 1974.

Curtis, Lynn A., *Violence, Race and Culture.* Lexington, Mass.: Lexington Books, 1975.

Curtis, Michael, et al., eds., *The Palestinians: People, History, Politics.*

Edison, N.J.: Transaction Books, 1975.

Da Cunha, Eueides, *Rebellion in the Backlands.* Chicago: University of Chicago Press, 1944.

Daigon, Arthur, *Violence—U.S.A.* New York: Bantam, 1975.

Dallin, Alexander, and George W. Breslauer, *Political Terror in Communist Systems.* Stanford: Stanford University Press, 1970.

Davies, James C., ed., *When Men Revolt and Why.* New York: Free Press, 1971.

Davis, Angela, *An Autobiography.* New York: Random House, 1974.

Davis, M., *Jews Fight Too!* New York: Jordan, 1945.

Davison, Phillips W., *International Political Communication.* New York: Praeger Publishers, 1965.

Debray, Régis, *Ché's Guerrilla War.* London: Penguin Books, 1975.

———, *Revolution on the Revolution.* New York: Monthly Review Press, 1967.

Dekel, Ephraim (Krasner), *Shai: Historical Exploits of Haganah Intelligence.* New York: Yoseloff, 1959.

Der Baader-Meinhoff Report. Mainz: Hase & Köhler Verlag, 1972.

Des Pres, Terrence, *An Anatomy of Life in the Death Camps.* New York: Oxford University Press, 1976.

Dewitt, Howard A., *Images of Ethnic and Radical Violence in California Politics, 1917-1930: A Survey.* San Francisco: R. and E. Research Associates, 1975.

Dillon, Martin, and Dennis Lehane, *Political Murder in Northern Ireland.* Baltimore, Md.: Penguin Books, 1974.

Dionisopoulog, P. A., *Rebellion, Racism and Representation.* DeKalb, Ill.: Northern Illinois University Press, 1970.

Dixon, C. A., and D. Heilbrunn. *Communist Guerrilla Warfare.* New York: Praeger Publishers, 1954.

Dobson, Christopher, *Black September: Its Short, Violent History.* New York: Macmillan, 1974.

Dobson, Christopher, and Roland Payne, *The Carlos Complex.* London: Hodder & Stoughton, 1977.

Donovan, Robert J. *The Assassins.* New York: Harper & Row, 1952.

Dortzbach, Karl and Debbie, *Kidnapped.* New York: Harper & Row, 1975.

Douglas, William O. *Points of Rebellion.* New York: Vintage, 1970.

Downton, J. V., *Rebel Leadership.* New York: Vintage, 1970.

Draper, Theodore, *Castro's Revolution: Myths and Realities.* New York: Praeger Publishers, 1962.

Drapkin, Israel, and Emilio Viano, eds., *Victimology: A New Focus:* Pt. 2: "Mass Violence and Genocide." Lexington, Mass.: Lexington Books, D. C. Heath, 1975.

Dror, Yehezkel, *Crazy States: A Counterconventional Strategic Problem.* Tel Aviv: Department of Defense, 1973.

Duff, Ernest A., and John F. McCamant, *Violence and Repression in Latin*

America: A Quantitative and Historical Analysis. New York: Macmillan, 1976.

Duncan, Patrick, *South Africa's Rule of Violence.* London: Methuen, 1964.

Eayrs, James, *Diplomacy and Its Discontents.* Toronto: University of Toronto Press, 1971.

Eckstein, Harry, ed., *Internal War.* New York: Free Press, 1964.

Edwardes, Michael, *Red Years: The Indian Rebellion of 1957.* London: Hamish Hamilton, 1973.

Edwards, Lyford P., *The Natural History of Revolution.* New York: Free Press, 1963.

Eggers, William, *Terrorism: The Slaughter of Innocents.* Chatsworth, Calif.: Sage Publications, 1971.

Einaudi, Luigi R., ed., *Beyond Cuba: Latin America Takes Charge of its Future.* New York: Crane, Russak, 1974.

Eliff, John T., *Crime, Dissent and the Attorney General.* Beverly Hills, Calif.: Sage Publications, 1971.

Ellis, Albert, and John Gulls, *Murder and Assassination.* New York: Lyle Stuart, 1971.

Ellul, Jacques, *Violence: Reflections from a Christian Perspective.* Translation by Cecilia Gaul. New York: Seabury, 1969.

El-Rayyes, Riad N., and Dunia Nahas, eds., *Guerrillas for Palestine: A Study of the Palestinian Commando Organization.* Beirut: An-Nahar Press Services, 1974.

Emerson, Rupert, *From Empire to Nation: The Rise to Self-Assertion of Asian and African Peoples.* Cambridge, Mass.: Harvard University Press, 1960.

Fanon, Frantz, *Towards the African Revolution: Political Essays.* Translated by Haakon Chevalier. New York: Grove Press, 1967.

Feierabend, Ivo, R. L. Feierabend, and T. R. Gurr, eds., *Anger, Violence, and Politics: Theories and Research.* Englewood Cliffs, N.J.: Prentice-Hall, 1972.

Felt, Edward, *Urban Revolt in South Africa, 1960-1964: A Case Study.* Evanston, Ill.: Northwestern University Press, 1971.

Ferguson, J. Halcro, *The Revolution of Latin America.* London: Thames & Hudson, 1963.

Ferreira, J. C., *Carlos Marighella.* Havana: Tricontinental, 1970.

Fitzgerald, Charles P., *Revolution in China.* New York: Praeger Publishers, 1952.

Forman, J., *The Making of Black Revolutionaries.* New York: Macmillan, 1972.

Fortas, Abe, *Concerning Dissent and Civil Disobedience.* New York: New American Library, 1968.

Franklin, W. M., *Protection of Foreign Interests.* New York: Greenwood, 1969.

Franzius, Enno, *History of the Order of Assassins.* New York: Funk &

Wagnalls Co., 1969.

Freedman, Robert Owen, *Soviet Policy towards the Middle East Since Nassar*. New York: Praeger Publishers, 1975.

Freeman, Thomas [pseud.], *The Crisis in Cuba*. Derby, Conn.: Monarch Books, 1963.

Friedlander, Robert A., *Terrorism: Documents of International and Local Control*. Dobbs Ferry, New York: Oceana, 1978.

Fromm, Erich, *The Anatomy of Human Destructiveness*. New York: Holt, Rinehart and Winston, 1973.

Gablonski, Edward, *Terror from the Sky: Air War*. Garden City, N.Y.: Doubleday & Co., 1971.

Galula, David, *Counterinsurgency Warfare: Theory and Practice*. New York: Praeger Publishers, 1964.

Gann, L. H., *Guerrillas in History*. Stanford: Hoover Institute, 1971.

Gaucher, Roland, *The Terrorists: From Tsarist Russia to the O.A.S.* Translated by P. Spurlin. London: Secker & Warburg, 1968.

Gellner, John, *Bayonets in the Streets: Urban Guerrilla at Home and Abroad*. Don Mills, Ont.: Collier MacMillan of Canada, 1974.

Gerassi, F., ed., *Venceremos!* New York: Simon & Schuster, 1968.

Giap, Vo-nguyen, *People's War, People's Army: The Viet-Cong Insurrection Manual for Underdeveloped Countries*. New York: Praeger Publishers, 1962.

_____, *The Tupamaro Guerrillas*. Translated by Anne Edmondston. New York: Saturday Review Press, 1972.

Goldberg, Yona, *Haganah or Terror*. New York: Hechalutz, 1947.

Gott, Richard, *Guerrilla Movements in Latin America*. London: Thomas Nelson, 1970.

Graham, Hugh Davis, and Ted Robert Gurr, eds., *The History of Violence in America*. New York: Bantam, 1970.

Green, G., *The Hostage Heart*. Chicago: Playboy Press, 1976.

_____, *Terrorism: Is it Revolutionary?* New York: Outlook Publications, 1970.

Greene, Thomas H., *Comparative Revolutionary Movements*. Englewood Cliffs, N.J.: Prentice-Hall, 1974.

Grivas, G., *Guerrilla Warfare and E.O.K.A.'s Struggle*. London: Longman's, 1964.

Groussard, Serge, *The Blood of Israel: The Massacre of the Israeli Athletes, The Olympics, 1972*. New York: William Morrow & Co., 1975.

Guillen, Abraham, *Philosophy of the Urban Guerrilla*. Translated by D. C. Hodges. New York: William Morrow & Co., 1973.

Gurr, Ted R., *Why Men Rebel*. Princeton, N.J.: Princeton University Press, 1971.

Hacker, Frederick J., *Crusaders, Criminals, Crazies*. New York: W. W. Norton & Co., 1976.

Haddad, George M., *Revolution and Military Rule in the Middle East*. New York: Speller, 1965.

Hansen, Emmanuel, *Franz Fanon: Social and Political Thought.* Columbus: Ohio University Press, 1976.

Harkabi, Yehoshafat, *The Arab's Position in Their Conflict with Israel.* Jerusalem: Israel Universities Press, 1972.

Havens, Murray C., Carl Leiden, and Karl M. Schmitt, *The Politics of Assassination.* Englewood Cliffs, N.J.: Prentice-Hall, 1970.

Hayden, Tom. *Rebellion in Newark.* New York: Random House, 1967.

Hodges, D. C., ed., *Philosophy of Urban Guerrilla, the Revolutionary Writings of Abraham Guillen.* New York: William Morrow & Co., 1973.

Hofstadter, Richard, and Michael Wallace, eds., *American Violence: A Documentary History.* New York: Alfred A. Knopf, 1970.

Horowitz, Irving L., ed., *The Anarchists.* New York: Dell Publishing Co., 1964.

Horrell, Muriel, *Terrorism in South Africa.* Johannesburg: South African Institute on Race Relations, 1968.

Hubbard, David G., *The Skyjacker: His Flights of Fantasy.* New York: Macmillan, 1971.

Huberman, L., and P. M. Sweezy, eds., *Regis Debray and the Latin American Revolution.* New York: Monthly Review, 1968.

Hunt, Sir David. *On the Spot.* London: Peter Davies, 1975.

Hussain, Mehmood, *The Palestine Liberation Organization: A Study in Ideology and Tactics.* New York: International Publications Service, 1975.

Hyams, Edward, *Terrorists and Terrorism.* New York: St. Martin's Press, 1974.

Hyde, Douglas Arnold, *The Roots of Guerrilla Warfare.* Chester Springs, Pa.: Dufour Editions, 1968.

Jackson, Sir Geoffrey, *Surviving the Long Nights—An Autobiographical Account of a Political Kidnapping.* New York: Vanguard Press, 1974.

Jenkins, Brian, *International Terrorism: A New Mode of Conflict.* Los Angeles: Crescent Publications, 1975.

Johnson, Chalmers A., *Revolutionary Change.* Boston: Little, Brown and Co., 1966.

Joyner, Nancy D., *Aerial Hijacking as an International Crime.* Dobbs Ferry, N.Y.: Oceana, 1974.

Kaplan, Morton A., ed., *Revolution in World Politics.* New York: Wiley, 1962.

Katz, Samuel, *Days of Fire.* Garden City, N.Y.: Doubleday & Co., 1968.

Kautsky, Karl, *Terrorism and Communism: A Contribution to the National History of Revolution.* Translated by W. H. Kerridge, London: Allen & Unwin, 1920.

Kedward, H. R., *Fascism in Western Europe, 1900-1945.* New York: New York University Press, 1971.

Khaled, Leila, *My People Shall Live.* New York: Bantam, 1974.

Kiernan, Thomas, *Arafat: The Man and the Myth.* New York: Norton & Co., 1976.

Kirkham, J. F., and S. Levy, *Assassination and Political Violence.* National

Commission on the Causes and Prevention of Violence, Washington, D.C.:
U.S. Government Printing Office, 1969.

Kirkham, James F., Sheldon G. Levy, and William J. Crotty, *Assassination
and Political Violence: A Staff Report to the National Commission on the
Causes and Prevention of Violence.* New York: Bantam, 1970.

Kiston, Frank, *Low Intensity Operations: Subversion, Insurgency, Peace-
Keeping.* London: Faber, 1972.

Kohl, J., and J. Litt, *Urban Guerrilla Warfare in Latin America.* Cambridge,
Mass.: M.I.T. Press, 1974.

Labrousse, Alain, *The Tupamaros: Urban Guerillas in Uruguay.* Harmondsworth: Penguin, 1973.

Laffin, J., *Fedayeen: The Arab-Israeli Dilemma.* New York: Free Press, 1973.

Lambrick, H. T., *The Terrorist.* London: Rowman, 1972.

Laqueur, Walter, *Guerrilla.* Boston: Little, Brown and Co., 1976.

_____, *The Guerrilla Reader: A Historical Anthology.* New York: New
American Library, 1977.

_____, *Terrorism.* Boston: Little, Brown and Co., 1977.

Lasswell, Harold, and Daniel Lerner, eds., *World Revolutionary Elites:
Studies in Coercive Ideological Movements.* Cambridge, Mass.: M.I.T.
Press, 1965.

Laushey, David M., *Bengal Terrorism and the Marxist Left.* Calcutta: Firma
K. L. Mukhopadhyay, 1975.

Leachman, Robert B., and Philip Althoff, eds., *Preventing Nuclear Theft:
Guidelines for Industry and Government.* New York: Praeger Publishers,
1972.

Leites, Nathan, and Charles Wolf, Jr., *Rebellion and Authority: An Analytic
Essay on Insurgent Conflicts.* Chicago: Markham, 1970.

Lineberry, William P., ed., *The Struggle Against Terrorism.* New York:
H. W. Wilson, 1977.

Liston, Robert A., *Terrorism.* New York: Thomas Nelson, 1977.

McGuirde, Maria, *To Take Arms: My Years with the IRA Provisionals.* New
York: Viking Press, 1973.

McKnight, Gerald, *The Mind of the Terrorist.* London: Michael Joseph,
1974.

McWhinney, Edward, *The Illegal Diversion of Aircraft and International
Law.* Leiden: Sijhoff, 1975.

McWhinney, Edward, and others, *Aerial Piracy and International Law.*
Dobbs Ferry, N.Y.: Oceana, 1971.

Mallin, Jay, ed., *Terror and Urban Guerrillas: A Study of Tactics and Documents.* Coral Gables, Fla.: University of Miami Press, 1971.

Malloy, James, *Bolivia: The Uncompleted Revolution.* Pittsburgh: University of Pittsburgh Press, 1970.

May, Rollo, *Power and Innocence: A Search for the Sources of Violence.*
New York: W. W. Norton & Co., 1972.

Mercader, A., and J. de Vera, *Tupamaros: Estrategia y Acción.* Montevideo:
Editorial Alfa, 1969.

Milner, Sheilagh Hodgins, and Henry Miller, *The Decolonization of*

Quebec: An Analysis of Left Wing Nationalism. Toronto: McClelland and Stewart, 1973.

Miron, Murray S., and Arnold P. Goldstein, *Hostage.* Kalamazoo, Mich.: Behaviordelia, 1978.

Momboisse, R. M., *Blueprint of Revolution: The Rebel, the Party, the Techniques of Revolt.* Springfield, Ill.: Charles C. Thomas, 1970.

⸻, *Riots, Revolts and Insurrections.* Springfield, Ill.: Charles C. Thomas, 1967.

Moore, Barrington M., Jr., *Terror and Progress in the U.S.S.R.* Cambridge, Mass.: Harvard University Press, 1954.

Morf, Gustave, *Terrorism in Quebec: Case Studies of the FLQ.* Toronto: Clark Irvin & Company, 1970.

Moss, Robert, *Counter Terrorism.* London: The Economist Brief Books, 1972.

⸻, *The War For the Cities.* New York: Coward, McCann & Geoghegan, 1972.

Naipaul, V. S., *Guerrillas.* New York: Alfred A. Knopf, 1975.

National Advisory Committee on Criminal Justice Standards and Goals, *Disorders and Terrorism.* Washington, D.C.: Report of the Task Force and Terrorism, 1976.

Nieburg, Harold L., *Political Violence: The Behavioral Process.* New York: St. Martin's Press, 1969.

Niezing, Johan, ed., *Urban Guerrilla: Studies on the Theory, Strategy and Practice of Political Violence in Modern Societies.* Rotterdam: Rotterdam University Press, 1974.

Oppenheimer, Martin, *The Urban Guerrilla.* Chicago: Quadrangle Books, 1969.

Paret, Peter, and John W. Shy, *Guerrillas in the 1960's.* New York: Praeger Publishers, 1962.

Parry, Albert, *Terrorism: From Robespierre to Arafat.* New York: Vanguard Press, 1976.

Pearsall, R. B., ed., *Symbionese Liberation Army—Documents and Communications.* Amsterdam: Rodopi N. V. Keizergracht, 1974.

Phillips, David, *Skyjack: The Story of Air Piracy.* London: Harrap, 1973.

Porzicanski, A. C., *Uruguay's Tupamaros: The Urban Guerrilla.* New York: Praeger Publishers, 1973.

Pryce-Jones, David, *The Face of Defeat: Palestinian Refugees and Guerrillas.* London: Weidenfeld and Nicholson, 1972.

Pye, Lucien, W., *Guerrilla Communism in Malaya: Its Social and Political Meaning.* Princeton: Princeton University Press, 1956.

Rapoport, David C., *Assassination and Terrorism.* Toronto: Canadian Broadcasting Corporation, 1971.

Reid, Malcolm, *The Shouting Signpainters: A Literary and Political Account of Quebec Revolutionary Nationalism.* Toronto and London: McClelland and Stewart, 1972.

Rojo, R., *My Friend Ché.* New York: Dial Press, 1969.

Sacks, A., *The Violence of Apartheid.* London: International Defense and

Air Fund, 1970.

Sarkesian, Sam C., ed., *Revolutionary Guerrilla Warfare*. Chicago: Precedent Publishing, 1975.

Saywell, John T., *Quebec 70: A Documentary Narrative*. Toronto: University of Toronto Press, 1971.

Schiff, Zeev, and Raphael Rothstein, *Fedayeen: The Story of the Palestinian Guerrillas*. London: Vallentine, Mitchell and Co., 1972.

Smith, Colin, *Carlos, Portrait of a Terrorist*. London: Sphere Books, 1976.

Sobel, Lester A., ed., *Political Terrorism*. New York: Facts on File, 1975.

Solzhenitsyn, Alexander, *The Gulag Archipelago*. New York: Harper & Row, 1973.

Sorel, Georges, *Reflections on Violence*. New York: Collier, 1961.

Stevenson, William, *90 Minutes at Entebbe*. New York: Bantam Books, 1976.

Storr, Anthony, *Human Destructiveness*. New York: Basic Books, 1972.

Tanham, George Kilpatrick, *Communist Revolutionary Warfare*. New York: Praeger Publishers, 1961.

Terrorism in India. New Delhi: Deep Publications, 1974.

Tinnin, David, *Hit Team*. London: Weidenfeld and Nicholson, 1976.

Trelease, Allen W., *White Terror: The Ku Klux Klan Conspiracy and Southern Reconstruction*. New York: Harper & Row, 1971.

Trotsky, Leon, *The Defence of Terrorism*. London: George Allen and Unwin, 1921.

Van den Haag, Ernest, *Political Violence and Civil Disobedience*. New York: Harper & Row, 1972.

Van Voris, William H., *Violence in Ulster: An Oral Documentary*. Amherst: University of Massachusetts Press, 1975.

Vallieres, Pierre, *White Niggers of America: The Precocious Autobiography of a Quebec Terrorist*. New York: Monthly Review Press, 1971.

Venturi, Franco, *Roots of Revolution*. New York: Grosset & Dunlap, 1966.

Walter, E. V., *Terror and Resistance: A Study of Political Violence*. New York: Oxford University Press, 1969.

Walzer, Michael, *The Revolution of the Saints: A Study of the Origins of Radical Politics*. Cambridge, Mass.: Harvard University Press, 1965.

Watson, Francis M., *Political Terrorism: The Threat and the Response*. Washington, D.C.: Robert B. Luce, 1976.

Whelton, Charles, *Skyjack!* New York: Tower Publications, 1970.

Wilkinson, Paul, *Political Terrorism*. New York: John Wiley & Sons, 1975.

————, *Terrorism and the Liberal State*. London: Macmillan, 1977.

Wilson, Colin, *Order of Assassins: The Psychology of Murder*. London: Rupert Hart-Davis, 1972.

Zweibach, Burton, *Civility and Disobedience*. New York: Cambridge University Press, 1975.

Articles

Aggarwala, Narinder, "Political Aspects of Hijacking," *International Conciliation*, no. 585, 1971, pp. 7-27.

Ahmad, Eqbal, "The Theory and Fallacy of Counterinsurgency," *Nation,* vol. 213, 1971, pp. 70-85.

"Airport Security Searches and the Fourth Amendment," *Columbia Law Review,* vol. 71, 1971, pp. 1039-58.

Akehurst, Michael, "Arab-Israeli Conflict and International Law," *New Zealand University Law Review,* vol. 5, 1973, p. 231.

Akers, E. R., and V. Fox, "The Detroit Rioters and Looters Committed to Prison," *Journal of Criminal Law, Criminology and Police Science,* vol. 35, 1964, p. 105.

Alexander, Yonah, "Communications Aspects of International Terrorism," *International Problems,* vol. 16, nos. 1-2, Spring 1977, pp. 55-60.

_____, "The Legacy of Palestinian Terrorism," *International Problems,* vol. 15, Fall 1976, pp. 57-64.

_____, "Some Perspectives on International Terrorism," *International Problems,* vol. 14, Fall 1975, pp. 24-29.

_____, "Terrorism, the Media, and the Police," *Journal of International Affairs,* vol. 32, no. 1, Spring-Summer 1978, pp. 72-83.

Alexander, Yonah, and Herbert M. Levine, "Prepare For the Next Entebbe," *Chitty's Law Journal,* vol. 25, September 1977, pp. 240-242.

Alsina, Geronimo, "The War and the Tupamaros," *Bulletin Tricontinental,* August 1972, pp. 29-42.

Alves, Márcio Moreira, "Kidnapped Diplomats: Greek Tragedy on a Latin Stage," *Commonweal,* vol. 92, 1970, pp. 311-14.

Anable, David, "Terrorists in New York Threatened U.S.-Soviet Links," *Christian Science Monitor,* April 5, 1976, p. 4.

Anderson, Jack, "Urban Guerrilla Operations Feared," *Washington Post,* April, 23, 1974.

"And Now, Mail-a-Death," *Time,* October 2, 1972, 28ff.

"Anti-Soviet Zionist Terrorism in the U.S.," *Current Digest of the Soviet Press,* vol. 23, 1971, pp. 6-8.

"Approaches to the Problem of International Terrorism—Symposium 10," *Journal of International Labour and Economics,* vol. 10, 1976, p. 483.

"Arab Terrorism," *Jewish Frontier,* vol. 36, 1969, pp. 13-16.

Archinard, André, "La Suisse et les infractions non aerliennes, commises à bord des aéronefs civils," *A.S.D.A. Bulletin S.V.I.R.,* no. 3, 1968, pp. 3-9; no. 1, 1969, pp. 2-10; no. 2, 1969, pp. 1-12.

Arendt, Hannah, "Reflections on Violence," *Journal of International Affairs,* vol. 23, no. 1, 1969, pp. 1-35.

"Argentina: Revolution within the Revolution," *Latin America,* vol. 5, no. 54, 1971, pp. 337-38.

Ashayb, Naim, "To Overcome the Crisis of the Palestine Resistance," *World Marxist Review,* vol. 15, no. 5, 1972, pp. 71-78.

"As Violence Spreads, United States Goes on Guard," *U.S. News and World Report,* November 2, 1970, p. 15.

Atwater, J., "Time to Get Tough with Terrorists," *Reader's Digest,* vol. 102, April 1973, pp. 89-93.

Baccelli, Guido Rinaldi, "Pirateria aerea: realtrà effettiva e disciplina giuridica," *Diritto aereo,* vol. 9, no. 35, 1970, pp. 150-60.

Barner, Don, "P.L.O. at U.N., What Now?" *New Outlook,* vol. 17, no. 9, 1974, pp. 62-66.

Barrie, G. N., "Crimes Committed Aboard Aircraft," *South African Law Journal,* vol. 83, 1968, pp. 203-8.

Bartos, M., "International Terrorism," *Review of International Affairs,* vol. 23, April 20, 1972, p. 25.

"Basques: Business and Bombs," *Time,* vol. 103, January 1974, pp. 48-49.

Bassiouni, Cherif M., "Ideologically Motivated Offenses and the Political Offense Exceptions in Extradition: A Proposed Judicial Standard for an Unruly Problem," *DePaul Law Review,* vol. 19, 1969, p. 217.

_____, "International Extradition: An American Experience and a Proposed Formula," *Revue Internationale de Droit Penal,* vol. 39, 1968, p. 3.

Bayer, Alan E., and Alexander W. Astin, "Violence and Disruption on the U.S. Campus, 1968-1969," *Educational Record,* vol. 50, 1969, p. 337.

Beaton, L., "Crisis in Quebec," *Round Table,* no. 241, 1971, p. 147-52.

Beckett, J. C., "Northern Ireland," *Journal of Contemporary History,* vol. 6, no. 1, 1971, pp. 121-34.

"Behind the Terror Bombings," *U.S. News and World Report,* March 30, 1970, p. 15.

Bell, J. Bowyer, "Assassination in International Politics: Lord Moyne, Count Bernadotte, and the Lehi," *International Studies Quarterly,* no. 1, 1972, pp. 59-82.

_____, "Transnational Terror and World Order," *South Atlantic Quarterly,* vol. 74, no. 4, Autumn 1975, pp. 404-417.

Bell, Robert G., "The U.S. Response to Terrorism Against International Civil Aviation," *Orbis,* vol. 19, Winter 1976, pp. 1326-1343.

Bennett, R. K., "Brotherhood of the Bomb," *Reader's Digest,* December 1970, pp. 102-6.

_____, "Terrorists Among Us: An Intelligence Report," *Reader's Digest,* October 1971, pp. 115-20.

Bennett, W. T., Jr., "U.S. Initiatives in the United Nations to Combat International Terrorism," *International Lawyer,* vol. 7, 1973, p. 752.

Beres, Louis Rene, "Guerrillas, Terrorists and Polarity: New Structural Models of World Politics," *Western Political Science Quarterly,* December 1974, pp. 624-636.

Besedin, Alexander, "Against Air Piracy," *New Times,* November 2, 1970, pp. 24-25.

"Biggest Blast," *Newsweek,* September 7, 1970, p. 33.

Binder, David, "U.S. Is Said to Plan a New Approach on Terrorism," *New York Times,* March 27, 1976, p. 3.

"Black Men and Bombs," *Ebony,* vol. 25, May 1970, pp. 49-50.

"Blowing Up Bridges," *Newsweek,* February 7, 1972, p. 28.

"Blown Up," *Economist,* January 16, 1971, p. 16.

"Bomb at the Golden Arch," *Washington Star-News,* August 20, 1975.

"Bombing Fallout," *Business Week,* November 22, 1969, p. 44.

"Bombing Incidents–1972," *F.B.I. Law Enforcement Bulletin*, April 1973, p. 21.

"Bombing Jitters," *Newsweek*, March 30, 1970, p. 23.

"Bombing Research Center," *New York Morning Telegraph*, December 8, 1971.

"Bombing Threats," *Environment*, October 1974, p. 21.

"Bomb Plots: Warning on Terror War," *U.S. News and World Report*, October 26, 1970, p. 36.

Bond, James, "Application of the Law of War to International Conflicts," *Georgia Journal of International and Comparative Law*, vol. 3, 1973, p. 345.

Bouthoul, G., "Le Terrorisme," *Etudes Polémologiques*, vol. 3, April 1973, pp. 37-46.

Boyle, Robert P. "International Action to Combat Aircraft Hijacking," *Lawyer of the Americas*, vol. 4, 1972, pp. 460-73.

Bozakis, Christos L., "Terrorism and the Internationally Protected Persons in the Light of the I.L.C.'s Draft Articles," *International and Comparative Law Quarterly*, vol. 23, 1974, p. 32.

Brach, Richard S., "The Inter-American Convention on the Kidnapping of Diplomats," *Columbia Journal of Transnational Law*, vol. 10, 1971, pp. 392-412.

Bradford, A. L., "Legal Ramifications of Hijacking Airplanes," *American Bar Association Journal*, vol. 48, 1962, pp. 1034-39.

Brandon, Henry, "Were We Masterful . . ." *Foreign Policy*, no. 10, 1973, pp. 158-70.

Bravo, Navarro M., "Apoderamiento ilícito de aeronaves en vuelo," *Revista española de derecho international*, vol. 22, 1969, pp. 788-809.

Buckley, W. F., "Politics of Assassination," *Esquire*, vol. 70, October 1968.

Burki, S. J., "Social and Economic Determinants of Political Violence: A Case Study of the Punjab," *Middle East Journal*, vol. 25, 1971, pp. 465-80.

Burnham, J., "Notes on Terrorism," *National Review*, October 13, 1972, p. 1116.

Callanan, Edward F., "Terror in Venezuela," *Military Review*, vol. 49, 1969, pp. 49-56.

Caloyanni, M. A., "The Proposal of M. Laval to the League of Nations for the Establishment of an International Permanent Tribunal in Criminal Matters," *Transaction of the Crotius Society*, vol. 21, 1936, p. 77.

Calvert, Peter, "The Diminishing Returns of Political Violence," *New Middle East*, vol. 56, May 1973, p. 25.

Charles, Russell, and Robert E. Hildner, "Urban Insurgency in Latin America: Its Implications for the Future," *Air University Review*, vol. 22, September-October 1971, pp. 561-64.

Chaturvedi, S. C., "Hijacking and the Law," *Indian Journal of International Law*, vol. 11, 1971, pp. 89-105.

Clark, Dennis, "Which Way the I.R.A.?" *Commonweal*, no. 13, 1973, pp. 294-97.

Clark, Leone S., "The Struggle to Cure Hijacking," *International Perspectives*, January-February 1973, pp. 47-51.

Clutterbuck, Richard, "Terrorist International," *Army Quarterly and Defence Journal*, vol. 104, January 1974, pp. 154-159.

Cobo, Juan, "The Roots of 'Violencia,'" *New Times*, August 5, 1970, pp. 25-27.

Colebrook, Joan, "Israel with Terrorists," *Commentary*, vol. 58, no. 1, July 1974, p. 30.

Collins, L., "Orgy of Killing: Algeria's European Secret Army Organization," *Newsweek*, vol. 59, January 29, 1962, p. 42.

"Comment, Constitutional and Statutory Basis of Governor's Emergency Powers," *Michigan Law Review*, vol. 64, 1965, p. 1290.

"The Convention for the Prevention and Punishment of Terrorism," *British Yearbook of International Law*, vol. 19, 1938, p. 214.

"Convention to Prevent and Punish the Acts of Terrorism Taking the Form of Crimes against Persons and Related Extortions that are of International Significance, *Serie Sobre Tratados*, vol. 37, Washington, D.C.: Pan American Union, February 2, 1971.

Cooley, John K., "China and the Palestinians," *Journal of Palestinian Studies*, vol. 1, no. 2, 1972, pp. 19-34.

Cooper, H.H.A., "Terrorism and the Intelligence Function," *Chitty's Law Journal*, vol. 73, March 1976, p. 24.

———, "Terrorism and the Media," *Chitty's Law Journal*, vol. 24, no. 7, 1976, pp. 226-232.

———, "The Terrorist and His Victims," *Victimology*, vol. 1, no. 2, June 1976.

Craig, Alexander, "Urban Guerrillas in Latin America," *Survey*, vol. 17, no. 3, 1971, pp. 112-28.

Cranston, Maurice, "Sartre and Violence," *Encounter*, July 1967.

"Curbing Terrorism," *Christian Science Monitor*, January 16, 1976, p. 32.

Czerniejewshi, H. J. "Guidelines for the Coverage of Terrorism," *The Quill*, 1977, pp. 21-23.

Dadrian, V., "Factors of Anger and Aggression in Genocide," *Journal of Human Relations*, vol. 19, 1971, pp. 394-417.

Davies, James C., "The Circumstances and Causes of Revolution: A Review," *Journal of Conflict Resolution*, June 1967, p. 11.

———, "Towards a Theory of Revolution," *American Sociological Review*, vol. 27, 1962, pp. 5-14.

Davis, Donald M., "Terrorism: Motives and Means," *Foreign Science Journal*, September 1962, p. 14.

Deakin, T. J., "Legacy of Carlos Marighella," *F.B.I. Law Enforcement Bulletin*, vol. 43, no. 10, October 1974, pp. 19-25.

"Death Penalty for Terrorists?" *Christian Century*, vol. 9, March 21, 1973, p. 333.

de Gramont, Sanche, "Moslem Terrorists in New Jobs," *New York Herald Tribune*, July 9, 1962, pp. 1-2.

Denaro, J. M., "In-flight Crimes, the Tokyo Convention and Federal Jurisdiction," *Journal of Air Law and Commerce,* vol. 35, 1969, pp. 171-203.

Derber, M., "Terrorism and the Movement," *Monthly Reviews,* vol. 22, February 1971, p. 36.

Dershowitz, Alan M., "Terrorism and Preventive Detention," *Commentary Report,* 1970, pp. 3-14.

Dinstein, Yoram, "Criminal Jurisdiction Over Aircraft Hijacking," *Israel Law Review,* vol. 7, 1972, pp. 195-206.

_____, "Terrorism and Wars of Liberation Applied to the Arab-Israeli Conflict: An Israeli Perspective," *Israel Yearbook of Human Rights,* vol. 3, 1973, p. 78.

"Dir Yassin," *West Asia Affairs,* Summer 1969, pp. 27-30.

"Document on Terror," *News from Behind the Iron Curtain,* vol. 1, 1952, pp. 44-57.

"Draft Convention for the Prevention and Punishment of Certain Acts of International Terrorism," *Department of State Bulletin,* vol. 67, October 16, 1972, p. 431.

Dugard, John, "International Terrorism: Problems of a Definition," *International Affairs,* vol. 50, no. 1, 1974, pp. 67-81.

_____, "Towards a Definition of International Terrorism," *American Journal of International Law,* vol. 67, no. 5, 1973, pp. 94-100.

Eave, L., "Political Terrorism: Hysteria on the Left," *New York Times Magazine,* April 12, 1970, pp. 25-27.

Eckstein, Harry, "On the Etiology of Internal War," *History and Theory,* vol. 4, 1965, pp. 133-163.

Epstein, D. G., "Combating Campus Terrorism," *Police Chief,* vol. 38, no. 1, January 1971, pp. 46-47, 49.

Erskine, Hazel, "Fear of Violence and Crime," *Public Opinion Quarterly,* vol. 38, 1974, p. 131.

Esson, D.M.R., "The Secret Weapon—Terrorism," *Army Quarterly,* vol. 78, 1959, p. 167.

Eustathiades, C., "La Cour pénale internationale pour le répression du terrorisme et le problème de la responsabilité internationale des états," *Revue Générale de droit international publique,* vol. 43, 1936, pp. 385-415.

Evans, Alona E., "Aircraft Hijacking: What Is to Be Done?" *American Journal of International Law,* vol. 66, 1972, pp. 819-22.

_____, "Its Cause and Cure," *American Journal of International Law,* vol. 63, 1969, pp. 695-710.

_____, "Jurisdiction-Fugitive Offender-Forcible Abduction-Ker-Frisbie Rule-Treaties-Extradition," *American Journal of International Law,* vol. 69, 1975, p. 406.

_____, "A Proposed Method of Control," *Journal of Air Law and Commerce,* vol. 37, 1971, pp. 171-81.

_____, "Reflections Upon the Political Offenses in International Practice," *American Journal of International Law,* vol. 57, 1963, p. 1.

Fadersori, Alberto S., "What Is an Urban Guerrilla?" *Military Review*, vol. 47, 1969, p. 94.

Falk, Richard A., "Terror, Liberation Movements, and the Process of Social Change," *American Journal of International Law*, vol. 63, 1969, pp. 423-27.

Fellaci, Oriana, "A Leader of Fedayeen: 'We Want a War Like the Vietnam War': Interview with George Habash," *Life*, June 12, 1970, pp. 32-34.

Feller, S. Z., "Comment on Criminal Jurisdiction Over Aircraft Hijacking," *Israel Law Review*, vol. 7, 1972, pp. 207-14.

Fenello, Michael J., "Technical Prevention of Air Piracy," *International Coalition*, no. 585, 1971, pp. 28-41.

Fenwick, C. C., "'Piracy' in the Caribbean," *American Journal of International Law*, vol. 55, 1961, pp. 426-28.

Fenyvesi, C., "Looking into the Muzzle of Terrorists," *The Quill*, 1977, pp. 16-18.

Firestone, Joseph M., "Continuities in the Theory of Violence," *Journal of Conflict Resolution*, vol. 18, 1974, p. 117.

Fitzgerald, G. F., "Development of International Rules Concerning Offenses and Certain Other Acts Committed on Board Aircraft," *Canadian Yearbook of International Law*, vol. 1, 1963, pp. 230-51.

————, "Towards Legal Suppression of Acts Against Civil Aviation," *International Conciliation*, no. 505, 1971, pp. 42-78.

Fitzgibbon, Russell H., "Revolution in Latin America: A Tentative Prognosis," *Virginia Quarterly Review*, Spring 1963, p. 39.

Flacks, R. "The Liberated Generation: An Exploration of the Roots of Student Protest," *Journal of Social Issues*, vol. 23, 1967, p. 52.

Franck, Thomas M., and Bert B. Lockwood, "Preliminary Thoughts Towards an International Convention on Terrorism," *American Journal of International Law*, vol. 68, 1974, p. 4.

Franjeck, S., "How Revolutionary Is the Palestinian Resistance: A Marxist Interpretation," *Journal of Palestine Studies*, vol. 1, no. 2, 1972, pp. 52-60.

Frank, Gerold, "The Moyne Case: A Tragic History," *Commentary*, December 1945, pp. 64-71.

Friedlander, R. A., "Terrorism," *Barrister*, vol. 2, Summer 1975, p. 10.

Friedmann, W., "Terrorists and Subversive Activities," *American Journal of International Law*, vol. 50, 1956, p. 475.

Fromkin, David, "The Strategy of Terrorism," *Foreign Affairs*, vol. 53, July 1975, p. 683.

Galyean, T. E., "Acts of Terrorism and Combat by Irregular Forces: An Insurance 'War' Risk," *California Western International Law Journal*, vol. 4, 1974, p. 314.

Garcia-Mora, Manuel R., "Crimes against Humanity and the Principle of Non-extradition of Political Offenders," *Michigan Law Review*, vol. 62, 1964, p. 927.

————, "The Crimes Against Peace," *Fordham Law Review*, vol. 34, 1965, p. 1.

————, "Criminal Jurisdiction over Foreigners for Treason and Offenses

Against the Safety of the State Committed Upon Foreign Territory," *University of Pittsburgh Law Review*, vol. 19, 1958, p. 567.

Gerassi, Marysa, "Uruguay's Urban Guerrillas," *Nation*, vol. 209, no. 10, 1969, pp. 306-10.

"Getting Away with Murder," *Economist*, November 4, 1972, pp. 15-16.

"The Girl Who Almost Killed Ford," *Time*, September 15, 1975, p. 8.

Glasser, S., "Terrorisme International et ses Divers Aspects," *Revue Internationale de Droit Comparé*, vol. 25, 1973, p. 825.

Gott, Richard, "Latin American Guerrillas," *Listener*, vol. 84, 1970, pp. 437-40.

"Greece Takes Tougher Stance Following Airport Terrorism," *Aviation Week*, vol. 99, August 13, 1973, p. 26.

Green, L. C., "International Law and the Suppression of Terrorism," edited by G. W. Bartholomew, *Malaya Law Review Legal Essays*, 1975.

_____, "International Terrorism and Its Legal Control," *Chitty's Law Journal*, vol. 21, 1973, pp. 289-301.

Gross, Leo, "International Terrorism and International Criminal Jurisdiction," *American Journal of International Law*, vol. 67, July 1973, pp. 508-511.

Hassel, Conrad V., "Terror: The Crime of the Privileged—An Examination and Prognosis," *Terrorism: An International Journal*, vol. 1, no. 1, 1977, pp. 1-16.

Hoffacker, Lewis, "The U.S. Government Response to Terrorism: A Global Approach," *Department of State Bulletin*, March 18, 1974, pp. 274-278.

Horchem, Hans Josef, "West Germany's Red Army Anarchists," *Conflict Studies*, June 1974.

Horowitz, Irving L., "Political Terrorism and State Power," *Journal of Political and Military Sociology*, vol. 1, Spring 1973, pp. 147-157.

Hoveyda, Fereydoun, "The Problem of International Terrorism at the United Nations," *Terrorism: An International Journal*, vol. 1, no. 1, 1977, pp. 71-84.

Hutchinson, Martha C., "The Concept of Revolutionary Terrorism," *Journal of Conflict Resolution*, vol. 16, September 1972, pp. 383-396.

Ingram, Timothy H., "Nuclear Hijacking: Now Within Grasp of Any Bright Lunatic," *Washington Monthly*, December 1972, pp. 26-28.

Iviansky, Ze'ev, "Individual Terror: Concept and Typology," *Journal of Contemporary History*, vol. 12, January 1977, pp. 43-63.

Jenkins, Brian, "International Terrorism: A Balance Sheet," *Survival*, vol. 17 (July-August 1975), pp. 158-164.

_____, "Research Note: Rand's Research on Terrorism," *Terrorism: An International Journal*, vol. 1, no. 1, 1977, pp. 85-96.

Karber, Philip A., "Urban Terrorism: Baseline Data and a Conceptual Framework," *Social Science Quarterly*, vol. 52, December 1971, pp. 521-33.

Krieger, David M., "Terrorists and Nuclear Technology: The Danger is Great, the Question is not whether the Worst will Happen but Where and How," *Bulletin of the Atomic Scientists*, June 1975, pp. 28-34.

Kupperman, Robert H., "Treating the Symptoms of Terrorism: Some Principles of Good Hygiene," *Terrorism: An International Journal*, vol. 1, no. 1, 1977, pp. 35-50.

Kuriyama, Y., "Young Palestinian Commandos in Political Socialization Perspectives," *Middle East Journal*, vol. 26, Summer 1972, pp. 325-50.

Kutner, Luis, "Constructive Notice: A Proposal to End International Terrorism," *New York Law Forum*, vol. 19, Fall 1973, pp. 325-50.

Laqueur, Walter, "Can Terrorism Succeed?" *Skeptic*, no. 11, pp. 24-29.

———, "Coming to Terms with Terror," *Times Literary Supplement*, April 2, 1976, p. 362.

———, "The Continuing Failure of Terrorism," *Harper's*, November 1976, pp. 69-74.

———, "The Futility of Terrorism," *Harper's*, March 1976, p. 99.

———, "Guerrillas and Terrorists," *Commentary*, October 1974, pp. 40-48.

———, "Interpretations of Terrorism: Fact, Fiction and Political Science," *Journal of Contemporary History*, vol. 12, January 1977, pp. 1-42.

Lasky, Melvin J., "Ulrike and Andreas: The Bonnie and Clyde of West Germany's Radical Subculture may have failed to make a Revolution, but they have bruised the Body Politic," *New York Times Magazine*, May 11, 1975, pp. 14ff.

Leiden, Carl, "Assassination in the Middle East," *Trans-Action*, vol. 6, May 1969, pp. 20-23.

Mallin, Jay, "Terrorism as a Political Weapon," *Air University Review* 22, July-August 1971, pp. 45-52.

———, "Terrorism in Revolutionary Warfare," *Strategic Review*, Fall 1974, pp. 48-55.

Mallison, W. T., Jr., and S. V. Mallison, "Concept of Public Purpose Terror in International Law," *Journal of Palestine Studies*, Winter 1975, pp. 36-51; also in *Howard Law Journal*, vol. 18, 1973, pp. 12-28.

Mazuri, Ali A., "Thoughts On Assassination in Africa," *Political Science Quarterly*, vol. 83, March 1968, pp. 40-58.

Means, John, "Political Kidnappings and Terrorism," *North American Review*, vol. 4, Winter 1970, pp. 16-19.

Mickolus, Edward, "Negotiating for Hostages: A Policy Dilemma," *ORBIS*, Winter 1976, pp. 1251-1269.

Moss, Robert, "International Terrorism and Western Societies," *International Journal*, vol. 28, Summer 1973, pp. 418-430.

Murphy, John F., "International Legal Control of International Terrorism: Performance and Prospects," *Illinois Bar Journal*, vol. 63, April 1975, p. 444.

"Organization of American States: Convention to Prevent and Punish Acts of Terrorism," *International Legal Materials*, vol. 10, March 1971, pp. 255-58.

Paust, J., "An Approach to Decision with Regard to Terrorism," *Akron Law Review*, vol. 7, 1974, pp. 397-403.

———, "Some Thoughts on 'Preliminary Thoughts' on Terrorism," *Ameri-*

can Journal of International Law, vol. 68, 1974, pp. 502-503.

————, "Survey of Possible Legal Responses to International Terrorism: Prevention, Punishment, and Cooperative Action," *Georgia Journal of International and Comparative Law*, vol. 5, 1975, pp. 431-469.

————, "Terrorism and the International Law of War," *Military Law Review*, vol. 64, 1974, pp. 1-36.

Pierre, Andrew J., "The Politics of International Terrorism," *ORBIS*, vol. 19, Winter 1976, pp. 1251-1269.

Price, H. Edward, Jr., "The Strategy and Tactics of Revolutionary Terrorism," *Comparative Studies in Society and History*, vol. 19, January 1977, pp. 52-66.

Romaniecki, Leon, "The Soviet Union and International Terrorism," *Soviet Studies*, vol. 26, no. 3, July 1974, pp. 417-40.

Roucek, J. S., "Sociological Element of a Theory of Terror and Violence," *American Journal of Economics and Sociology*, vol. 21, April 1962, pp. 165-172.

Rozakis, Christos L., "Terrorism and the Internationally Protected Persons in the Light of the ILC Draft Articles," *International and Comparative Law Quarterly*, vol. 23, January 1974, pp. 32-72.

Russell, Charles A., and Bowman H. Miller, "Profile of a Terrorist," *Terrorism: An International Journal*, vol. 1, no. 1, 1977, pp. 17-34.

Schwarzenberger, G., "Terrorists, Hijackers, Guerrilleros, and Mercenaries," *Current Legal Problems*, vol. 24, 1971, pp. 257-282.

Segre, D. V., and J. H. Adler, "The Ecology of Terrorism," *Encounter*, vol. 40, February 1973, pp. 17-24.

Shapley, Deborah, "Plutonium: Reactor Proliferation Threatens a Nuclear Black Market," *Science*, vol. 172, April 9, 1971, pp. 143-46.

Silverstein, Martin Elliot, "Emergency Medical Preparedness," *Terrorism: An International Journal*, vol. 1, no. 1, 1977, pp. 51-70.

Smart, I.M.H., "The Power of Terror," *International Journal*, vol. 30, Spring 1975, pp. 225-237.

Stern, Geoffrey, "The Use of Terror as a Political Weapon," *Journal of International Studies*, vol. 4, Winter 1975-76, pp. 263-267.

Stevenson, John R., "International Law and the Export of Terrorism," *The Record of the Association of the Bar of the City of New York*, vol. 27, December 1972, pp. 716-29.

Taylor, Theodore B., "Nuclear Terrorism: A Threat of the Future," *Science Digest*, August 1974, pp. 12-16.

Thompson, W. Scott, "Political Violence and the 'Correlation of Forces,'" *ORBIS*, vol. 19, Winter 1976, pp. 1270-1288.

Wilkinson, Paul, "Terrorism versus Liberal Democracy—The Problem of Response," *Conflict*, vol. 67, January 1976.

————, "Three Questions on Terrorism," *Government and Opposition*, vol. 8, no. 3, 1973, pp. 290-312.

Wohlstetter, Roberta, "Kidnapping to Win Friends and Influence People,"

Survey, vol. 20, no. 4, Autumn 1974, pp. 1-40.

Wolf, John B., "Controlling Political Terrorism in a Free Society," *ORBIS*, vol. 19, Winter 1976, pp. 1289-1308.

Other Sources

Aines, R. C., "The Jewish Underground Against the British Mandate in Palestine." Thesis, Union College, 1973.

Cardillo, L. M., "The Tupamaros: A Case of Power Duality in Uruguayan Politics." Manuscript on deposit at Fletcher School of Law and Diplomacy, Tufts University, 1975.

Chishol, Henry J., "The Function of Terror and Violence in Revolution." Thesis, Georgetown University, 1948.

Green, L. C., "The Nature and Control of International Terrorism." University of Alberta, Edmonton, 1974 (occasional paper).

Horowitz, Irving L., "Profile of the Terrorist: Some Propositions," in *Political Terrorism and Personal Deviance*, a summary of remarks at a conference sponsored by the U.S. Department of State, February 15, 1973, pp. 2-5.

Hutchinson, Martha Crenshaw, "Implications of the Pattern of Transnational Terrorism." Paper presented to the International Studies Association Convention, Washington, D.C., February 20, 1975.

————, "Transnational Terrorism as a Policy Issue." Paper presented to the American Political Science Association Convention, Chicago, Ill., August 29–September 2, 1974.

International Association of Chiefs of Police, Professional Standards Division, *Civil Disorders: After-action Reports*. A report to the Attorney General of the United States reviewing the experience of eight American cities during the civil disorders of March–April 1968. Washington, D.C., 1968.

International Terrorism: Proceedings of an Intensive Panel at the 15th Annual Convention of the International Studies Association, St. Louis, Mo., March 23, 1974. Milwaukee: University of Wisconsin, 1974, 96 pp.

Jenkin, Brian Michael, "Hostage Survival: Some Preliminary Observations." Paper presented to United States Information Agency International Terrorism Seminar, August 11, 1975.

Jenkins, R., *England—Prevention of Terrorism (Temporary Provisions)—A Bill*. London: Her Majesty's Stationery Office, 1974.

Jureidini, Paul A., "The Relationship of the Palestinian Guerrilla Movement With the Government of Jordan, 1967-1970." Ph.D. dissertation, American University.

Kelley, C. M., "Terrorism—A Phenomenon of Sickness." Claremont Men's College, 1974.

Kelley, J., and G. Pellatier, *Legal Control of the Populace in Subversive Warfare*, Judge Advocate General's School Text, 1966.

Kreiger, David, "Nuclear Power: A Trojan Horse for Terrorists." Paper presented at Stockholm International Peace Research Institute Symposium, June 15-18, 1973.

MacNamara, Donal E. J., "Political Terrorism: Crime or Tactic (The Case of the Irish Republican Army)." Paper presented at the annual meeting of the American Society of Criminology, Toronto, October 30–November 2, 1975.

Middendorff, W., *New Developments in the Taking of Hostages and Kidnapping—A Summary.* Washington, D.C.: U.S. Law Enforcement Assistance Administration, National Institute of Law Enforcement and Criminal Justice, National Criminal Justice Reference Service, 1975.

Milbank, David L., "International and Transnational Terrorism: Diagnosis and Prognosis." Paper prepared for delivery to the U.S. Department of State Conference on International Terrorism, March 25-26, 1976, 41pp. + appendixes.

Pereny, Peter S., *Summary of State Department Conference on Terrorism.* External Research Study, December 29, 1972, pp. 1-10.

Ramon, Zvia, "A Study of the Offense of Skyjacking." Master's thesis, John Jay College of Criminal Justice, 1973.

Redlick, Amy, "The Impact of Transnational Interactions on Separatism: A Case Study of the Quebec Separatist Movement." Ph.D. dissertation, Fletcher School of Law and Diplomacy, Tufts University, 1977.

Schmitt, Karl, "Targets of Terrorists." Paper presented at the U.S. Department of State Conference on Terrorism, October 1972.

"Task Force on Kidnapping." Transcript of an interview by the editors of *Canada Today* with Claude Roquet and Allen Rowe on the operations of the Special Task Force created by the Canadian Department of External Affairs, *External Affairs* 23 (January 1971), pp. 6-11.

Taylor, Theodore B., W. R. VanCleave, and E. M. Kinderman, "Preliminary Survey of Non-National Nuclear Threats." Stanford Research Institute, September 1968.

U.S., Congress, House, Committee on Foreign Affairs, Subcommittee on the Near East and South Asia, *International Terrorism: Hearings,* 93rd Cong., 2d sess., June 11, 18-19, 24, 1974.

U.S., Congress, House, Committee on Internal Security, *Political Kidnappings, 1968-1973: A Staff Study,* 93rd Cong., 1st sess., 1973.

————, *Terrorism: Hearings,* 93rd Cong., 2d sess., February–March 1974, pt. 1.

————, *Terrorism: Hearings,* 93rd Cong., 2d sess., May–June 1974, pt. 2.

————, *Terrorism: Hearings,* 93rd Cong., 2d sess., June–July 1974, pt. 3.

————, *Terrorism: Hearings,* 93rd Cong., 2d sess., July–August 1974, pt. 4.

————, *Terrorism—A Staff Study,* 93rd Cong., 2d sess., August 7, 1974.

U.S., Congress, House, Committee on Interstate and Foreign Commerce, Subcommittee on Transportation and Aeronautics, *Anti-hijacking Act of 1973: Hearings,* 93rd Cong., 1st sess., February 27-28 and March 1, 6-8, 9,

1973, H.R. 3858, H.R. 670, H.R. 3853, and H.R. 4287, pts. 1, 2.

U.S., Congress, Senate, Aircraft Piracy Amendments of 1973: Debate and Vote. *Congressional Record,* 93rd Cong., 2d sess., 1974, pp. S3502-3506.

U.S., Congress, Senate, Committee on Commerce, Subcommittee on Aviation, *The Administration's Emergency Anti-hijacking Regulations: Hearings,* 93rd Cong., 1st sess., January 9-10, 1973.

U.S., Congress, Senate, Committee on Foreign Relations, *Aircraft Hijacking Convention: Hearings,* 92d Cong., 1st sess., on Executive A, June 7, 20, 1971.

U.S., Congress, Senate, Committee on the Judiciary, *Terroristic Activity: The Cuban Connection in Puerto Rico; Castro's Hand in Puerto Rican and U.S. Terrorism: Hearings before the Subcommittee to Investigate the Administration of the Internal Security Act and Other Internal Security Laws,* 94th Cong., 1st sess., July 30, 1975, pt. 5.

————, *Terroristic Activity: Hearings before the Subcommittee To Investigate the Administration of the Internal Security Act and Other Internal Security Laws,* 93rd Cong., 2d sess., September 23, 1974, pt. 1.

————, *Terroristic Activity: Hostage Defense Measures: Hearings before the Subcommittee To Investigate the Administration of the Internal Security Act and Other Internal Security Laws,* 94th Cong., 1st sess., July 25, 1975, pt. 5.

————, *Terroristic Activity: Inside the Weatherman Movement: Hearings before the Subcommittee To Investigate the Administration of the Internal Security Act and Other Internal Security Laws,* 93rd Cong., 2d sess., October 18, 1974, pt. 2.

————, *Terroristic Activity: International Terrorism: Hearings before the Subcommittee To Investigate the Administration of the Internal Security Act and Other Internal Security Laws,* 94th Cong., 1st sess., May 14, 1975, pt. 4.

————, *Terroristic Activity: Testimony of Dr. Frederick Schwarz: Hearings before the Subcommittee To Investigate the Administration of the Internal Security Act and Other Internal Security Laws,* 93rd Cong., 2d sess., July 5, 1974, pt. 3.

U.S., Department of Justice, *Domestic Terrorist Matters.* Washington, D.C.: FBI, 1974.

————, *Hostage Situations—Bibliography.* Quantico, Va.: FBI Academy, 1973.

————, *Terrorist Activities—Bibliography.* Quantico, Va.: FBI Academy, 1975.

U.S., National Commission on the Causes and Prevention of Violence, *To Establish Justice, To Insure Domestic Tranquility: A Final Report.* Washington, D.C.: Government Printing Office, 1969.

United Kingdom, *Report of the Committee of Privy Counselors Appointed To Consider Authorized Procedures for the Interrogation of Persons Suspected of Terrorism.* London: Her Majesty's Stationery Office, 1972.

Violence Against Society. Washington, D.C.: Chamber of Commerce of the United States, 1971.

Williams, Shahron G., "The Transnational Impact of Insurgency Terrorism: A Quantitative Approach." Ph.D. dissertation, Queens College, City University of New York.

Wolf, John B., "Black September: A Description of an International Terrorist Organization and an Assessment of its Implications for Urban Law Enforcement Agencies of the United States." Master's thesis, John Jay College of Criminal Justice, 1974.

Index